BEST *of the* BEST
from the
MID-ATLANTIC
COOKBOOK

Selected Recipes from the Favorite Cookbooks
of MARYLAND, DELAWARE, NEW JERSEY
and WASHINGTON, D.C.

Sailing is a popular sport in the Mid-Atlantic region, as well as a favorite recreational pastime. Situated on picturesque Chesapeake Bay, Annapolis, Maryland, is often referred to as the Sailing Capital of the United States.

BEST *of the* BEST
from the
MID-ATLANTIC
COOKBOOK

Selected Recipes from the Favorite Cookbooks
of MARYLAND, DELAWARE, NEW JERSEY
and WASHINGTON, D.C.

EDITED BY

Gwen McKee

AND

Barbara Moseley

Illustrated by Tupper England

QUAIL RIDGE PRESS
Preserving America's Food Heritage

Recipe Collection©2001 Quail Ridge Press, Inc.

Reprinted with permission and all rights reserved under the name of the cookbooks, organizations or individuals listed below.

The Best of Friends ©2000 Friends of Baltimore Parent's Association; *Beyond Peanut Butter and Jelly: Time for Cooking with the International Nanny Association* ©2000 International Nanny Association; *Breakfast at Nine, Tea at Four* ©1998 Callawind Publications, Inc.; *Capital Celebrations* ©1997 The Junior League of Washington, DC; *Capital Classics* ©1989 The Junior League of Washington, DC; *The Chesapeake Collection* ©1983 Woman's Club of Denton, Inc.; *Chesapeake's Bounty* ©2000 Conduit Press; *Coastal Cuisine* ©1999 Connie Correia Fisher; *Collected Recipes—Yours, Mine, Ours* ©1995 Linda D. Channell; *The Congressional Club Cookbook* ©1998 The Congressional Club; *Conveniently Vegan* ©1997 Debra Wasserman; *A Cook's Tour of the Eastern Shore* ©1948 by Easton Maryland Memorial Hospital Junior Auxiliary; *Cooking Secrets* ©2000 Bon Vivant Press; *Dr. John's Healing Psoriasis Cookbook...Plus!* ©2000 by John O. A. Pagano; *Food Fabulous Food* ©1997 The Women's Board to Cooper Health System; *The Glen Afton Cookbook* ©1999 The Glen Afton Women's Club; *Hoboken Cooks* ©1998 United Synagogue of Hoboken; *In the Kitchen with Kendi, Vol. 1* ©1999 Kendi O'Neill; *Lambertville Community Cookbook* ©1995 Kalmia Club of Lambertville; *Maryland's Historic Restaurants and their recipes* ©1995 by Dawn O'Brien and Rebecca Schenck; *Maryland's Way* ©1963 Hammond-Harwood House Association; *A Matter of Taste* ©1989 The Junior League of Morristown, NJ, Inc.; *Meatless Meals for Working People* ©1998 Debra Wasserman and Charles Stahler; *Mrs. Kitching's Smith Island Cookbook* ©1981 Tidewater Publishers; *My Favorite Maryland Recipes* ©1964 Helen Avalynne Tawes; *Of Tide & Thyme* ©1995 The Junior League of Annapolis; *PB&J USA* ©1998 Connie Correia Fisher; *The Queen Victoria® Cookbook* ©1992 by Joan and Dane Wells; *Simply Vegan* ©1999 Debra Wasserman; *A Taste of Catholicism* ©1996 Cathedral Foundation Press; *Vegan Meals for One & Two* ©2001 The Vegetarian Resource Group; *What's Cookin'* ©1993 Arlene Luskin; *Where There's A Will...* ©1997 Evelyn Will; *Why Not for Breakfast?* ©1993 Nancy J. Hawkins; *Winterthur's Culinary Collection* ©1983 The Henry Francis du Pont Winterthur Museum, Inc.

Library of Congress Cataloging-in-Publication Data

Best of the best from the Mid-Atlantic : selected recipes from the favorite cookbooks of
    Maryland, Delaware, New Jersey and Washington D.C. / edited by Gwen McKee and
    Barbara Moseley ;
    illustrated by Tupper England.
        p. cm.
    Includes index
    ISBN 1-893062-28-7
        1. Cookery, American. I. McKee, Gwen. II. Moseley, Barbara.

TX715.B4856485 2001
641.5973—dc21   2001034913

Front cover photo courtesy of Annapolis & Anne Arundel County Conference & Visitors Bureau.
Back cover photo by Greg Campbell.
Design by Cynthia Clark.
Printed in Canada.

QUAIL RIDGE PRESS
P. O. Box 123 • Brandon, MS 39043 • 1-800-343-1583
e-mail: info@quailridge.com • www.quailridge.com

CONTENTS

Editors Gwen McKee and Barbara Moseley enjoy a morning stroll on the beach at picturesque Cape May, New Jersey, which holds the distinction of being the oldest seashore resort in the United States.

PREFACE

From the shores of the Atlantic in New Jersey, throughout Delaware, to the Chesapeake Bay in Maryland, and inland to the bustling streets of our Nation's capitol, we followed the food . . . and it lead us to so many delightful places. The *Best of the Best from the Mid-Atlantic Cookbook* captures this vast array of food within its pages, bringing it all together . . . deliciously. Come with us and discover this delectable cuisine.

The abundance of crabs from the Chesapeake Bay has a decided influence on Mid-Atlantic cooking and eating. Maryland chefs find a plethora of ways to spice it up in fancy dishes, fold it into omelets, stuff it into fish, or mix it into sauces. Delaware, too, boasts superior crab harvests from the western shore of the Delaware Bay, while the inland areas are well known for the production of broiler chickens. Clams may be the cook's choice in New Jersey, where massive clam beds extend from Barnegat Bay to Cape May.

The culinary influences from the Mid-Atlantic states converge in Washington D.C., as do favorites from the United States and many foreign countries. Even the most particular palates will find these recipes irresistible. The Nation's capitol graciously offers a little something for everyone.

In our travels, we find that cooking and cookbooks are a sure-fire way to get to know people, a nice "entree," as most everybody likes to talk about food. Sampling our way through delicious Maryland, we met waitress Hazel in Frederick, who was proud to have us try some of her own special seasoning. We chatted with Bill on Main Street in New Market, who not only guided us to friendly Karen, proprietor of the General Store, but gave us a personal tour of his historic National Register home. In the low-ceilinged kitchen, we imagined many a pot of simmering stew warmly welcoming guests for generations.

When you think of New Jersey, do you think urban? Think again. We discovered why it is called The Garden State. Farms are everywhere, with crops as far as the eye can see. Stopping at local markets revealed not only a tremendous variety of fresh produce (the tomatoes are unbelievable), but jars of delicious preserved goodies from recent orchard harvests. Yum!

On the ferry from Cape May, New Jersey to Lewes, Delaware, we met a young couple who were just getting into cooking, and then chatted with some experienced chefs on the boardwalk in Ocean City, Maryland. In contrast to a winter trip we had taken earlier in the year, when clam chowder in Princeton was a welcome respite from the snow, the stuffed French toast and early morning coffee in Cape May in June was equally incredible. Traveling up through Delaware, we enjoyed the farms, the food, the flowers (Longwood and Winterthur are feasts for the eyes), as well as the history in the nation's first state. A billboard said it, and we agree, Delaware is indeed a "small wonder."

Traveling this magnificent region, we've collected 79 of Delaware, Maryland, New Jersey, and Washington D.C.'s most popular cookbooks, gleaning their best-loved recipes and gathering them together in this cookbook, the 32nd volume in our BEST OF THE BEST STATE COOKBOOK SERIES. You can treat yourself to the same fare we enjoyed: Annapolis Harbor Boil, Tomatoes Stuffed with Crab Salad, Lockhouse Punch, Cape May French Toast Casserole, Delaware Succotash, Washington Red Skins, Best Maryland Crabcakes, Bal'More Rhubarb Pie, etc., etc., etc.

We've added photographs and quips about Mid-Atlantic history and food to make you feel right at home. Following each recipe is the name of its contributing cookbook; additional details about each book are provided in a special catalog section of the book. This section shows a photograph of each contributing book and furnishes ordering information, price, and other items of particular interest to cookbook collectors (see page 255).

We are thankful to so many for their contributions. Thank you to Tupper England, who does such an outstanding job capturing the character of each state with her illustrations. We also appreciate the willingness of food editors to help us with our research and to bookstore and gift shop managers who imparted their wisdom concerning their region's cookbooks. We also thank each state's tourism departments for supplying us with photographs and useful tid-bits about their state. And to all the fine folks we met along the way that shared their invaluable knowledge of the region's taste, thank you for smiling back...we couldn't have done it without you.

We believe you will enjoy preparing these recipes and experiencing the sheer delight of Mid-Atlantic cuisine.

Gwen McKee and Barbara Moseley

CONTRIBUTING COOKBOOKS

Around the Table: Recipes & Reflections
Atlantic Highlands Historical Society Cookbook
Barineau-Williams Family Cookbook Vol. II
Bayside Treasures
Best of Friends
Beyond Peanut Butter and Jelly
Bountiful Blessings
Bread of Life
Breakfast at Nine, Tea at Four
Cape May Fare
Capital Celebrations
Capital Classics
The Chesapeake Collection
Chesapeake's Bounty
Coastal Cuisine: Seaside Recipes from Maine to Maryland
Collected Recipes: Yours, Mine, Ours
Come, Dine With Us!
Conducting in the Kitchen
The Congressional Club Cookbook
Conveniently Vegan
A Cookbook of Treasures
Cooking Along the Susquehanna
Cooking Secrets: Mid-Atlantic & Chesapeake
Cooking Through the Years
Cooking with the Allenhurst Garden Club
A Cook's Tour of the Eastern Shore
Country Chick's Home Cookin
DAPI's Delectable Delights
Dr. John's Healing Psoriasis Cookbook...Plus!
Fair Haven Fare
A Family Tradition
Favorite Recipes Home-Style
Flavors of Cape Henlopen
Food Fabulous Food
Gardeners in the Kitchen: A Second Helping
The Glen Afton Cookbook: Recipes in Good Taste
Good Things to Eat
The Great Gourmet
The Happy Cooker 3

CONTRIBUTING COOKBOOKS

Hoboken Cooks: Favorite Recipes from the Mile-Square City
In the Kitchen with Kendi, Volume 1
In the Komondor Kitchen
Jaycee Cookin'
La Cucina Casalinga: Italian Home Cooking
Lambertville Community Cookbook
Let's Cook Swiss
Maryland's Historic Restaurants and their Recipes
Maryland's Way: The Hammond-Harwood House Cook Book
A Matter of Taste
Meatless Meals for Working People
Mid-Day Magic
More Favorites from the Melting Pot
Mrs. Kitching's Smith Island Cookbook
My Favorite Maryland Recipes
Of Tide & Thyme
Our Favorite Recipes
Our Favorite Recipes: Book Three
Out of the Frying Pan Into the Fire!!!
PB&J USA
The Queen Victoria® Cookbook
Recipes from the Skipjack Martha Lewis
Restaurant Recipes from the Shore and More...
Sealed with a Knish
A Second Helping
Simple Pleasures: Healthful Everyday Kosher Recipes for Body & Soul
Simply Vegan: Quick Vegetarian Meals
South Coastal Cuisine
Steppingstone Cookery
A Taste of Catholicism
A Taste of GBMC
A Taste of Heaven
A Taste of Tradition
A Tasting Tour Through the 8th District
225 Years in Pennington & Still Cooking
Vegan Meals for One & Two: Your Own Personal Recipes
What's Cookin'
Where There's a Will...
Why Not for Breakfast?
Winterthur's Culinary Collection

BEVERAGES & APPETIZERS

Once the 175-room country estate of Henry Francis du Pont, Winterthur, Delaware, is now world renowned for its vast woodland gardens and unrivaled collection of American decorative arts.

Spice Russian Tea

2⅓ cups Tang
1¼ cups instant tea
½ cup sugar

6 ounces instant lemonade mix
1½ teaspoons cinnamon
1½ teaspoons ground cloves

Mix all ingredients together. Add 2 teaspoons per cup with hot water. Can add more or less to taste.

The Glen Afton Cookbook

Creamsicle Cooler

1 (16-ounce) can frozen orange
    juice
1 cup cold milk
1 cup cold water

¼ cup sugar
1 teaspoon vanilla
10 ice cubes, crushed (about ½
    cup)

Whip together orange juice, cold milk, water, sugar, vanilla, and crushed ice in blender and serve. A fresh mint leaf is a nice garnish with this juice.

DAPI's Delectable Delights

Lockhouse Punch

1 cup sugar
2 cinnamon sticks
1 whole nutmeg
4 whole allspice

2 cups apple cider, or apple juice
6 cups orange juice
2 cups vodka, optional

Mix all ingredients except vodka in a crockpot and stir well. Cover and cook on low setting for 4–10 hours. Cook on high setting for 2–3 hours. Just before serving, you may add 2 cups vodka. This is the punch served at the Lockhouse during the Candlelight Tour (without the vodka).

Cooking Along the Susquehanna

Taco Salsa Dip

2 (8-ounce) packages Neufchâtel
  cream cheese, softened
3 tomatoes, diced
1 (1-pound) jar of salsa (hot,
  medium, or mild)

½ head of lettuce, shredded, then
  chopped
1 (1-pound) bag shredded
  Monterey Jack or Cheddar
  cheese

Spread cream cheese evenly on the bottom of a 9x13x2-inch glass pan. Layer the remaining ingredients as follows: tomato, salsa, lettuce, shredded cheese. Keep refrigerated until 1 hour before serving to allow for softening of the cream cheese. Serve with tortilla chips.

Conducting in the Kitchen

Black Bean Salsa

1 can black beans, rinsed and
  drained
2 tablespoons fresh lime juice
4 tablespoons minced cilantro
4 scallions, finely chopped
2 cloves garlic, minced
2 tablespoons apple cider vinegar

4 large plum tomatoes, seeded and
  chopped
Salt and pepper to taste
½ teaspoon cumin
2 seeded and minced jalapeño
  peppers

Mix black beans, lime juice, cilantro, scallions, garlic, vinegar, tomatoes, salt, pepper, cumin, and jalapeño peppers together and chill for 2–3 hours. Serve with tortilla chips.

A Taste of Tradition

Roedown races, as the steeplechase is known locally in horse country south of Annapolis, Maryland, are races in which the horses jump over different types of fences on a grass course. Tailgate parties, from simple picnics to elaborate buffets decorated with silver, candles and flowers, are a major part of the hospitality along the course fence.

Hot Asparagus Dip

1½ cups freshly grated Parmesan
  cheese (about 7 ounces)
2 (15-ounce) cans cut asparagus
  spears, drained

1½ cups mayonnaise
1 clove garlic, crushed
Pepper to taste

Grate (chop) cheese in food processor. Add other ingredients and process until blended. Pour into baking dish and bake for 20–30 minutes at 350°, or until slightly brown and bubbling. Serve hot with crackers or large corn chips.

Around the Table

Mushroom Dip

This dip is great on Challah!

1 (15-ounce) can mushrooms,
  drained
3–4 cloves garlic
½ cup plus 2 tablespoons grated
  Parmesan cheese, divided

1 tablespoon lemon juice
¼ cup mayonnaise
¼ cup cream cheese
2 tablespoons bread crumbs

Blend or process the mushrooms and garlic. Add ½ cup Parmesan cheese, lemon juice, mayonnaise, and cream cheese. Mix well. Put in a small ovenproof pan. Sprinkle with bread crumbs and remaining 2 tablespoons Parmesan. Bake at 350° for 20–25 minutes.

Hoboken Cooks

Pumpkin Dip

This is a great fall snack that you can make all year long.

1 (8-ounce) package cream cheese
1 (16-ounce) can pumpkin pie
  filling
1 teaspoon cinnamon

½ teaspoon ginger
Ginger cookies, apple or pear
  slices, for dipping

Blend cream cheese, pumpkin, and spices. Serve with ginger cookies or fruit.

Around the Table

Mexican Corn Dip

Cool and delightful.

2 (11-ounce) cans Mexican corn, drained
4 ounces chopped green chiles
2 jalapeño peppers, chopped
5 green onions, chopped

1 tablespoon sugar
1 cup mayonnaise
1 cup sour cream
2 cups shredded sharp Cheddar cheese

Combine all the ingredients, mixing well, in a mixing bowl. Refrigerate overnight. Serve with tortilla chips. Keeps in the refrigerator for 5 days. Yields 16 servings.

Capital Celebrations

Sesame Chicken with Honey Dip

Served by popular request each year at an annual tailgate party.

CHICKEN:

½ cup mayonnaise
1½ teaspoons dry mustard
2 teaspoons instant minced onion

1 cup fine dry bread crumbs
½ cup sesame seeds
2 cups uncooked cubed chicken

Preheat oven to 400°. Mix mayonnaise, mustard, and minced onion in a shallow dish or pie pan; set aside. Mix crumbs and sesame seeds. Toss chicken in mayonnaise mixture, then roll in crumb mixture. Place on baking sheet. Bake at 400° for 12 15 minutes, or until lightly browned. Serve hot or at room temperature with dip. Yields 2 dozen.

HONEY DIP:

2 tablespoons honey

1 cup mayonnaise

Combine honey with mayonnaise.

A Matter of Taste

Chafing Dish Crab Dip

Easy, and can be made ahead. Perfect for a party!

1 pound fresh backfin crabmeat, picked
1 (8-ounce) package cream cheese, softened
2 tablespoons milk
1 medium onion, chopped
2 tablespoons horseradish
Dash hot pepper sauce
Salt and white pepper to taste
4 tablespoons mayonnaise
3 tablespoons sherry/wine
Pinch seafood seasoning
Dash paprika
Toasted almonds
Crackers

Combine all ingredients except almonds and crackers. Bake at 375° for 10–15 minutes. Sprinkle with toasted almonds, and serve in chafing dish with crackers. Serves 10–12.

Of Tide & Thyme

Tilghman Island Crab Melt

1 (8-ounce) jar Cheez Whiz
2 tablespoons mayonnaise
1 stick margarine, room temperature
½ teaspoon garlic powder
1 pound crabmeat
9 English muffins, split

Mix together Cheez Whiz, mayonnaise, margarine and garlic powder. Fold in crabmeat. Spread on English muffin halves. Toast in toaster oven or broiler until hot and bubbly. Cut each muffin into 4 pieces.

These freeze well; place on cookie sheet to freeze, then store in Ziploc freezer bags. Yields 18 muffin halves.

Best of Friends

Crabmeat Ramekins

1 pound crabmeat, cooked, flaked
6 slices bacon, cooked crisp
1½ cups mayonnaise
½ cup chili sauce
1 teaspoon tarragon

1 teaspoon vinegar
1 teaspoon dry English mustard
½ teaspoon Tabasco
Paprika and salt to taste

Divide cooked crabmeat into 6 lightly buttered ramekins (individual baking dishes). Heat in preheated oven at 400° for 5 minutes. Top each portion with one slice of bacon (cooked crisp).

In a large bowl, combine mayonnaise, chili sauce, tarragon, vinegar, dry mustard, Tabasco, paprika and salt to taste. Top the crabmeat with this mixture. Put ramekins under a preheated broiler for 2–3 minutes, or until topping is bubbling. Makes 6 servings.

Cooking Through the Years

Crab Tassies

These tarts have a rich crab filling.

½ cup butter, softened
3 ounces cream cheese, softened
1 cup flour
¼ teaspoon salt
1 pound crabmeat
½ cup mayonnaise
1 tablespoon lemon juice

¼ cup finely chopped celery
2 small scallions, finely chopped
½ cup grated Swiss cheese
½ teaspoon Worcestershire sauce
¼ teaspoon seasoned salt
Dash of Tabasco

Cream butter and cream cheese. Stir in flour and salt. Roll into 24 small balls and chill 1 hour. Press into tiny muffin tins, about 1¾ inches in diameter.

Mix crab with remaining ingredients. Spoon into unbaked shells and bake at 350° until golden, approximately 30 minutes. Yields 24.

Capital Classics

Shrimp Mousse

This looks great, tastes great, and never fails to get raves! Best of all, it can be done ahead of time.

1 can tomato soup	⅓ cup chopped green onions
1 package unflavored gelatin	1 or 2 cans tiny shrimp, drained
1 (8-ounce) package cream cheese,	Leafy lettuce
softened	Lemon wedges
1 cup mayonnaise	Green olives

Bring soup to a boil. Stir in gelatin and cream cheese. Stir until smooth; the lumps will stir out. Remove from heat and cool slightly. Add mayonnaise, green onions, and shrimp. Pour into oiled mold. Chill 3 hours or more.

Unmold onto a bed of leafy green lettuce and garnish with lemon wedges and green olives. Serve with party-size rye or pumpernickel bread or crackers.

Lambertville Community Cookbook

Coconut Shrimp

This is a great "do-ahead" hors d'oeuvre.

1 pound medium shrimp	2 tablespoons cream
¼ cup flour	¾ cup flaked coconut
½ teaspoon salt	⅓ cup dry bread crumbs
½ teaspoon dry mustard	3 cups vegetable oil
1 egg	Chinese Mustard Sauce

Shell and devein shrimp, but leave tails intact. Combine flour, salt, and dry mustard in a small bowl. Beat egg and cream in another small bowl. Combine coconut and bread crumbs in shallow dish. Dip shrimp in flour mixture, then in egg-cream and finally in coconut-crumb mixture (coat well). At this point shrimp can be arranged in single layer and refrigerated.

When ready to cook, pour oil in medium saucepan (or wok) to 2-inch depth. Heat oil to 350°. Fry shrimp (6 or less at a time) for about 2 minutes. Turn once, cooking until golden brown. Remove with slotted spoon and drain on paper towels or paper bag. Keep warm in slow oven until all shrimp are cooked. Serve with Chinese Mustard Sauce and duck sauce.

Note: Can freeze and reheat in 350–370° oven for about 10 minutes. Serve on doilies to absorb any remaining grease.

CHINESE MUSTARD SAUCE:

⅓ cup dry mustard	1 tablespoon honey
2 teaspoons vinegar	¼ cup cold water (maybe less)

Mix all ingredients until well blended. Refrigerate.

Jaycee Cookin'

On December 25, 1776, George Washington made his famous overnight crossing of the Delaware River from Pennsylvania to surprise the British in New Jersey.

Lobster Cocktail

2 tablespoons balsamic vinegar
6 (1-pound) lobsters
6 small bunches mache
  (also known as lamb's lettuce)
4 celery stalks
24 orange segments
1 very ripe papaya, peeled and
  seeded

2 tablespoons lemon juice
½ teaspoon salt
¼ teaspoon white pepper
10 tablespoons extra virgin cold
  pressed olive oil
6 sprigs lemon thyme

In a large pot of salted boiling water, add vinegar and lobsters. Simmer for 6 minutes. Drain and rinse under cold water. Set aside. When cool enough to handle, crack shell and remove the tail and claw meat. Slice each tail, on the bias, into 6 pieces.

Gently clean mache with a damp paper towel. Arrange mache in 6 oversized martini glasses. Shave each celery stalk to expose the tender core. Make 24 shavings from the 4 stalks, 4 shavings per glass. Alternate the celery shavings and orange segments around the glasses. Mound lobster chunks in the center of the glasses. Dice papaya into ½-inch cubes (about 24–30 pieces). Place papaya on top of mache and lobster.

Whisk together lemon juice, salt and white pepper. Add the olive oil in a stream. Combine thoroughly and drizzle a bit over each lobster cocktail. Finish with a sprig of lemon thyme. Serves 6.

Recipe from Executive Chef/Owner Adolfo de Martino,
Green Gables Restaurant and Inn, Beach Haven, New Jersey

Coastal Cuisine

All-Purpose Wine Cheese

¾–1 pound sharp Cheddar cheese
½ cup butter
1 (8-ounce) package cream cheese

½ cup cream sherry or port wine
2 tablespoons fresh Parmesan
 (optional)

Shred Cheddar in processor; add butter and cream cheese, cut in pieces. Add wine gradually and process until smooth. Scrape sides of container, add Parmesan and blend thoroughly. Spoon into containers, cover and refrigerate. Keeps for about a month; firm when cold, softens at room temperature. Yields about 3 cups.

Mid-Day Magic

Freiburger Käsefondue Moitie-Moitie
(Cheese Fondue Half-Half)

Bread cubes
1 pound (450 g) Gruyère cheese,
 shredded
1 pound (450 g) Vacherin cheese,
 shredded

1 pint (5 dl) white wine
5 cloves garlic, sliced
1 tablespoon lemon juice
1 tablespoon cornstarch, dissolved
 in some white wine

Prepare 1-inch (2.5 cm) cubes of white or dark bread. Combine all remaining ingredients except cornstarch in a fondue pot and slowly bring to a boil, stirring frequently with a wooden spoon. When cheese is melted, add the cornstarch and cook gently for some more minutes until the mixture is smooth. To serve, transfer fondue pot to a fondue burner or chafing dish on the table. Spear bread pieces with fondue forks and dip into fondue, stirring the mixture thoroughly as you dip. Fondue should cook very gently during the whole meal. Adjust burner, if fondue is boiling too much or too little.

Let's Cook Swiss

Liptauer Cheese

Best made a day ahead of serving.

1 (8-ounce) package cream cheese
½ cup butter or margarine
3 tablespoons thick sour cream
2 anchovy filets (or 1 teaspoon paste)
1 small onion, finely chopped
1½ tablespoons Hungarian paprika

½ teaspoon salt
1 tablespoon gin (optional)
1 teaspoon capers
1 tablespoon Dijon mustard
1 teaspoon caraway seeds
Several dashes Maggi seasoning

Put cheese, butter, and sour cream into mixer and beat until reasonably fluffy. Add all the other ingredients and mix until everything is very well blended. Mound in a bowl and serve with rye or pumpernickel slices.

Note: Some people like to add garlic (fresh). Just make sure it is well mashed before blending in with all the other ingredients.

In the Komondor Kitchen

Chäschüechli
(Cheese Pies)

Typical Swiss fast food, these little pies are served at fairs and festivities throughout the year. Use a mixture of well-matured Swiss cheese (e.g. Gruyère, Sbrinz, Emmental and Appenzeller).

8 ounces (250 g) short crust (basic pie) or puff pastry
8 ounces (250 g) Swiss cheeses, grated
7 fluid ounces (200 ml) heavy whipping cream

10 fluid ounces (300 ml) milk
2 tablespoons flour
3 eggs
Salt and pepper
Grated nutmeg

Heat the oven to 400° (200°C). Gas mark 6. Roll out the pastry and line buttered foil molds 4 inches (10 cm) in diameter.* Sprinkle cheese into tartlet molds. Whisk together cream, milk, flour, eggs, salt, pepper, and nutmeg. Divide the custard between the molds. Bake at once for about 20 minutes or until golden brown and beautifully risen. Serve immediately, as they sink rather fast.

*For one large pie, use an 11-inch (28 cm) quiche pan and bake for 30 minutes.

Let's Cook Swiss

Goat Cheese Appetizer

1 package goat cheese, chilled
½ cup olive oil
2 cloves garlic, crushed
¼ cup sun-dried tomatoes
½ cup chopped black olives
2 teaspoons fresh basil, chopped

1½ teaspoons fresh parsley, chopped
1 teaspoon whole peppercorns
½ teaspoon rosemary
½ teaspoon thyme
¼ teaspoon red chile flakes

Slice goat cheese ¼-inch thick and place in a serving dish, such as a quiche dish or a large bowl with low sides. It will be crumbly. Drizzle oil over it and add garlic. Plump tomatoes in water, drain, chop, and sprinkle over cheese. Sprinkle on olives, basil, parsley, peppercorns, rosemary, thyme, and chile flakes. Marinate at room temperature 4–6 hours. Remove garlic.

Serve with slices of French bread, preferably the small baguette size. Serves 10–12.

Recipe by Mrs. Tom Allen, wife of Representative from Maine
The Congressional Club Cookbook

Cheese Pumpkin

2 loaves round French bread
1 (2½-ounce) package chipped beef
3 cups shredded sharp Cheddar cheese
1 (8-ounce) package cream cheese, softened

1 cup sour cream
¾ cup canned pumpkin
½ cup chopped parsley
1 tablespoon Worcestershire sauce
2 green onions, chopped
Dash hot pepper sauce

Preheat oven to 300°. Slice the top of one loaf of bread; set aside to be used as lid. Hollow out bread, leaving a ½-inch rim to support the filling. Chop beef into small pieces and set aside. Mix Cheddar cheese, cream cheese, sour cream, pumpkin, and parsley in a medium bowl. Add beef, Worcestershire sauce, onions, and hot pepper sauce; blend well. Pour into hollowed-out bread. Cover with "lid" and wrap loaf with aluminum foil. Bake 2 hours. While appetizer is baking, cube second loaf of bread and use for dipping. Serve appetizer hot.

Cooking Along the Susquehanna

Swiss Cheese-Spinach Spread

1 (8-ounce) package Neufchâtel
  cheese, softened
4 ounces Swiss cheese, shredded
4 cups loosely packed fresh
  spinach leaves
½ teaspoon finely chopped fresh
  garlic

¼ teaspoon salt
⅛ teaspoon ground red pepper
2 tablespoons olive or vegetable
  oil
½ cup chopped walnuts, toasted
2½ ounces (½ cup) cooked ham,
  finely chopped

In food processor bowl with metal blade, place cream cheese and Swiss cheese; cover. Process until smooth (30–60 seconds); set aside. In clean processor bowl with metal blade, place spinach, garlic, salt and red pepper; cover. With processor running, slowly add oil until well mixed. By hand, stir in walnuts; set aside. Line 1-quart bowl with plastic food wrap, extending wrap 3–4 inches over edge.

Spread half of cheese mixture in bottom of bowl; top with half of ham, the spinach mixture, remaining ham and remaining cheese mixture. Fold plastic wrap over top to cover. Refrigerate until firm (4 hours or overnight).

Remove plastic food wrap from top of spread. Invert molded spread onto serving plate. Remove remaining plastic food wrap. Serve spread with crackers, crusty French bread or breadsticks. Makes 3 cups.

Bountiful Blessings

Cheese Crock

1 pound Cheddar cheese, shredded
1 (3-ounce) package cream cheese
1–2 tablespoons oil

1 teaspoon each dry mustard and
  garlic salt
2 tablespoons brandy

Let cheeses stand at room temperature until soft. Then add oil, mustard, garlic salt, and brandy; beat until well blended. Pack into container, cover and refrigerate for about a week before using the first time. Makes about 3 cups.

Note: Cheese Crock can be kept going by adding cheese to it as follows: Firm cheese, such as Swiss, Jack, or any Cheddar-type are fine. Shred and beat in, adding small amount of oil or cream cheese for good consistency. Also add brandy, sherry, port, beer, or kirsch, keeping the total not larger than the original proportion of brandy—then let mixture age a few days before serving. Use it every week or two, and save part of the original mixture to keep crock going.

What's Cookin'

Sun-Dried Tomato Spread

3 ounces sun-dried tomatoes
2 large garlic cloves
1 teaspoon dried basil
½ teaspoon salt
½ cup olive oil

2 parsley sprigs
¼ teaspoon red pepper
1 green onion, chopped
6 ounces cream cheese
2 ounces butter, softened

Cover dried tomatoes with boiling water and let stand for 20 minutes to rehydrate. Drain. Combine all but cream cheese and butter in processor, then let marinate for 2 hours.

Combine cream cheese and butter. Whip until smooth. In small bowl lined with plastic wrap, layer cheese, tomato, cheese, tomato, and cheese. This keeps for several days in refrigerator. Serve with Cayenne Toast.

CAYENNE TOAST:

½ teaspoon sugar
½ teaspoon pepper
½ cup olive oil
½ teaspoon cayenne pepper

½ teaspoon salt
½ teaspoon paprika
½ teaspoon garlic powder
1 loaf French bread

Whisk ingredients (except bread) together. Cut bread into ¼-inch slices. Spread oil mixture on each slice with a pastry brush. Bake on ungreased sheet in a 200° oven for 1 hour.

Steppingstone Cookery

Layered Pesto Spread

1 cup whole fresh basil leaves,
   plus extra for garnish
⅓ cup grated Parmesan cheese
   (1⅓ ounces)

2 tablespoons olive oil
½ cup pine nuts
1 (8-ounce) container whipped
   cream cheese

Line a small bowl with plastic wrap. Chop 1 cup of basil in a food processor. Blend in Parmesan cheese and olive oil. Stir in the pine nuts by hand. Layer whipped cream cheese and basil pesto alternately in lined bowl, beginning and ending with cream cheese. Refrigerate for 60 minutes. Invert onto a serving plate and remove plastic wrap. Garnish with extra basil leaves and serve with crackers. Yields 1½ cups.

Note: This can be refrigerated in a tightly sealed container for up to 2 weeks.

Breakfast at Nine, Tea at Four

Basil and Tomato Tart

1 refrigerated pie crust, unbaked
6 ounces mozzarella cheese,
   shredded (1½ cups), divided
8 plum or 4 medium tomatoes
1 cup fresh basil, loosely packed

4 garlic cloves
½ cup mayonnaise
¼ cup grated Parmesan cheese
⅛ teaspoon white pepper

Prebake pie crust according to directions. Remove from oven. Sprinkle with ½ cup mozzarella cheese. Preheat oven to 375°. Cut tomatoes into wedges, seed, and drain on paper towels. Arrange tomato wedges on top of melted cheese.

In a food processor, combine basil and garlic. Process and sprinkle over tomato wedges. In medium bowl, combine remaining mozzarella cheese, mayonnaise, Parmesan cheese, and pepper. Spoon cheese mixture over basil and spread evenly to cover the top of pie. Bake 375° for 35–40 minutes, or until top is golden and bubbly. Serve warm.

Food Fabulous Food

Hot Asparagus Roll-Ups

20 slices thin white bread
1 (3-ounce) package bleu cheese, softened
1 (8-ounce) package cream cheese, softened
1 egg, beaten
¼ teaspoon garlic salt
⅛ teaspoon cayenne pepper
½ cup finely chopped green onions
20 canned asparagus spears
¾ cup melted butter
½ cup finely chopped fresh parsley (optional)

Preheat oven to 400°. Trim crust from bread and flatten slices with a rolling pin. Mix cheeses, egg, garlic salt, and cayenne. Fold in onions. Spread bread slices generously and evenly with cheese mixture. Roll an asparagus spear in each slice of bread, sealing well by using a little cheese mixture to bind edges to roll. At this point, they can be frozen, then thawed as needed. Roll each canape in butter and place on an ungreased baking sheet. Bake 15–20 minutes or until lightly browned. Garnish with parsley, if desired.

Fair Haven Fare

Zucchini Squares

4 eggs, slightly beaten
½ teaspoon seasoned salt
½ teaspoon dried oregano (rubbed between palms of your hands)
½ cup vegetable oil
½ cup chopped onions
½ cup Parmesan cheese
2 tablespoons snipped parsley
1 cup Bisquick Baking Mix
4 cups thinly sliced, unpared zucchini

Beat eggs with seasonings; stir in oil. Mix with all remaining ingredients, adding zucchini last. Bake in greased 9x13-inch dish, 350° for 35 minutes, or until a cake tester or toothpick comes out clean. It should be golden brown. Slice in small squares to serve. This will keep several days, refrigerated, and can be reheated in the microwave.

Conducting in the Kitchen

Onion Strips

1 loaf sliced bread
1 package onion soup mix

1 cup butter or margarine,
   softened

Cut crust from bread. Mix dry onion soup with butter or margarine. Spread mixture on each slice of bread. Cut each slice into 4 strips. Toast in 350° oven for 10 minutes. Serves 20.

Note: These freeze well before baking. Can be made ahead and kept on aluminum foil baking sheet in freezer until ready to bake and serve.

Cape May Fare

Onion Ring Loaf

This is better than Blooming Onions!

4–6 mild white onions or sweet
   onions
1 cup milk
3 eggs, beaten

Salt to taste
Approximately 2 cups pancake
   mix, like Bisquick Baking Mix
Oil for deep frying

Slice onions crosswise and separate into rings. Soak rings in mixture of milk, eggs, and salt to taste in bowl for 30 minutes. Dip each onion ring in pancake mix and fry in oil heated to 375° until golden brown. Pack fried onion rings solidly but without pressing, into an 8x4-inch loaf pan. Bake at 400° for 10–15 minutes. Turn onto serving plate. Makes 4 servings.

Country Chic's Home Cookin

 The clustered spires of Frederick are still the most prominent and recognizable feature on the skyline of this Western Maryland city. Built in the 1850s, the graceful buildings were featured in John Greenleaf Whittier's Civil War poem, "Barbara Fritchie," in which he describes the town as a crossroads of history: "The clustered spires of Frederick stand, Green-walled by the hills of Maryland . . . On that pleasant morn of the early Fall, When Lee marched over the mountain-wall; Over the mountains winding down, Horse and foot, into Frederick town."

Artichoke Nibbles

These are amazingly easy to make, so of course I serve them at practically every party I have. The nibbles taste better when they're hot.

1 (12-ounce) can marinated	Salt (optional)
artichoke hearts	Pepper to taste
1 small onion, finely chopped	Oregano to taste
1 clove garlic, minced	Tabasco
4 eggs	2 cups shredded Cheddar cheese
¼ cup dry bread crumbs	2 tablespoons minced parsley

Drain the marinade from the artichoke hearts, and chop them well. Add onion and garlic. Sauté until onion is limp, but not browned.

Beat eggs well. Add bread crumbs, salt, pepper, oregano, and a couple of drops of Tabasco—or more if you're brave. Stir in the Cheddar, parsley, and artichoke and onion mixture.

Bake in a 7x11-inch or 8x8-inch pan at 350° for 30 minutes. Serve with any kind of cracker or pita. Serves 6–8.

Hoboken Cooks

Hot Spinach Balls

2 (10-ounce) packages frozen chopped spinach, thawed and squeezed dry
2 cups herb stuffing mix, crushed
1 cup Parmesan cheese, firmly packed

½ cup melted butter or margarine
¼ cup finely chopped green onions
3 eggs, lightly beaten
Dash nutmeg
Mustard Sauce

Combine spinach with stuffing mix, Parmesan cheese, butter, onions, eggs, and nutmeg; mix well. Shape mixture into 1-inch balls; place on cookie sheet. (May be made ahead of time to this point, and refrigerated or frozen until ready to use.) Bake at 375° for 10 minutes. Serve hot with Mustard Sauce.

MUSTARD SAUCE:
¼ cup dry mustard
½ cup white vinegar

¼ cup sugar
1 egg yolk

Combine mustard and vinegar in small bowl; cover with plastic wrap and let stand 4 hours at room temperature. Combine sugar and egg yolk in saucepan. Stir in mustard and vinegar mixture. Cook, stirring constantly over low heat, until thick and smooth. Cover and refrigerate until ready to serve. Serve at room temperature. Saves well.

Conducting in the Kitchen

Union Street Spinach Balls

This very popular North Union Street get-together dish would keep well as next-day snacks, if there were ever any left.

½ cup grated Parmesan
2 cups Italian bread crumbs
2 cups chopped spinach, cooked and drained
1 onion, diced
½ teaspoon garlic powder

½ teaspoon thyme
4 eggs, beaten
½ teaspoon pepper
½ teaspoon salt
¾ cup butter, melted

Mix all ingredients and refrigerate ½ hour. Make into small balls and put on greased cookie sheet. Bake at 350° for 15–20 minutes. Serve warm or cool.

Lambertville Community Cookbook

Swiss-Stuffed Mushrooms

1 pound medium mushrooms
Salt
2 tablespoons butter, melted
½ cup fine, dry bread crumbs
½ cup (2 ounces) shredded Swiss
  cheese

1 egg, beaten
1 teaspoon dried parsley flakes
1 teaspoon crushed, dried dill
  weed
¼–½ teaspoon grated lemon rind
2 tablespoons lemon juice

Clean mushrooms with damp paper towel. Remove stems and set aside. Sprinkle inside of caps with salt. Chop stems finely and sauté in butter over medium heat for 3–4 minutes. Add remaining ingredients, except mushroom caps, mixing well. Spoon mixture into mushroom caps.

Place stuffed mushrooms on ungreased baking sheet. Bake at 350° for 5–8 minutes or until thoroughly heated. Serve hot. Yields 1½ dozen.

Note: May microwave on HIGH for 3–4 minutes, while sitting on flat, glass plate, 9 at a time.

Our Favorite Recipes

Kennett Square Mushrooms

20–25 fresh medium-sized
  mushrooms (approximately
  ½ pound)
2 tablespoons butter
1 small onion, minced
1 tablespoon Worcestershire sauce

⅓ cup soft, fine bread crumbs
½ cup shredded sharp Cheddar
  cheese
Salt and pepper to taste
Parsley
2 tablespoons water

Select mushrooms with closed caps. Pull stems from mushrooms and chop finely. Melt butter in skillet and add stems and onion. Sauté until tender and translucent. Stir in remaining ingredients except water. If preferred, parsley may be sprinkled on top instead of mixed in with other ingredients. Fill mushroom caps with mixture, mounding over top. Arrange mushrooms in ovenproof serving dish. At this point mushrooms can be refrigerated up to 24 hours. Before serving, add 2 tablespoons of water to dish. Bake at 350° for 20 minutes. Serve hot. Yields 20–25 mushrooms.

Winterthur's Culinary Collection

Party-Thyme Meatballs

SAUCE:

3 cans jellied cranberry sauce   3 bottles chili sauce

Combine cranberry sauce and chili sauce in a 6- to 8-quart pot. Allow to simmer while you make the meatballs.

MEATBALLS:

4 pounds lean ground beef	2 teaspoons onion powder
1 cup grated Parmesan cheese	Salt and pepper to taste
1 cup plain bread crumbs	Milk (enough to moisten mixture
4 eggs	only)
4 teaspoons dried parsley	Fresh thyme, for garnish

Combine all ingredients except thyme, and mix thoroughly. Form into 1-inch balls. Add meatballs to sauce. Cook, uncovered, for approximately one hour over medium heat, stirring occasionally. When ready to serve, spoon into shallow serving dish and garnish with fresh thyme.

Meatballs can be prepared in advance and frozen until the day of the party. Allow an additional 30 minutes of simmering in sauce when using frozen meatballs.

If you prefer to brown meatballs before adding to sauce, place on a broiler rack and bake in oven for 10 minutes at 400°.

This recipe can be adapted to a slow cooker as follows: Simmer sauce on HIGH while preparing meatballs. Once meatballs are added to sauce, turn to LOW, cover, and cook 4–6 hours. Serves a large party.

Collected Recipes

 New Jersey rocks! The famous Les Paul invented the first solid body electric guitar in Mahwah in 1940.

Cucumber Sandwiches

2 cucumbers, sliced thin
Salt
1 (8-ounce) carton cream cheese
  with chives

1 loaf whole wheat bread, sliced

Spread cucumber slices on paper towels and sprinkle with salt. Cover with more paper towels. Let it sit for at least one hour or longer (can be kept in refrigerator).

Spread all the slices of bread with cream cheese. Place a layer of cucumbers on each slice. Put 2 slices together to make your sandwich. Cut off crusts and cut into finger sandwiches. Cover with a damp towel until ready to serve to prevent them from drying out.

Variation: Can make more attractive by adding green food coloring to cream cheese and decorating each sandwich.

A Tasting Tour Through the 8th District

Hot Pepper Jelly Appetizers

2 cups shredded Cheddar cheese
6 tablespoons (¾ stick) butter,
  chilled, chopped

1 cup flour
½ cup hot pepper jelly

Combine Cheddar cheese, butter, and flour in a food processor and process until mixture resembles coarse meal. Process for an additional 5–6 seconds or until mixture forms a ball. Chill, wrapped in plastic wrap, for 30 minutes. Shape into 2-inch balls. Arrange 1 inch apart on an ungreased baking sheet. Bake at 400° for 5 minutes.

Make a small indention on the top of each ball. Spoon one teaspoon of the hot pepper jelly into each indention. Bake for 5 minutes longer or until golden brown. Cool on the baking sheet for 2 minutes; remove to a wire rack to cool completely. Yields 24.

Beyond Peanut Butter and Jelly

Nutty-O's Snack

½ cup brown sugar, packed
½ cup dark corn syrup
¼ cup butter or margarine
½ teaspoon salt

6 cups Cheerios cereal
1 cup pecan halves, walnut halves
  or peanuts
½ cup slivered almonds

Heat oven to 325°. Brush jellyroll pan, 15½x10½x1-inch, with butter. Heat brown sugar, corn syrup, butter, and salt in 3-quart saucepan over medium heat, stirring constantly, until sugar is dissolved, about 5 minutes; remove from heat. Stir in cereal and nuts until well coated. Spread mixture in pan. Bake 15 minutes. Cool 10 minutes; loosen mixture with metal spatula. Let stand until firm, about 1 hour. Store in covered container. Makes about 8 cups.

Bread of Life

BREAD & BREAKFAST

The entire town of New Market, Maryland, is considered an historic district. The town has welcomed travelers since it was founded in 1793. In those days, the hotels lining Main Street offered a night's lodging for only 25 cents.

Biscuits

These just melt in your mouth.

6 tablespoons softened butter
2 cups flour
2 teaspoons baking powder

½ teaspoon salt
¾ cup half-and-half

Preheat oven to 450°. Put the butter in a food processor and soften. Add flour, baking powder, and salt. Slowly add half-and-half. On floured cutting board, gently pat down the dough. Using a small lip glass or round cutter, cut dough into round shapes and place on a cookie sheet. Bake 10 minutes, or until just browned. Makes 6–8 biscuits.

Note: Another version of this is to add ½ cup sharp Cheddar cheese. You may also use ½ cup sour cream and ¼ cup water in place of the milk.

Chesapeake's Bounty

Maryland Biscuits

There are various ways of beating these biscuits. One man recalls the sound of the cook beating biscuits with the nose of a hammer out on a tree stump behind the kitchen. The flat of an axe, the heel of a sadiron, the heel of your hand . . . all these are mentioned in old recipes. You must beat them until the dough blisters and is smooth-looking. You must beat them at least 30 minutes, and 45 minutes for company.

LARGE QUANTITY:
3 pounds flour
6 ounces lard
1 heaping tablespoon salt

½ teaspoon baking powder
1 pint water

SMALL QUANTITY:
3 cups flour
⅓ cup lard

½ teaspoon salt
½ cup water or milk

Blend flour and lard. Add salt and baking powder. Mix in the liquid. Beat the dough with a hammer for 30 minutes. Form into small biscuits, prick top with fork, and bake in a hot oven (500°).

A Cook's Tour of the Eastern Shore

Sweet Potato Rolls

1 cup mashed sweet potatoes
3 tablespoons butter, melted
1 package active dry yeast
1¼ cups warm water, divided
1 egg

1 teaspoon salt
4 tablespoons sugar
5 cups sifted flour
Additional melted butter

Combine sweet potatoes and butter. Dissolve the yeast in ½ cup very warm water and add to sweet potatoes. Add egg, salt, and sugar. Blend well. Add flour alternately with remaining water. Mix well. Turn onto floured board. Knead well. Place in greased bowl. Turn greased-side up. Cover with a towel and allow to rise until double in volume, about 2 hours. Roll out onto a floured board and form into desired shapes. Brush with melted butter. Place on greased cookie sheet or in greased muffin tins. Cover and let rise again until double. Bake at 425° for about 15 minutes.

TOPPING:
1 cup confectioners' sugar
3 tablespoons orange juice

1 tablespoon grated orange rind
Dash salt

Combine the powdered sugar, orange juice, orange rind, and a dash of salt and spread over rolls as soon as they come out of the oven.

Country Chic's Home Cookin

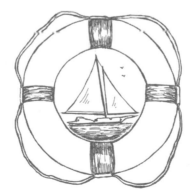

Classic Bruschetta

Use a good, dense, crusted loaf of bread, sliced thin, but thick enough to hold as finger food.

1 loaf bread   **Parmesan cheese**

Cut bread into ½-inch slices. Brush both sides with olive oil. Place on an ungreased baking sheet and bake at 425° for 5 minutes, or until crisp and lightly browned, turning once. (Can be covered and stored for up to 24 hours at room temperature.)

Spread each toast with a thin layer of Olive Paste. Top with Tomato Topping; sprinkle with Parmesan cheese. Return to baking sheet and bake at 425° for 2–3 minutes, or until cheese melts and toppings are heated through.

OLIVE PASTE:

1 cup pitted, ripe olives   **1 teaspoon olive oil**
1 teaspoon balsamic vinegar   **2 cloves garlic, minced**
1 teaspoon capers, drained

Blend the above ingredients until nearly smooth paste forms. (If desired, can be made ahead and refrigerated up to 2 days.)

TOMATO TOPPING:

2 medium red tomatoes, chopped   **½ cup chopped green pepper**
2 medium yellow tomatoes,   **½ cup chopped yellow pepper**
** chopped**   **1 tablespoon olive oil**
⅓ cup sliced green onions   **1 tablespoon chopped fresh basil**
½ cup chopped red pepper   **⅛ teaspoon black pepper**

Combine tomatoes, onions, peppers and olive oil. Add basil and black pepper. (Can be covered and chilled for up to 2 days.)

Where There's a Will...

Bannoch

Most definitely the popular bread of the house. We must have given the recipe out hundreds of times. It is so easy and tastes out of this world.

3 cups all-purpose flour
1 tablespoon baking powder
1 teaspoon baking soda
1 tablespoon sugar

1 teaspoon salt
1½ cups buttermilk
½ cup sour cream or plain yogurt

Preheat oven to 350°. Sift flour, baking powder, baking soda, sugar, and salt into mixing bowl. Repeat twice. Add buttermilk and sour cream and mix well. Form dough into ball and transfer to lightly floured surface (dough will be sticky). Roll dough into a 12x7x1-inch oval; score top carefully and transfer to ungreased baking sheet. Bake until loaf is brown, about 30 minutes. Serve warm. Makes 1 loaf.

Why Not for Breakfast?

Cheese Bread

1 loaf French or Italian bread
Soft margarine
Garlic powder
Parmesan cheese

Oregano
6 slices provolone cheese
1 large onion, thinly sliced
2 cups shredded sharp cheese

Split bread loaf in half, longways. Spread margarine on both sides of bread. On one side of bread, sprinkle garlic powder, Parmesan cheese, and oregano. Arrange slices of provolone cheese, sliced onion, and sharp cheese. Put top of loaf together, wrap in foil, and bake in oven at 350° for 15 minutes, or until warmed.

A Second Helping

 In 1785, Oliver Evans of Newport, Delaware, invented the automatic flour-milling machinery that revolutionized the industry.

Pesto

1½ cups fresh basil leaves
10 cloves garlic, peeled
⅔ cup pine nuts, roasted (or walnuts)
½ cup Romano cheese

1 Vitamin C tablet (keeps pesto nice and green)
Salt and pepper to taste
1¼ cups olive oil

Blend all in blender till mixed finely and completely. Will keep well in refrigerator. Freezes well. Put in small plastic containers, like butter tubs.

Spread on bread and place in 350° oven for 15 minutes.

Our Favorite Recipes–Book Three

Knishes I

¼ cup oil
¼ cup water
2 cups flour
½ teaspoon baking powder

Pinch of salt
2 eggs
Potato Filling

Boil together the oil and water. Mix the flour, baking powder, and salt. Make a well in the flour mixture and drop in the eggs and oil/water mixture. Mix well. Knead the dough until it is soft enough to handle. Keep well covered until ready to use. Prepare the filling. Roll the dough out thinly. Spread filling on dough. Roll jellyroll-style. Cut into 2-inch pieces, pinching the ends closed. Grease a cookie sheet with vegetable cooking spray; place pieces on the sheet. Bake 30 minutes at 350°, or until golden brown.

POTATO FILLING:
1 onion, chopped
4 tablespoons margarine

2 eggs, beaten
2 cups mashed potatoes

Sauté the onion in margarine until golden. Combine with remaining ingredients. Spread on dough.

Sealed with a Knish

Easy Banana Bread

2 cups flour
2 teaspoons cinnamon
¾ cup vegetable oil
¼ teaspoon baking powder
3 medium-size ripe bananas
1 teaspoon salt
2 teaspoons baking soda

3 eggs (or equivalent egg
  substitute), beaten
1 cup sugar
2 teaspoons vanilla extract
½ cup chopped walnuts
  (optional)
½ cup raisins (optional)

Preheat oven to 350°. Mix all ingredients (if using electric mixer, 5–7 minutes on medium speed). Pour into greased loaf pan. Bake for 40 minutes (or until you get a clean fork on testing). Cool and serve. Serves 10–12.

Cooking Through the Years

Blueberry-Banana Bread

1 cup butter, softened
2 cups sugar
4 eggs
5 medium bananas, mashed
4 cups flour, divided
2 cups blueberries

1 teaspoon baking powder
2 teaspoons baking soda
½ teaspoon salt
3 teaspoons allspice
2 teaspoons vanilla

Cream together butter and sugar. Beat in eggs, followed by mashed bananas. Mix 2 tablespoons flour with the blueberries. Stir 2 cups flour into banana mixture. Sift remaining flour with dry ingredients and fold in together with vanilla. Add berries. Spoon into 2 greased and floured 9x5-inch loaf pans. Bake in preheated 325° oven for about one hour. Yields 2 loaves. May be frozen.

Mid-Day Magic

Pumpkin Spice Bread

3½ cups unsifted flour
2½ cups sugar
2 teaspoons baking soda
1½ teaspoons salt
1 teaspoon cinnamon

1 teaspoon nutmeg
1 (1-pound) can pumpkin
1 cup corn oil
4 eggs

Grease and flour 2 (9x5x3-inch) loaf pans. In large bowl, combine first 6 ingredients and set aside. Stir together pumpkin and oil. To this add eggs, one at a time, beating well after each addition. Make a well in the center of the flour mixture. Add pumpkin mixture; stir until flour is just moistened. Pour into prepared pans. Bake at 350° for one hour or until cake tester inserted in center comes out clean. Cool in pan 10 minutes. Remove and cool on racks. Yields 2 loaves.

Winterthur's Culinary Collection

Lemon Black Walnut Bread

2 sticks sweet butter, softened,
  divided
1½ cups sugar, divided
4 eggs, separated
⅔ cup lemon juice, divided
2 tablespoons grated lemon rind
3 cups cake flour

4 teaspoons baking powder
1 cup milk
Pinch of salt
1 cup shelled, chopped black
  walnuts
¼ cup water

Preheat oven to 350°. Butter 2 (9x5x3-inch) loaf pans using 3 tablespoons butter. In mixing bowl, cream together remaining butter and 1 cup sugar. Beat in egg yolks, one at a time, then stir in ⅓ cup lemon juice, and grated rind. Combine flour with baking powder. Add ⅓ of flour mixture to the creamed butter, then add half the milk, another ⅓ flour, remaining milk and remaining flour. Do not overmix. In another bowl, beat the egg whites and salt until stiff. Fold egg whites and black walnuts gently into batter. Pour batter into prepared pans. Bake 45–50 minutes. Cool bread slightly. Remove from pans. Boil remaining ⅓ cup lemon juice, water, and ½ cup sugar together for 2 minutes. Drizzle lemon syrup over cooled loaves.

More Favorites from the Melting Pot

Strawberry Nut Bread

A year 'round favorite, Strawberry Nut Bread is easy to make with frozen strawberries, and gives a taste of summertime.

6 eggs, beaten
2 cups salad oil
3 cups sugar
2 teaspoons vanilla
4 cups frozen strawberries, thawed, mashed, not drained

6 cups flour
2 teaspoons baking soda
½ teaspoon baking powder
2 teaspoons salt
1 cup chopped walnuts or pecans

Combine eggs, oil, sugar, and vanilla. Beat well. Add strawberries. Combine dry ingredients and gradually add to strawberry mixture. Stir in nuts. Pour into 4 greased loaf pans and bake at 325° for one hour, or until pick inserted in center comes out clean. Makes 4 loaves.

The Queen Victoria® Cookbook

Cranberry Nut Bread

2 cups flour
1 cup sugar
1½ teaspoons baking powder
½ teaspoon baking soda
1 teaspoon salt
¼ cup shortening

¾ cup orange juice
1 tablespoon grated orange rind
1 egg
½ cup chopped nuts
1 cup coarsely chopped fresh
  cranberries

Sift together flour, sugar, baking powder, baking soda, and salt. Cut in shortening until like oatmeal. Add orange juice and rind with well-beaten egg. Pour all at once into dry ingredients, mixing just enough to dampen. Carefully fold in nuts and cranberries. Spoon into greased loaf pan. Bake at 350° about 1 hour. Cool and remove from pan.

The Glen Afton Cookbook

Very Berry Streusel Muffins

2 cups all-purpose flour
½ cup sugar
2 teaspoons baking powder
½ teaspoon baking soda
½ teaspoon salt
1 (8-ounce) container lemon
  yogurt

½ cup vegetable oil
1 teaspoon grated lemon zest
2 eggs
½ cup fresh raspberries (scant
  ¼ pint)
½ cup fresh blueberries (scant
  ¼ pint)

Preheat oven to 400°. Grease 12 muffin cups. In a large bowl, combine flour, sugar, baking powder, baking soda, and salt. Mix well. In a small bowl, combine yogurt, oil, lemon zest, and eggs. Mix well. Add to the flour mixture, stirring just until the dry ingredients are moistened. Gently stir in the raspberries and blueberries. Fill the prepared muffin cups.

TOPPING:
⅓ cup sugar   2 tablespoons butter
¼ cup all-purpose flour

In a small bowl, combine the sugar and flour. Using a pastry blender, or two knives, cut in the butter until the mixture is crumbly. Sprinkle the topping over the muffins and bake for 18–20 minutes, or until a wooden toothpick inserted in the center comes out clean. Turn out on a wire rack to cool. Serve warm or at room temperature.

Breakfast at Nine, Tea at Four

Pumpkin Chocolate Chip Muffins

Chocolate Chips make these irresistible.

1⅔ cups flour
1 cup sugar
1 teaspoon pumpkin pie spice
1 teaspoon cinnamon
1 teaspoon baking soda
¼ teaspoon baking powder

¼ teaspoon salt
2 large eggs
1 cup canned pumpkin
½ cup butter, melted
1 cup chocolate chips

Thoroughly mix flour, sugar, pie spice, cinnamon, baking soda, baking powder, and salt in a large bowl. Beat together eggs, pumpkin, and butter. Pour over dry ingredients and mix until just moistened. Add chocolate chips. Spoon batter evenly into greased muffin tins. Bake at 350° for 20–25 minutes. Yields 1 dozen muffins.

Capital Classics

Feta Cheese Cups

8 slices firm white bread
¼ cup melted butter (⅛ pound)
1 large egg, beaten

3 ounces cream cheese, softened
¾ cup crumbled feta cheese
　(3 ounces)

Preheat oven to 350°. Grease 24 miniature muffin cups. Using a 2-inch cookie cutter, cut the bread into rounds to fit the muffin cups. Brush one side of the bread with the melted butter and fit it into the muffin cup buttered-side-down. Combine the egg, cream cheese, and feta cheese. Drop 1 teaspoon of the cheese mixture into each muffin cup. Bake for 20 minutes, or until puffy and lightly browned. Yields 24 cheese cups.

Breakfast at Nine, Tea at Four

Sausage and Onion Squares

1 pound mild bulk sausage
1 large onion, chopped
2 cups Bisquick Baking Mix
⅔ cup milk
2 eggs, divided

2 teaspoons caraway seeds
1½ cups sour cream
¼ teaspoon salt
¼ teaspoon paprika

Cook sausage and onion until brown and onion is tender. Drain well. Combine Bisquick, milk, and 1 egg; mix well. Spread mixture in a greased 9x13x2-inch baking dish. Sprinkle with caraway seeds. Top with sausage and onion mixture. Combine sour cream, salt, and remaining egg and blend well. Pour over sausage mixture and sprinkle with paprika. Bake at 350° for 25–30 minutes. Cut into squares. Makes 4 servings.

Atlantic Highlands

Mexi-Mix Eggs

1 tablespoon margarine
2 eggs
¼ cup milk
3 tablespoons salsa (with onion
    and garlic)

1 pinch salt and pepper (optional)
1–2 tablespoons chopped green
    pepper (optional)
3 slices any cheese

Heat small frying pan with margarine. Beat eggs, milk, salsa, salt, pepper, and green pepper; pour in pan and place lid on pan. Cook for 2–3 minutes; turn and add cheese; cover and cook 2 minutes. Serve with toast.

A Taste of Heaven

 Delmar is popularized as the little town too big for one state. The community has the distinction of being located partly in Delaware and partly in Maryland—its name is a combination of the first three letters of both states. The Mason-Dixon Line also divides Delmar, which is recognized as the official beginning of the Mason-Dixon Line.

Baked Eggs in Pepper Rings

1 large green pepper
1 tablespoon butter
4 eggs
¼ teaspoon salt
⅛ teaspoon pepper
⅛ teaspoon oregano

⅛ teaspoon basil
4 tablespoons cream
4 tablespoons fresh bread crumbs
2 teaspoons Parmesan cheese
2 tablespoons butter, melted

Cut pepper into 4 rings ½-inch thick. Cook in lightly salted water for 3–5 minutes. Drain. Melt 1 tablespoon butter in a 1-quart shallow casserole in oven. Place pepper rings in casserole. Break 1 egg into each ring. Sprinkle with seasonings. Pour 1 tablespoon cream over each. Combine crumbs, Parmesan, and butter; sprinkle over. Bake at 350° for 15–20 minutes, or until eggs are set. This doubles, triples, and more for a large brunch. Can easily be prepared ahead.

Flavors of Cape Henlopen

Baked Eggs with Three Cheeses

7 eggs, beaten
1 cup milk
2 teaspoons sugar
1 pound small curd cottage cheese
4 ounces cream cheese, cubed

1 pound shredded Monterey Jack
   or muenster cheese
⅔ cup butter or margarine, melted
½ cup flour
1 teaspoon baking powder

Beat together eggs, milk, and sugar. Add cheeses and melted butter and mix well. Mix in flour and baking powder, then pour into a 3-quart baking dish sprayed with non-stick pan coating. Bake 45–50 minutes at 350°, or until knife inserted in center comes out clean. May be prepared in advance and refrigerated, covered. If put in oven directly from refrigerator, uncover, and bake up to 60 minutes. Cut into rectangles to serve. Serves 12.

The Queen Victoria® Cookbook

Stovetop Cheese Soufflé

Dynamite and impressive. Allow plenty of time to make. It holds a long time after making. A wonderful side dish.

2 tablespoons butter or margarine	1 cup milk
2 tablespoons all-purpose flour	1 cup shredded sharp cheese
½ teaspoon dry mustard	(4 ounces)
½ teaspoon salt	4 eggs, separated

Melt butter or margarine in a medium saucepan over medium heat. Stir in flour, dry mustard, and salt until mixture bubbles. Gradually stir in milk until sauce bubbles and thickens. Cook one minute longer. Stir in cheese until melted. Remove from heat. In a medium bowl, beat egg whites with electric mixer at high speed until soft peaks form; set aside.

Beat egg yolks in a large bowl. Slowly beat cheese sauce into beaten egg yolks. Fold in beaten egg whites by hand until no streaks of white remain. Pour water, 2 inches deep, into bottom of double boiler. Turn egg mixture into top of double boiler; cover. Bring water to a boil. Turn down heat until water just simmers. Without lifting cover, cook soufflé over simmering water one hour. At the end of one hour, a knife inserted in center of soufflé should come out clean. If knife does not come out clean, cook 10 minutes longer. Makes 4 servings.

Why Not for Breakfast?

Sweet Blintz Soufflé

Lower in calories and cholesterol than the traditional soufflé, but no less delicious.

Cooking spray	2 cups low-fat yogurt or sour
12 frozen blintzes (cheese, cherry	cream or combination
or blueberry or combination)	¼ cup sugar
Cinnamon sugar, for sprinkling	2 teaspoons vanilla
4 egg whites (or 3 eggs)	¼ cup orange juice

Spray a 9x13-inch pan with non-stick cooking spray. Lay blintzes in a single layer in pan. Lightly spray top of blintzes with cooking spray and sprinkle with cinnamon sugar. Then mix together the remaining ingredients and pour over blintzes. Sprinkle with additional cinnamon sugar, if desired. Bake at 350°, uncovered, for 40 minutes to 1 hour.

Simple Pleasures

Puffed Seafood Omelet

OMELET:

Butter, for pan
1 cup (2 sticks) unsalted butter
1 cup all-purpose flour
2 cups milk

8 eggs, beaten to blend
½ teaspoon salt
¼ teaspoon freshly grated nutmeg

Butter jellyroll pan; line with kitchen parchment. Butter and flour paper. Melt 1 cup butter in heavy medium-size saucepan over medium-low heat. Whisk in flour and cook 3 minutes.

Increase heat; whisk in milk and cook until thick and smooth, about 2 minutes. Remove from heat. Beat in eggs, salt, and nutmeg. Pour batter into prepared pan. Bake until omelet is puffed and golden, 20–30 minutes.

FILLING:

2 tablespoons (¼ stick) unsalted
    butter
2 tablespoons all-purpose flour
1⅓ cups heavy (whipping) cream
2 tablespoons dry sherry

¾ pound seafood (crab, shrimp,
    lobster, or any combination)
Salt
Cayenne pepper

Melt butter in heavy medium-size saucepan over medium-low heat. Whisk in flour and cook 3 minutes. Whisk in cream and boil until thick and smooth, about 2 minutes. Add sherry and boil one minute. Add seafood and heat through. Season with salt and cayenne.

Line work surface with kitchen towel. Invert omelet on to it. Remove paper from bottom of omelet. Spread omelet with filling. Starting at short end and using towel as aid, roll omelet up as for jellyroll. Transfer to platter. Slice and serve. Serves 6–8.

Why Not for Breakfast?

Frittata with Pasta, Vegetables, and Crab

½ pound capellini
⅓ cup finely chopped zucchini
⅓ cup finely chopped red or
   yellow pepper
⅓ cup finely chopped sweet onion

3 tablespoons butter
6 large eggs, whisked
½ cup grated provolone cheese
¼ cup Parmesan cheese
⅔ cup flaked crabmeat

Cook capellini al dente in boiling salted water. Drain and rinse with cold water. Sauté vegetables in melted butter. Do not overcook. Mix pasta with beaten eggs. Add vegetables, cheeses, and crab. Pour mixture into greased 9x13-inch pan. Cover with foil and bake in preheated 350° oven for ½ hour, or until frittata is golden. Serves 8.

Cooking with the Allenhurst Garden Club

Crab Frittata

Good for brunch or a light supper.

1 clove garlic, mashed
⅔ cup chopped onion
1 cup chopped zucchini
½ cup sliced mushrooms
2 tablespoons butter
1½ teaspoons salt

¼ teaspoon pepper
3 eggs
½ cup non-fat milk
½ cup grated Parmesan cheese
1 can crabmeat, drained
Parsley

Sauté vegetables in butter; add salt and pepper. Cook, covered, for 5–7 minutes. Meanwhile, beat together eggs, milk, and cheese. Combine crab, vegetables, and egg mixture in buttered casserole. Sprinkle with parsley. Bake at 350° for 20 minutes, or until firm. Serves 2–4.

Winterthur's Culinary Collection

Peanut Butter and Almond Strudel with Strawberry Glaze

6 phyllo dough sheets
1 cup melted butter
2 cups peanut butter
1 cup sliced almonds, toasted
1½ cups coconut, toasted

1 cup marshmallow spread
1 (8-ounce) jar strawberry
    preserves
1 pint fresh strawberries, cleaned
    and cut in half

Follow thawing instructions on phyllo pastry box.

When ready to assemble strudel, preheat oven to 350°. On working surface, place enough parchment paper, foil, or plastic wrap to border phyllo dough. One sheet at a time, butter phyllo dough with pastry brush, placing another sheet of dough on top. Continue until all 6 sheets have been buttered. Spread peanut butter on phyllo dough. Sprinkle toasted almonds and coconut on peanut butter. Spread marsh-mallow spread on almonds and coconut.

To roll strudel, grab corners of parchment paper, foil, or plastic base, lift, and fold several times until all dough is rolled. Brush strudel with melted butter and bake until golden and crisp to your satisfaction.

In medium saucepan, heat preserves until slightly warmed. To serve, slice 2 (1-inch) pieces of very warm strudel and put them on a serving plate. Drizzle with glaze. Place 2 strawberries on top.

Note: Fun for kids, but can be messy. Use caution, peanut butter will be hot.

PB&J USA

Bird's Nest Apple Strudel

Fantastic for a large group.

1 pound phyllo dough
3 slices firm white bread
6 medium tart apples (about
  3 pounds total), peeled, cored
  and cut into eighths
1 cup walnut pieces
1 cup sugar
1 teaspoon ground cinnamon

½ teaspoon freshly ground
  nutmeg
2 tablespoons cornstarch
1 cup golden raisins
2 sticks unsalted butter
Confectioners' sugar, for
  sprinkling
Whipped cream

Remove frozen phyllo dough from the box but leave it in the plastic wrapper. Thaw until you can easily remove the plastic, about 30 minutes. The outer sheets will be soft, but the interior ones will still be firm. When ready to assemble the strudel, cut the dough into 6 equal sections. Stack 2 or 3 at a time upright in the large feed tube of a food processor, using firm pressure, process with the thick (6mm) slicing disc (see Note). Transfer the shreds to 2 large mixing bowls.

Preheat oven to 300°. Butter a 9x13x2-inch glass baking dish. Toast the bread in the oven just until dry, about 10 minutes. Let cool, then process with the metal blade of food processor until finely chopped, about 30 seconds. Reserve. Raise the oven temperature to 350°.

Process the apples in 4 batches until coarsely chopped, 4–6 pulses for each batch. Set aside. Process the walnuts until coarsely chopped, 6–8 pulses. Combine sugar, cinnamon, nutmeg, cornstarch, and bread crumbs. Add raisins, chopped apples, and walnuts. Set the mixture aside.

Melt 1 stick butter and slowly pour it over the phyllo in one mixing bowl, tossing gently. Repeat with remaining butter and second bowl of phyllo. Distribute half the phyllo shreds in an even layer in the baking dish. Spread the apple-nut mixture over them. Distribute the remaining phyllo on top. Cover loosely with aluminum foil and bake for 30 minutes. Remove foil and bake until phyllo is golden and crispy, 25–30 minutes. Remove strudel from oven and let cool. Cut into squares and dust with sifted confectioners' sugar. Serve warm or cool with whipped cream. Serves 12–20.

Note: If you do not have a thick (6mm) slicing disk, you may cut the phyllo dough (at room temperature) with a sharp knife into ¼-inch (6mm) wide strips.

Why Not for Breakfast?

Sour Cream Coffee Cake

½ pound butter or margarine
2 cups sugar
4 eggs
2 teaspoons vanilla

1 pint sour cream
4 cups sifted flour
2 teaspoons baking powder
2 teaspoons baking soda

FILLING:
1 teaspoon cinnamon
¼ cup brown sugar

½ cup finely chopped nuts
½ cup granulated sugar

Cream butter, sugar, eggs, and vanilla together. Add sour cream, flour, baking powder, and baking soda. Mix Filling ingredients. Pour ½ the batter into a greased 9- or 10-inch Bundt pan. Add ½ the filling and swirl with knife. Repeat with remaining batter and filling. Bake at 350° for 1 hour, or a little longer.

Jaycee Cookin'

Austrian Coffee Cake

1 cup butter or margarine
2 cups sugar
6 eggs, separated
1½ cups all-purpose flour,
   sifted

½ teaspoon salt
2 teaspoons baking powder
6 tablespoons milk
1 teaspoon vanilla
Confectioners' sugar

Cream butter, add sugar slowly while creaming. Beat in egg yolks (one at a time). Mix and sift flour, salt, and baking powder. Combine milk and flavoring. Add flour mixture and milk alternately to butter mixture, stirring gently but thoroughly. Beat egg whites until stiff, but not dry. Fold thoroughly into batter. Spoon into well greased tube pan. Bake at 350° 1 hour and 10 minutes (or until cake tests done). Cool 10 minutes before inverting. Sprinkle with confectioners' sugar.

Cooking Through the Years

Anne's Blueberry Coffeecake

4 cups flour
1½ cups sugar
1 tablespoon plus 2 teaspoons
   baking powder
1½ teaspoons salt

1½ cups milk
2 eggs
½ cup shortening
4 cups fresh or frozen blueberries
Topping and Glaze

Mix flour, sugar, baking powder, salt, milk, eggs, and shortening in large bowl until moistened; beat vigorously for one minute. Carefully stir in blueberries. Spread batter in greased 9x13-inch pan. Sprinkle with Topping. Bake at 350° for 45–50 minutes, or until wooden toothpick inserted in center comes out clean. Cool slightly; drizzle Glaze on top.

TOPPING:

1 cup sugar
⅔ cup flour

1 teaspoon cinnamon
½ cup soft butter

Combine all ingredients; sprinkle over batter.

GLAZE:

2 cups powdered sugar
¼ cup butter, softened

1 teaspoon vanilla
Milk

Mix sugar, butter, and vanilla. Add milk, about 2 tablespoons at a time, until glaze is the consistency to drizzle over coffeecake.

A Taste of GBMC

Eggless Banana Pancakes

½ cup rolled oats
½ cup whole wheat pastry flour
  or unbleached white flour
½ cup cornmeal (white or yellow)
1 tablespoon baking powder

1½ cups water
2 large ripe bananas, sliced or
  mashed
2 teaspoons oil

Mix all the ingredients together in a bowl. Use about ¼ cup of batter per pancake, poured into lightly oiled preheated frying pan. Fry over low heat on one side until light brown, then flip over and fry on the other side until done. Serves 2.

Variations: Add chopped apples, raisins, or blueberries to the batter before frying.

Total Calories Per Serving: 482; Fat 8g; Total fat of Daily Value 12%; Prot 12g; Iron 4mg; Carbo 97g; Cal 306mg; Dietary fiber 9g.

Meatless Meals for Working People

Apple Puffed Pancake

6 eggs
1½ cups milk
1 cup flour
3 tablespoons sugar
1 teaspoon vanilla
½ teaspoon salt

¼ teaspoon cinnamon
¼ pound (1 stick) butter
  or margarine
2 apples, peeled and thinly sliced
2–3 tablespoons brown sugar

Preheat oven to 425°. In a blender or large bowl, mix eggs, milk, flour, sugar, vanilla, salt, and cinnamon until blended. If using a mixer, batter will remain slightly lumpy. Melt butter in a 12-inch fluted porcelain quiche dish or 9x13-inch baking dish in oven. Add apple slices to baking dish. Return to oven and immediately pour batter over apples. Sprinkle with brown sugar. Bake in middle of oven 20 minutes, or until puffed and brown. Serve immediately. Makes 6–8 servings.

The Great Gourmet

Kaiserschmarren
(The Emperor's Pancakes)

1 cup flour
2 tablespoons sugar, divided
1 teaspoon baking powder
2 eggs, beaten
1 cup milk

4 tablespoons butter
2 apples, peeled and sliced
½ teaspoon cinnamon
3 tablespoons confectioners' sugar

Combine flour, 1 tablespoon sugar, and baking powder into a large bowl. Combine eggs and milk; pour into dry ingredients and stir well. Melt butter in a large skillet. Sauté apple slices in butter until lightly browned. Mix cinnamon and sugar; sprinkle over apples. Pour all the pancake batter over the apples and cook until lightly browned on bottom, then turn over with a spatula, as for scrambled eggs. Continue cooking until lightly browned on other side. Remove to a serving platter and sprinkle with confectioners' sugar. Serves 4.

Note: Sauté means to cook quickly in a small amount of fat over medium-high heat.

Good Things to Eat

Cape May French Toast Casserole

1 cup brown sugar
1 stick butter (½ cup)
2 tablespoons corn syrup
2 tart apples, peeled and sliced
1 loaf French bread, cut into
   ¾-inch slices

5 eggs, beaten
1½ cups milk
1 teaspoon vanilla

Cook sugar, butter, and corn syrup until syrupy. Pour into 9x13-inch dish. Spread apple slices on syrup. Place bread on apples. Whisk together eggs, milk, and vanilla. Pour over bread. Cover and refrigerate overnight.

Heat oven to 350°. Bake, uncovered, for 30–40 minutes. Serve with your choice of syrup. Makes 8 servings.

Cooking with the Allenhurst Garden Club

Stuffed Baked French Toast

A spectacular, puffy dish right when it comes out of the oven, this sinks as it stands, but still tastes delicious. This recipe is another way to offer French Toast without having to stand over the griddle all morning. A popular favorite of our guests, this recipe is one of our most requested.

20–24 slices bread, any variety
   (white, raisin, cinnamon or egg
   are good)
6 eggs

4 cups half-and-half
2 teaspoons vanilla
1 cup sugar
Dash nutmeg

FILLING:
16 ounces cream cheese, softened
1 teaspoon vanilla
2 eggs

½ cup sugar
Applesauce, sliced fresh fruit or
   berries (optional)

Trim crusts from bread. Spray a 3-quart baking dish with non-stick pan coating. Arrange half bread in pan so that entire bottom is covered. In a separate bowl, mix eggs, half-and-half, vanilla, and sugar. Pour half of this liquid over bread. In a separate bowl, combine Filling ingredients, except optional fruits, together until creamy. Pour Filling over moistened bread, then layer with fruit, if desired. Arrange other half of bread over top of Filling and pour rest of egg mixture over top. Sprinkle top with a dash of nutmeg. Cover and let stand in refrigerator overnight.

Bake in a preheated 350° oven for 60 minutes. Let stand 10 minutes before cutting into 12 rectangles to serve. Serve with warmed maple or fruit syrup or fresh fruits of the season, if desired.

The Queen Victoria® Cookbook

Eggnog French Toast with Cranberry Syrup

The French toast must be prepared the night before, then baked just before serving time.

4 ounces softened cream cheese
¼ cup dried cranberries (1 ounce)
1 (1-pound) loaf French bread,
    cut into 12–14 (1-inch) slices
2½ cups half-and-half
6 tablespoons melted butter

8 eggs
¼ teaspoon ground nutmeg
¼ cup sugar
1 teaspoon vanilla
1 teaspoon rum extract

Grease a 9x13x2-inch glass baking dish. In a food processor, combine cream cheese and cranberries. Cut part way through each slice of bread to form a pocket. Fill with cheese mixture and arrange in the baking dish.

In a large bowl, whisk half-and-half, butter, eggs, nutmeg, sugar, vanilla, and rum extract. Pour evenly over bread slices. Cover and refrigerate for at least 8 hours, or overnight; then preheat the oven to 350° and bake for 30 minutes, or until golden brown.

CRANBERRY SYRUP:

1 cup frozen raspberry-cranberry
    juice concentrate, thawed
1 cup whole-berry cranberry
    sauce

⅓ cup sugar
2 tablespoons cornstarch

Combine all the ingredients in a small saucepan. Whisk over medium-low heat until dissolved and slightly thickened. Separate the French Toast slices with a knife and serve immediately with Cranberry Syrup.

Breakfast at Nine, Tea at Four

 One day, Elizabeth Lee, one of the few cranberry growers living in New Egypt, New Jersey, decided to boil some damaged berries instead of throwing them away. She liked the tasty jelly so much she started a business selling "Bog Sweet Cranberry Sauce." That was the beginning of the Ocean Spray company that still sells cranberry products today.

Blueberry-Stuffed French Toast

12 slices of homemade-type white bread, crusts discarded and bread cut into 1-inch cubes
2 (8-ounce) packages cold cream cheese, cut into 1-inch cubes
1 cup blueberries, picked over and rinsed
12 large eggs
⅓ cup maple syrup
2 cups milk

Arrange half the bread cubes in a buttered 9x13-inch glass baking dish, scatter cream cheese over bread, and sprinkle blueberries over cream cheese. Arrange remaining bread cubes over blueberries. In a large bowl, whisk together eggs, syrup, and milk, and pour egg mixture evenly over bread mixture; chill, covered, overnight. Bake, covered with foil, in the middle of a preheated 350° oven for 30 minutes; remove foil and bake 30 minutes more, or until puffed and golden.

SAUCE:

1 cup sugar
2 tablespoons cornstarch
1 cup water
1 cup blueberries, picked over and rinsed
1 tablespoon unsalted butter

In a small saucepan stir together sugar, cornstarch, and water and cook over moderately-high heat, stirring occasionally, for 5 minutes, or until thickened.

Stir in blueberries and simmer, stirring occasionally, for 10 minutes or until the berries have burst. Add butter and stir until butter has melted. Serve with French Toast. Makes 6–8 servings.

Around the Table

Blueberry Grunt

During New Jersey blueberry season, this is our number one fruit treat.

BLUEBERRIES:

½ cup sugar
½ cup water
2 tablespoons lemon juice

½ teaspoon allspice
2 pints blueberries

Combine sugar, water, lemon juice, and allspice in large frying pan and bring to a boil. Add blueberries and reduce to bare simmer.

DUMPLINGS:

1 egg
⅓ cup heavy cream
⅔ cup all-purpose flour

2 tablespoons sugar
1 teaspoon baking powder
¼ teaspoon salt

Beat egg with cream in small bowl, whisk in remaining ingredients to make heavy batter. Drop rounded tablespoons of batter over blueberries. Cover and simmer gently without peeking for 15 minutes. Uncover and test for doneness. Grunts should have risen like mushroom caps and blueberries reduced to a sauce. Test with wooden toothpick. If it does not come out clean, cover and cook another 5 minutes. Serves 6.

Why Not For Breakfast?

SOUPS

The USS Constellation *was the last all sail warship built by the U.S. Navy. It is the only Civil War era vessel still afloat, and is now preserved as a museum at Baltimore's Inner Harbor.*

Chesapeake Bouillabaisse

¼ cup olive oil
4 cups thinly sliced potatoes
2 cups crushed tomatoes
2 cloves garlic, minced
½ cup minced shallots or onion
2 cups fish stock
2 teaspoons parsley, divided

1 tablespoon salt
1 teaspoon Old Bay Seasoning
1 pound rockfish fillets, chunked
1 pound flounder or seabass,
  chunked
1 pound lump crabmeat

Place olive oil in stock pot. Add potatoes and tomatoes and toss. Add garlic and shallots; sauté until soft. Add preheated fish stock, 1 teaspoon parsley, salt, and Old Bay. Simmer. Place fish and crab on top and add the rest of the parsley. Simmer 10–15 minutes and serve.

Note: To make fish stock, boil 2 cups water, fish trimmings, and 1 teaspoon salt; strain.

Recipes from the Skipjack Martha Lewis

Crab and Asparagus Soup

½ cup margarine
½ cup flour
8 cups skim milk
2 tablespoons finely chopped
  onion
2 teaspoons instant chicken
  bouillon

½ teaspoon pepper
1 teaspoon salt
2 teaspoons parsley flakes
10 ounces frozen asparagus,
  cut in thirds
1 pound Maryland crabmeat,
  cartilage removed

Melt margarine in large saucepan over medium heat. Gradually blend in flour. Stir in milk. Add onion, bouillon, seasonings, and parsley. Continue stirring until mixture thickens slightly. Add asparagus and cook over medium-low heat for 20–30 minutes, stirring often. Add crabmeat and cook over medium heat for approximately 5 minutes. Serve hot. Yields 6 servings.

Gardeners in the Kitchen

South River Club Crab Soup

2 tablespoons butter
1½ tablespoons flour
2½ cups milk
1 teaspoon salt
¼ teaspoon black pepper
⅛ teaspoon red pepper

1 pound crabmeat
1 cup cream
2 hard-boiled eggs
Sherry to taste (about a wine
   glass)

Melt butter and stir in flour; add milk, salt, black and red pepper. Stir until well-heated and thickened. Add crabmeat and cream. Heat well. Add eggs which have been pressed through a sieve, then sherry. Serves 4.

Maryland's Way

Indian Crab Soup

4 tablespoons butter
½ cup finely chopped onion
1 clove garlic, minced
1 medium apple, peeled and diced
2 teaspoons curry powder
3 tablespoons flour
1 medium tomato, peeled and
   chopped

3 cups chicken broth
Salt and pepper to taste
½ pound crabmeat
½ cup heavy cream
Dash of Tabasco sauce
Sour cream

Melt butter and add onion, cooking until transparent. Stir in garlic and apple. Sprinkle with curry and flour. Add tomato and chicken broth. Whisk. When thickened and smooth, add salt and pepper and crabmeat, and simmer 10 minutes. Add cream and bring to a boil. Add Tabasco sauce. Garnish with sour cream. Serves 6.

Winterthur's Culinary Collection

 Mmm, mmm good! Campbell's Soup originated from the first "condensed" soup cooked and canned in Camden County, New Jersey in 1897.

Crab and Corn Bisque

½ cup chopped celery
½ cup chopped green onions
¼ cup chopped green pepper
    (optional)
½ cup butter or margarine
2 (10¾-ounce) cans cream of
    potato soup, undiluted
1 (17-ounce) can cream-style corn
1½ cups half-and-half
1½ cups milk

2 bay leaves
1 teaspoon dried whole thyme
1 teaspoon garlic powder
¼ teaspoon white pepper
Dash of hot sauce
¼ teaspoon white pepper
¼ teaspoon Old Bay Seasoning
1 pound crabmeat, or ½ pound
    shrimp and ½ pound crab
Chopped parsley

Sauté celery, green onions, and green pepper in butter in Dutch oven. Add soup, corn, half-and-half, milk, bay leaves, thyme, garlic powder, white pepper, hot sauce and seasoning; cook until thoroughly heated. Gently stir in crabmeat and heat thoroughly. Discard bay leaves and garnish with parsley.

Bountiful Blessings

Cream of Crab Soup

1 pound crabmeat
1 vegetable bouillon cube
1 cup boiling water
¼ cup chopped onion
¼ cup margarine or butter
2 tablespoons flour

1 teaspoon celery salt
⅛ teaspoon pepper
1 quart milk
Few drops hot sauce
Parsley flakes (garnish)

Remove cartilage from crab. Dissolve bouillon in water. In 4-quart saucepan, cook onion in margarine until tender. Blend in flour and seasonings. Add milk and bouillon gradually. Cook over medium heat; stir constantly until mixture thickens enough to coat spoon. Add crabmeat and hot sauce; do not boil. Garnish with parsley before serving.

Note: Soup improves upon standing, so it is good to prepare ahead. Cool to room temperature, refrigerate until ready to use. Reheat over very low heat; stir often until hot, but do not boil.

A Taste of Catholicism

Fish Chowder, Jersey Shore

1½–2 pounds Jersey Shore fish
   fillets
Cold salted water
2 ounces salted pork (or bacon)
1 large onion, chopped fine
8 medium potatoes, diced
2 cups boiling water

Salt and pepper to taste
1 quart milk, scalded
2 tablespoons butter
1 cup oyster or other crackers,
   crumbled
1 small can corn (optional)

Place fish in saucepan; cover with cold salty water. Bring to boil and boil for 5 minutes. Save stock. Remove any skin on the fish. Fry the salt pork (or bacon) until fat is rendered. Remove pork and drain on paper towels. Sauté onion in fat; add potatoes and boiling water. Boil for 5 minutes. Add fish and reserved stock. Simmer another 15 minutes. Check potatoes for doneness. Season with salt and pepper. Add milk, butter, and crackers. (In Belford, the cooks always added a small can of corn.) Makes 4 servings.

Atlantic Highlands

Seafood Chowder

6 tablespoons butter
6 tablespoons flour
1½ cups milk
½ cup dry sherry
8 drops Worcestershire sauce
½ teaspoon pepper

¼ cup chopped leeks (or green
   onions)
1 cup sliced fresh mushrooms
3 cups cooked seafood (shrimp,
   scallops, clams, crab)

In a heavy-gauge saucepan, melt butter. Mix in flour and slowly add milk. Stir frequently to keep lump-free. Cook over medium heat until liquid boils and becomes thickened. Add sherry, Worcestershire, and pepper. Simmer for 2 minutes. In another pan, sauté leeks and mushrooms. Add to liquid. Add cooked seafood and heat until warmed. Serve 4–6.

Cape May Fare

Atlantic Coast Fish Chowder

2 tablespoons butter or margarine
1 large onion, diced
½ cup diced celery
1 garlic clove, minced
2 cups water
2 cups peeled, diced potatoes,
  about 2 medium
2 teaspoons salt
1 teaspoon lemon juice

¾ teaspoon dry dill weed
¼ teaspoon ground pepper
1 pound cod or scrod fillets, cut
  into 1-inch pieces
1 (8½-ounce) can whole kernel
  corn, drained
2 cups milk or light cream
2 teaspoons cornstarch
Chopped fresh parsley for garnish

In Dutch oven or large saucepan, melt butter over medium heat. Stir in onion, celery, and garlic. Cook 5 minutes, stirring often. Add water, potatoes, salt, lemon juice, dill weed, and pepper; bring to a boil. Reduce heat to low. Cover and simmer 10–15 minutes, until potatoes are almost tender. Add fish, cover, and cook 5–10 minutes longer until fish flakes easily. Stir in corn; heat through. In cup, blend milk and cornstarch until smooth; stir into soup. Increase heat to medium and bring to a boil; boil one minute until soup thickens, stirring constantly. To serve, garnish with fresh parsley or fresh dill weed. Makes 4–6 servings.

Cooking with the Allenhurst Garden Club

Soft Shell Clam Chowder

1 pint fresh shucked soft shell
  clams (save liquor)
1 cup chopped celery
½ cup chopped onion
½ cup chopped green pepper
¼ cup melted fat (or oil)
1 cup clam liquor and water
1 cup diced potatoes

1 teaspoon salt
½ teaspoon Worcestershire sauce
¼ teaspoon garlic salt
¼ teaspoon thyme
1 small bay leaf
Dash of pepper
1 (28-ounce) can tomatoes

Drain clams, reserving liquor. Chop clams. Cook celery, onion, and green pepper in fat until tender. Add clam liquor and potatoes and seasonings. Cover and bring to the boiling point. Reduce heat and simmer for 15 minutes or until potatoes are tender. Break up tomatoes with a fork. Add tomatoes and clams to vegetable mixture. Simmer for 5 minutes longer or until heated. Serves 6.

A Family Tradition

Quahog "Chowdah"

½ pound butter
1 cup scallops
3 cups white corn
1 cup diced onion
1 cup diced celery
1 pound red potatoes, diced

1 teaspoon thyme
¼ cup parsley
1 quart clam juice
3 cups shucked top neck clams
3 ounces Worcestershire sauce
1 cup heavy cream

Melt butter in large pan and lightly sauté scallops, corn, onion, celery, potatoes, thyme, and parsley. Add juice and bring to a boil. Lower heat and simmer 15 minutes. Add clams and Worcestershire sauce and simmer for 5 minutes. Remove from heat and add cream. Serves 4.

Recipe from Chef/Owner David Twining, Nantuckets, Fenwick Isle, Delaware

Coastal Cuisine

Delmarva Style Clam Chowder

3 ounces bacon, diced
½ cup diced celery
½ cup diced onions
1 tiny jalapeño pepper, diced
1 tablespoon flour
1½ cups clam broth
1½ cups water
2 teaspoons clam base
2 teaspoons white pepper

½ teaspoon rosemary
1 teaspoon thyme
2 dashes garlic powder
2 teaspoons Tabasco sauce
2 small or 1 large potato, cooked
    and diced
2 ounces diced pimentos
2 ounces canned clams, strained
1 cup heavy cream

Sauté bacon until ¾ cooked. Add celery, onion, and jalapeño; sauté just until soft. Add flour; reduce heat and cook about 10 minutes. Add clam broth, water, and clam base; stir well. Bring to a boil, then reduce heat to low again and add all spices, Tabasco, potatoes, pimentos, and clams; simmer for 20 minutes. Remove from heat and stir in the heavy cream. Serves 4.

Come, Dine With Us!

Corn Chowder

¼ pound salt pork, finely minced
   in processor
4 cups corn, cut from cob
1½ cups thinly sliced celery
2 cups thinly sliced onions
5 potatoes, pared and cut into
   ½-inch cubes
¼ teaspoon baking soda
1 teaspoon sugar

1 teaspoon Worcestershire sauce
4 cups chicken broth
1 cup heavy cream
1 cup light cream
3 cups half-and-half or milk
Salt to taste
Pepper to taste
Chopped parsley

In a large Dutch oven over medium heat, brown the salt pork lightly. Add corn, celery, onions, and potatoes. Sauté 8–10 minutes, stirring occasionally. Add soda, sugar, Worcestershire, and chicken broth. Bring to a boil, then turn to a low heat. Simmer until potatoes are tender. Add heavy cream, light cream, and the half-and-half or milk; do not boil. Salt and pepper to taste. Serve in warmed soup bowls. Garnish with chopped parsley. Serves 8–10.

Conducting in the Kitchen

Corn Chowder

1 onion, chopped
1 tablespoon oil
2 cups water
2 stalks celery, chopped
2 carrots, chopped
2 (17-ounce) cans vegan
   creamed corn

1 cup soy milk
1 potato, chopped
1½ teaspoons garlic powder
¼ teaspoon nutmeg
Salt and pepper to taste

Sauté onion in oil over medium-high heat until soft. Add water and chopped celery and carrots. Cook 10 minutes. Add creamed corn, soy milk, chopped potato, and spices. Continue cooking for another 10 minutes. Serve hot. Serves 5.

Total calories per serving: 166; Total fat: 8% of daily value; Fat 5g; Prot 5g; Carbo 30g; Cal 40mg; Iron 1mg; Sod 315mg; Fiber 4g.

Simply Vegan

One Pot Beef Stew

2 pounds stew meat
Flour
2–3 tablespoons oil
2 medium onions, chopped

6–7 potatoes, chopped
4 carrots, chopped
2 (8-ounce) cans beef broth

Coat meat with flour. Brown meat in oil in pot. Add onions and cook until tender. Add potatoes, carrots, and beef broth; cover. Cook over medium heat until meat is tender. If more water is needed, add some. Time varies depending on pot size.

Out of the Frying Pan Into the Fire!!!

White Chili

2 pounds boneless chicken breasts, cooked and diced into ½-inch cubes
1 tablespoon olive oil
2 medium onions, chopped
4 garlic cloves, minced
2 (4-ounce) cans chopped mild chiles
2 teaspoons cumin

¼ teaspoon cayenne
3 pounds cooked Great Northern beans (canned)
4 cups chicken stock or canned broth
20 ounces Monterey Jack cheese, divided
Sour cream (optional)
Chopped jalapeños (optional)

Cook and cube chicken; save stock. In same pan, when chicken is done, add oil and sauté onions. Stir in garlic, chiles, and spices. Add chicken, beans, stock, and 12 ounces of the cheese. Simmer for 15 minutes. Ladle into big bowls and top with remaining cheese. Serve with sour cream and chopped jalapeños, if desired.

A Taste of GBMC

Barratt's Chapel in Kent County, Delaware, is known as the Cradle of Methodism. It was built in 1780 and is the oldest surviving church built by and for Methodists in the United States.

Market Soup

Flavor improves with age and is best made the day before.

Bouquet Garni*
1 (15-ounce) can Great Northern
  beans, or more, if desired
3 quarts water
1 (28-ounce) can tomatoes,
  chopped
2 cups chopped celery
2 cups chopped onions

2 garlic cloves, minced
1 pound smoked sausage, diced
2 boneless, skinless chicken
  breasts, cubed, uncooked
1 ham hock
½ cup red wine (optional)
Salt to taste
Tabasco to taste

Place all ingredients except salt and Tabasco in a stockpot and boil gently, uncovered, for 3–4 hours. Stir occasionally and skim off fat if necessary. Add more water if soup appears too thick. Add salt and Tabasco. Remove Bouquet Garni. Serve with rice.

*Bouquet Garni: Combination of 2 sprigs fresh parsley, 1 bay leaf, 1 sprig fresh thyme, and 1 sprig tarragon. Wrap parsley around other herbs and tie securely with string. Can be put in a cheesecloth bag and tied.

Where There's a Will...

Beer Cheese Soup

¾ cup finely chopped carrots
½ cup finely chopped celery
¼ cup finely chopped onion
½ cup butter or margarine
1 cup Bisquick Baking Mix
½ teaspoon paprika
⅛ teaspoon pepper
⅛ teaspoon ground red pepper

3 (10-ounce) cans undiluted
  chicken broth
2 cups half-and-half (low-fat milk
  may be substituted)
2 cups shredded sharp Cheddar
  cheese
4–8 ounces beer

In a skillet, cook the chopped vegetables in butter until soft. Stir in the baking mix, paprika, and black and red pepper. Gradually stir in the chicken broth. Heat to boiling over medium heat, stirring constantly. Boil and stir 1 minute; reduce heat and gradually stir in the half-and-half, cheese, and beer. Cook gently, stirring until cheese is melted.

Cooking Along the Susquehanna

Chicken Noodle Soup

HOMEMADE NOODLES:

1 egg, slightly beaten
½ egg shell of water

½ teaspoon salt
All-purpose flour

In a small bowl, slightly beat egg. Add water and salt. Add flour, a little at a time, mixing thoroughly. When the dough holds together, roll out on a floured cloth very thin. Let set until it is almost dry. Roll up like a jellyroll and slice very thin. Separate all the dough and let set until ready to put in the soup.

SOUP:

⅓ cup chicken soup base
1 gallon water
1 medium onion, chopped
2 stalks celery, chopped
2 medium carrots, cut up
1 large chicken breast

1 bay leaf
1 tablespoon parsley
½ teaspoon celery seed
½ teaspoon thyme
1 tablespoon salt

Combine all the above ingredients. Bring to a boil and turn down heat to simmer and cook for 1–2 hours. Remove chicken breast and cut in small pieces. Return to pot and simmer for another hour. Add homemade noodles that have been dried and cut up. Cook for another hour.

Note: You can use ready-made noodles instead of making your own.

Favorite Recipes Home-Style

French Onion Soup

10 medium onions, sliced
¼ cup melted butter
¼ cup sherry
2 (12-ounce) cans beer
5 cups water
2 tablespoons Worcestershire
2 cloves garlic, minced
1 teaspoon salt and pepper
½ teaspoon dill weed

⅛ teaspoon marjoram
3 tablespoons parsley
9 beef-flavored bouillon cubes
½ teaspoon dry mustard
½ teaspoon celery seeds
1 bay leaf
2 cups croutons
2 cups shredded Swiss cheese

Separate onions into rings; cook in butter 25–30 minutes. Add sherry to onions and cook 5 minutes. Add remaining ingredients except croutons and cheese and bring to a boil. Cover, reduce heat, and simmer 1 hour. Remove bay leaf. Ladle into bowls; top with 2 tablespoons croutons. Sprinkle cheese over croutons. Yields 4 quarts.

Jaycee Cookin'

Mexican Tortilla Soup

1 tablespoon vegetable oil
1 cup chopped red onion
1 red bell pepper, chopped
2 cloves garlic, minced
2 boneless, skinless chicken
　breasts
1 teaspoon cumin

7 cups chicken stock
1 (9-ounce) package frozen corn,
　thawed
Tortilla chips, broken
1 cup shredded Monterey Jack
　cheese
Sour cream

In a large soup pot, heat the oil, then sauté the red onion, red pepper, and garlic until slightly softened. Add the chicken breasts, sauté 4–5 minutes each side until just cooked through. Remove chicken and put to one side to cool. Add cumin and broth to the pot and heat until simmering. Add corn and simmer for 10 minutes. Shred chicken with a fork and return to the soup pot; simmer 1 minute. Place a handful of tortilla chips in each bowl, add a sprinkle of cheese, ladle in the soup, and top with a dollop of sour cream.

Around the Table

Tortilla Soup

Even better reheated the next day.

1 small onion, chopped
1 (4-ounce) can chopped green
　chiles
4 cloves garlic, crushed
2 tablespoons olive oil
1 cup peeled, chopped tomatoes
1 can beef broth
1 can chicken broth
1½ cups water
1½ cups tomato juice

1 teaspoon ground cumin
1 teaspoon chili powder
1 teaspoon salt
⅛ teaspoon pepper
2 teaspoons Worcestershire
1 tablespoon A.1. Sauce
3 corn tortillas, cut in ½-inch
　strips
¼ cup shredded Cheddar

Sauté onion, chiles, and garlic in oil until soft. Add tomatoes, broths, water, tomato juice, cumin, chili powder, salt, pepper, Worcestershire, and A.1. Bring to boil; lower heat and simmer, covered, for one hour. Add tortillas and cheese; simmer 10 minutes longer.

Lambertville Community Cookbook

Carrot Soup II

2 tablespoons butter or margarine
½ cup roughly chopped onions
1 pound carrots, peeled, trimmed
  and cut in rounds
1 pound potatoes, peeled and
  cubed
6 cups chicken broth
1 bay leaf

1 stalk celery, chopped
2 sprigs parsley
½ teaspoon thyme
1 cup cream + 1 cup milk
  (or 2 cups milk)
½ teaspoon sugar
Salt and pepper to taste
Dash Tabasco

Melt butter; add onions and cook until limp. Add carrots and potatoes and cook until coated with butter. Add broth, bay leaf, celery, parsley, and thyme. Bring to boil and cook, uncovered, until carrots are tender, about 20 minutes. Remove bay leaf and parsley, and purée the mixture in several batches. Return to pot and add cream and/or milk, sugar, and remaining seasonings. Can be served hot or cold. May be frozen.

Mid-Day Magic

Lentil Soup

½ pound lentils
1 medium onion
1 clove garlic
2 stalks celery
¼ cup olive oil
2 quarts water

Salt and pepper to taste
Chopped parsley to taste
¼ pound spaghetti or other small
  pasta
Grated Italian cheese

Wash lentils. Chop onion, garlic, and celery. Sauté in oil in saucepan until lightly browned. Add lentils and water. Add salt, pepper, and parsley. Cook until lentils are tender, about 1½ hours. Break spaghetti into small pieces or use small pasta. Cook with lentils on very low heat until tender. Serve with grated Italian cheese.

Note: If you have leftover lentil soup and it's dry, or you would like, cook some frozen chopped spinach and mix together.

La Cucina Casalinga

Italian Wedding Soup

2 tablespoons olive oil
2–3 cloves fresh garlic
6–8 cups chicken stock or canned
  broth
1 box frozen spinach, broken into
  2-inch pieces, or fresh spinach
  or escarole
Approximately 6 ounces cheese
  tortellini (fresh or frozen)

Approximately 1¼ cups slivered
  cooked breast of chicken
2 teaspoons chopped parsley
Salt and freshly ground pepper
Grated Parmesan or Romano
  cheese

Heat olive oil and garlic until slightly brown. Add chicken stock to garlic and bring to a boil. Strain, if desired. Add spinach and cook approximately 10 minutes. Add tortellini and cook approximately 10–12 minutes. Add slivered chicken and heat thoroughly. Add parsley and salt and pepper the last 2 minutes of cooking. Serve with Parmesan or Romano cheese.

La Cucina Casalinga

Sweet Red Pepper Soup

2 tablespoons unsalted butter
2 large onions, chopped
2 medium carrots, peeled and
  sliced
6 cups chicken stock
2½ pounds sweet red peppers,
  chopped

1 cup skim milk
Salt and pepper to taste
¼ teaspoon thyme
Sour cream or yogurt, for garnish

Melt butter in large saucepan and sauté onions over low heat until soft. Add carrots and chicken stock and bring to a boil. Reduce heat and simmer for 20 minutes. Add chopped red peppers and cook for 20 minutes, until peppers are soft. Remove from heat and add milk, salt, pepper, and thyme. When soup is cool, purée in batches in blender or food processor. To serve, reheat, but do not boil. Add a dollop of sour cream or yogurt, if desired. Yields 6 adult servings.

Best of Friends

Strawberry Soup

1 pint fresh strawberries, hulled
   (reserve 4 for garnish)
2 cups plain, low-fat yogurt
¾ cup sour cream

¼ cup honey
1 ounce strawberry schnapps
Sour cream, for garnish

Combine all ingredients in a blender and purée until smooth. Refrigerate at least 1 hour before serving. Garnish each bowl with a dollop of sour cream and a strawberry.

Cooking Secrets

SALADS

Lewes, Delaware, is situated where the Delaware Bay and Atlantic Ocean meet at Cape Henlopen. Founded as a whaling station by Dutch settlers in 1631, Lewes also holds the distinction of being "the first town in the first state."

Avocado Crab Salad

1 head lettuce
2 ripe avocados
½ pound crabmeat (imitation
  works well, too)
2 apples

⅓ cup mayonnaise
1 teaspoon catsup
Pinch of paprika
Juice of ½ lemon

Separate the leaves of the lettuce; wash and let drain. Remove skins of avocado and cut into segments. Cut the crabmeat into chunks, if necessary. Peel and dice apples. Mix mayonnaise, catsup, paprika, and lemon juice. Toss salad with dressing. Place on lettuce leaves.

Recipes from the Skipjack Martha Lewis

Tomatoes Stuffed with Crab Salad

This is perfect for a lady's luncheon on a hot summer day.

1 pound crabmeat
½ cup chopped celery
Juice of ½ lemon
½ cup mayonnaise
2 tablespoons chopped onion

2 tablespoons chopped basil
4 tomatoes
Lettuce
Lemon slices, for garnish

Combine the ingredients, except for tomatoes, lettuce, and lemon. Core the tomatoes. Spoon the crabmeat mixture into each tomato. Serve on a bed of lettuce. Garnish with lemon slices. Half an avocado can be substituted for the tomato. Serves 4.

Chesapeake's Bounty

Crab Salad

1 pound fresh backfin crabmeat	1 tablespoon sour cream
½ small red onion, diced fine	2 tablespoons mayonnaise
1 stalk celery, diced fine	Ground black pepper to taste
Juice of 1 lemon	Old Bay Seasoning to taste
1 rounded tablespoon Grey	
Poupon Mustard	

Inspect crabmeat, removing any shell. Mix remaining ingredients. Pour over crab and mix gently. Serve as salad on bed of lettuce or to stuff a tomato or as an appetizer on crackers. Serves 4.

South Coastal Cuisine

Crab Salad

This is for crab lovers. It has a mild flavor so as not to cover up the crab. Also great for a luncheon or light dinner.

1 pound lump crabmeat	1 teaspoon Worcestershire sauce
4 cups shredded lettuce	1 small jar pimento, diced
½ cup minced celery	1 teaspoon chopped fresh parsley
¼ cup minced scallions	1 teaspoon chopped fresh chives
2 hard-boiled eggs, chopped	½ teaspoon salt
¼ cup mayonnaise	2 teaspoons Old Bay Seasoning
¼ cup sour cream	2 tomatoes, cut into wedges
½ teaspoon dry mustard	

Pick through crabmeat and set aside. Soak shredded lettuce in ice water; set aside. Add celery, scallions, and eggs to crabmeat; set aside. In small bowl mix mayonnaise, sour cream, dry mustard, Worcestershire sauce, pimento, parsley, chives, salt, and Old Bay until well combined. Drain lettuce well. Mix mayonnaise mixture and crab mixture together. Chill lettuce and crab salad (separately) for 1 hour. To serve place lettuce on plate and top with ¼ of crab salad. Arrange tomato wedges around. Serves 4.

A Taste of Tradition

Vickie's Crab Salad

4 stalks celery
1 large green pepper
1 pound crabmeat

2 tablespoons mayonnaise
5 tablespoons French dressing

Chop celery and green pepper. Combine all ingredients. Chill for 2 hours or more. Serve on lettuce, tomatoes or crackers.

Bayside Treasures

Tropical Seafood Salad

DRESSING:
⅓ cup reserved pineapple juice*
2 tablespoons white wine vinegar
1½ teaspoons sugar
¼ teaspoon shredded lime peel

1½ teaspoons lime juice
1 teaspoon cornstarch
⅛ teaspoon ground cinnamon
⅛ teaspoon ground cumin

Combine pineapple juice, white wine vinegar, sugar, lime peel, lime juice, cornstarch, cinnamon, and cumin in a small saucepan. Cook and stir until mixture is thick and bubbly. Cook and stir 2 minutes more. Remove from heat; cool.

1 cup sugar snap or snow peas
½ pound sea or bay scallops
½ pound small shrimp
1 medium head Boston or bibb
  lettuce (6–7 ounces)

1 (15¼-ounce) can pineapple
  spears, reserve juice*
1 medium mango, peeled, seeded,
  and sliced
½ medium carrot, finely shredded

Cook sugar snap or snow peas in a small amount of boiling water for 30–60 seconds. Drain and cool. Thaw scallops, if frozen. Rinse scallops and shrimp. If scallops are large, cut into quarters. Peel shrimp (devein if large). Cook shrimp and scallops separately in lightly salted boiling water, 1–4 minutes, until opaque. Drain.

Line 4 plates with lettuce leaves. Arrange cooked shrimp and scallops on one side of the plate. From seafood, fan out pineapple spears, mango slices and peas. Drizzle with Dressing. Sprinkle with shredded carrot. Makes 4 servings.

Restaurant Recipes from the Shore and More...

Charlton Tuna Salad

1 (6-ounce) can tuna in water,
  drained and flaked
½ cup low-fat or nonfat plain
  yogurt
1 teaspoon dried dill weed
1 teaspoon dried mint

¼ teaspoon black pepper
4 lettuce leaves
¼ pound white seedless grapes,
  divided, for garnish
2 slices lemon, for garnish

In a medium bowl, mix together tuna, yogurt, herbs and pepper. Cover and chill for one hour. To serve, place on lettuce leaves and garnish with grapes and lemon. Serve with a whole grain roll. Serves 1–2.

Dr. John's Healing Psoriasis Cookbook...Plus!

Beach Club Salad

DRESSING:
½ cup raspberry vinegar
1 tablespoon Dijon mustard
1 medium clove garlic, minced

¼ teaspoon salt
Ground pepper to taste
¾ cup olive oil

Whisk together vinegar, mustard, garlic, salt and pepper. Slowly pour in oil, whisking until emulsified. Set aside ¾ cup.

SALAD:
4 boneless chicken breasts
4 cups spinach leaves, rinsed and
  dried
1 head romaine, rinsed and dried
¾ pound strawberries, hulled and
  sliced

1 cup bleu cheese, crumbled
3 tablespoons slivered almonds,
  toasted

Place chicken in a single layer in a non-reactive bowl. Pour remaining Dressing over chicken. Marinate 4 hours or overnight.

   Cook chicken over medium-hot coals until cooked through, 6–7 minutes per side. Slice across grain into thin strips. At serving time, tear spinach and lettuce into bite-sized pieces. Add chicken, strawberries, bleu cheese, and almonds. Drizzle with reserved Dressing.

Cooking with the Allenhurst Garden Club

Boiled Dressing for Chicken Salad

Just add the cooked chicken . . .

½ cup plus 1 tablespoon sugar
¼ cup plus 2 tablespoons flour
¾ tablespoon salt
¾ tablespoon dry mustard
4 eggs
¾ cup vinegar

¾ cup water
1 cup milk
2 tablespoons butter
¼ cup mayonnaise
Cayenne pepper

Mix sugar, flour, salt, and mustard. Beat eggs. Add beaten eggs, vinegar, and water to dry ingredients. Cook over medium heat, stirring constantly, until thickened. Use electric mixer, if lumpy. When it starts to thicken, add milk and butter. Continue cooking and stirring until thick. Remove from heat. Add mayonnaise and cayenne. Yields 1 quart.

The Chesapeake Collection

Orange Cashew Chicken Salad

A departure from traditional chicken salad.

¼ cup chopped cilantro or parsley
¼ cup safflower oil
¼ cup orange juice
2 teaspoons red wine vinegar
1½ teaspoons Dijon mustard
1 egg
1 tablespoon sugar
½ teaspoon salt

Dash Tabasco
4 boned chicken breast halves,
  poached
1 head romaine lettuce, torn
3 celery stalks, julienned
3 scallions, sliced
½ cup cashews
Orange slices (optional)

Blend cilantro, oil, orange juice, vinegar, mustard, egg, sugar, salt, and Tabasco in a blender or food processor.

Cut chicken into ¼-inch slices and toss with dressing. Refrigerate 4–6 hours or overnight. When ready to serve, toss chicken and dressing with vegetables and cashews. Garnish with orange slices, if desired.

Capital Classics

Fruity Chicken Salad

1 (15½-ounce) can pineapple
  tidbits, undrained
4 cups chopped cooked chicken
1 (11-ounce) can mandarin oranges
1 cup chopped celery
1 cup seedless grapes, halved
1 (8-ounce) can sliced water
  chestnuts, drained

1½ cups mayonnaise
1 tablespoon soy sauce
1 teaspoon curry powder
1 (2½-ounce) package sliced
  almonds, toasted
1 (3-ounce) can chow mein noodles
Lettuce leaves (optional)

Drain pineapple, reserving 2 tablespoons juice. Combine with chicken, oranges, celery, grapes, and water chestnuts; mix well. Combine 2 tablespoons pineapple juice with mayonnaise, soy sauce, and curry powder. Stir well and add to chicken mixture. Chill. Stir in almonds and noodles just before serving on lettuce, if desired. Serves 8–10.

Recipe by Mrs. Mac Collins, wife of Representative from Georgia
The Congressional Club Cookbook

Curried Chicken Salad

3 cups cubed cooked chicken
1 (8-ounce) can sliced water
  chestnuts, drained

1¾ cups chopped seedless grapes
1 cup finely chopped celery

DRESSING:
¾ cup mayonnaise or salad
  dressing
1 teaspoon curry powder
2 teaspoons soy sauce

2 teaspoons lemon juice
Salt to taste
1 (11-ounce) can mandarin orange
  sections, drained (optional)

In a large bowl combine chicken, water chestnuts, grapes, and celery. Prepare Dressing in small bowl. Stir together mayonnaise, curry powder, soy sauce, lemon juice, and salt. Mix well. Stir dressing into chicken mixture; add mandarin oranges, then toss to coat. Cover and chill up to 5 hours. Makes 6–8 servings.

Best of Friends

Curry Brown Rice Salad

2 tablespoons lemon juice
1 tablespoon vegetable oil
1 teaspoon curry powder
½ cup raisins

1 cup thinly sliced zucchini
½ cup thinly sliced carrots
½ cup thinly sliced green pepper
2½ cups cooked brown rice

Stir together lemon juice, oil, and curry powder; set aside. Mix together remaining ingredients. Mix in dressing. Chill at least one hour before serving. Makes 10 servings.

Sealed with a Knish

Tortellini Salad

DRESSING:
¼ cup red wine vinegar
¾ cup olive oil
1 tablespoon Dijon mustard

1 tablespoon dried parsley
2 teaspoons dill
1½ teaspoons basil

SALAD:
1 pound tri-color tortellini, cooked
¼ pound prosciutto, diced
¼ pound provolone, cubed

2 red peppers, chopped
¼ cup grated Parmesan cheese

Mix ingredients for Dressing in a large bowl. Use a wire whisk and blend for 1 minute. Add tortellini, prosciutto, provolone, red peppers, and Parmesan cheese. Toss well, cover, and refrigerate overnight.

Collected Recipes

Tofu Eggless Salad

1 pound tofu, drained and
   crumbled (firm tofu is best)
1 stalk celery, finely chopped
1 large carrot, grated

3 tablespoons sweet pickle relish
2 tablespoons eggless mayonnaise
Salt, pepper, and dill weed to taste

In a medium-size bowl, mix all the ingredients together. Serve on a bed of lettuce or on whole grain toast with lettuce and sprouts. Serves 6.

Total Calories Per Serving: 117; Fat 6g; Total Fat of Daily Value 9%; Prot 9g; Iron 1mg; Carbo 6g; Cal 139mg; Dietary fiber 1g.

Meatless Meals for Working People

The Manor Tavern's Tuscany Bread Salad

3 cups mixed salad greens
5–6 Roma tomatoes, chopped
4 ounces mozzarella cheese, cubed

¾ cup herb croutons
Balsamic Vinaigrette

Toss first 4 ingredients in a mixing bowl. Add Balsamic Vinaigrette to taste. Serves 4.

BALSAMIC VINAIGRETTE:
2 egg yolks
1 cup olive oil
¼ cup balsamic vinegar

1 tablespoon diced garlic
1 tablespoon sugar
1 teaspoon honey

Whip egg yolks until stiff. Slowly drizzle in oil, beating continuously. Add vinegar and beat until well mixed. Add garlic, sugar, and honey and mix until incorporated. (May be prepared in food processor.) Yields 1½ cups.

Recipe from The Manor Tavern, Monkton, Maryland
Maryland's Historic Restaurants and their Recipes

Salad with Warm Brie Dressing

The dressing tastes best when made with a young Brie, not quite ripe, with the rind snowy white.

CROUTONS:

5 slices whole wheat or
   multi-grain bread

3 tablespoons butter
1 clove garlic

Remove crusts from bread and cut into cubes. Melt butter in a heavy skillet. Put garlic through a garlic press and add to butter. Stir. Fry bread cubes in garlic butter until golden. Remove from skillet and drain on paper towels.

SALAD:

1 head romaine lettuce

1 bunch watercress

Wash and dry romaine. Slice vertically through the center spine of each leaf. Then slice each piece horizontally into 1½-inch strips. Wash, dry, and remove tough stems from watercress. Toss with romaine and arrange on individual plates.

WARM BRIE DRESSING:

½ cup vegetable oil
4 tablespoons chopped onion
1 tablespoon chopped garlic
⅓ cup tarragon vinegar

1 tablespoon lemon juice
3 teaspoons Dijon mustard
7 ounces Brie cheese

Heat oil in a heavy skillet and fry onion and garlic until limp and slightly golden. Turn heat to warm. Add vinegar, lemon juice, and mustard. Combine well. Remove the thin layer of rind from the Brie. Discard the rind. Cut cheese into chunks. Turn up the heat under the skillet. Add the Brie and stir with a wooden spoon until melted. Pour dressing over greens and top with croutons. Serve immediately while still warm. Yields 6 servings.

A Matter of Taste

Romaine, Spinach & Arugula

1 pound spinach
2–3 leaves romaine lettuce
1 bunch arugula

1 can mandarin oranges, drained
1 red onion

Wash and clean spinach, lettuce, and arugula. Drain well; break into pieces. In a large bowl, mix greens and mandarin oranges. Add onion, cut into rings.

DRESSING:
¾ cup olive oil
¼ cup balsamic vinegar
1 tablespoon sugar

1 teaspoon salt
1 teaspoon freshly ground pepper

Mix Dressing in a jar; pour over salad. Mix and serve. Serves 6.

Cooking Through the Years

Greek Salad

1 (10-ounce) package salad greens
    or make your own mix
1 cup black olives
3 plum tomatoes, chopped
½ cup thinly sliced red onion

½ medium cucumber, peeled and
    cut into chunks
⅔ cup Greek or Italian dressing
1 (4-ounce) package crumbled feta
    cheese

Toss greens, olives, tomatoes, onion, and cucumber in large bowl. Drizzle with dressing and sprinkle with feta cheese. Makes 6 servings.

Out of the Frying Pan Into the Fire!!!

Valentine Salad

CREAMY VINAIGRETTE DRESSING:

1 egg yolk
2 tablespoons red wine vinegar
1 tablespoon Dijon mustard

1 cup salad oil
Salt and pepper to taste

Blend egg yolk, vinegar, and mustard. Gradually whisk in oil. Add salt and pepper.

SALAD:

1 Belgian endive
½ bunch watercress
½ head soft lettuce

1 red apple
½ cup chopped walnuts
Salt and pepper to taste

Slice endive. Remove stems from watercress and tear lettuce into small pieces. Core apple and slice. Combine with Creamy Vinaigrette Dressing, nuts, and salt and pepper to taste.

The Glen Afton Cookbook

Caribbean Salad

This recipe is as authentic as they come—from a friend who got it from her Jamaican housekeeper!

DRESSING:

½ cup oil
⅓ cup vinegar (white or cider)
1 clove garlic, crushed
2 tablespoons brown sugar

1 small scallion, chopped
½ tablespoon curry powder
1 teaspoon tamari

Prepare the Dressing and chill.

SALAD:

1 package mixed salad greens
1 small can mandarin orange
   slices, drained
Handful seedless green grapes

1 large ripe avocado, sliced
Handful blanched, slivered
   almonds

Combine Salad ingredients. Before serving, toss with chilled Dressing.

Simple Pleasures

Magnificent Spring Salad

1 (16-ounce) can grapefruit
   segments, drained (reserve
   juice)
1 (10.5-ounce) can mandarin
   oranges, drained (reserve juice)
1 medium cucumber, sliced thin
1 small onion, thinly sliced and
   separated into rings

Orange juice
⅔ cup wine vinegar
⅓ cup sugar
¼ teaspoon salt
Pepper to taste
2 avocados, seeded, peeled, and
   sliced
Lettuce

In a large bowl, combine grapefruit, oranges, cucumbers, and onions.
Measure reserved juices and add enough orange juice to make 1 cup.
Combine juice mixture, vinegar, sugar, salt and pepper; pour over fruit.
Cover and marinate in refrigerator for 2–3 hours. At serving time, add
avocado slices and toss to coat. Remove ingredients from marinade and
arrange on lettuce-lined plates. Drizzle some marinade on top. Serves
8–10.

Where There's a Will...

Cherry Fruit Mold

2 (3-ounce) packages cherry
  gelatin
1 cup boiling water
1 (20-ounce) can crushed
  pineapple, drained

1 cup coarsely chopped walnuts
3 medium bananas, mashed
1 (30-ounce) can pitted dark sweet
  cherries
1 pint sour cream

Dissolve gelatin in boiling water. Add everything except the sour cream, including the cherry juice. Pour half of this mixture into a trifle dish. Chill until almost set. Spoon sour cream on top gently. Add remainder of mixture, gently and neatly. The sour cream will be in the middle. Continue to chill until fully set and then serve.

The Happy Cooker 3

Carrot Raisin Salad

¼ cup orange juice
1 tablespoon brown sugar
1 teaspoon prepared spicy brown
  mustard

3 cups shredded carrots
¾ cup chopped apple
¼ cup raisins

In a small bowl combine orange juice, brown sugar, and mustard. In large bowl, combine remaining ingredients. Pour dressing over and toss well. Cover; refrigerate until chilled.

A Tasting Tour Through the 8th District

 The Chesapeake Bay has enriched the land surrounding it, providing ideal growing conditions for many crops such as sweet corn and berries, crisp ripe apples and peaches, fresh beans and other vegetables. Combined with the fish and shellfish of the Bay, colonists and Native Americans were provided with a healthy diet.

Pea Salad

1 (20-ounce) package frozen peas,
    thawed
1 pound bacon, fried, drained,
    and crumbled (or 1 jar real
    bacon bits)
¼ cup chopped green onions

1 teaspoon salt
1 teaspoon sugar
1 teaspoon pepper
¾ cup mayonnaise
7 ounces slivered almonds or
    cashews

Combine all ingredients. Refrigerate until chilled. Best to be eaten the day it's made. Makes 10 servings.

Fair Haven Fare

Farmers' Market Coleslaw

This is a good "clean out the fridge" salad. Use any combination of fresh herbs, throw in some shredded zucchini or yellow squash, extra tomato, or whatever you have!

1½ cups mayonnaise
¾ cup sugar
¼ cup red wine vinegar
¼ teaspoon celery seeds
1 clove garlic, finely chopped
Salt and freshly ground black
    pepper to taste
1 large cabbage (about 5 pounds),
    shredded or chopped
½ cup finely chopped green bell
    pepper

½ cup finely chopped red bell
    pepper
¼ cup shredded carrot
¾ cup diced tomato
½ cup finely chopped onion
½ cup finely chopped celery
2 tablespoons finely chopped
    fresh dill
2 tablespoons finely chopped
    fresh parsley

In a bowl, whisk together the mayonnaise, sugar, vinegar, celery seeds, garlic, and salt and pepper. In a large bowl, combine the cabbage, bell peppers, carrot, tomato, onion, celery, dill, and parsley. Pour dressing over the mixture, tossing to coat. Chill the coleslaw, covered, for at least 4 hours or overnight. Serves 8.

In the Kitchen with Kendi

Linda's Own Salad Dressing

¾ cup extra virgin olive oil
¼ cup red wine vinegar
2 teaspoons sugar

1 teaspoon Worcestershire sauce
1 teaspoon garlic paste

In a small bowl, combine all ingredients. Using a wire whisk, blend for 1 minute. Refrigerate for approximately 1 hour before serving. I recommend using this dressing with romaine, endive, or spinach salad.

Collected Recipes

Chipparelli's Salad Dressing

Over the years, the secret of this famous Baltimore salad has come to surface.

2 cloves garlic, crushed
3 hard-boiled eggs, crushed
2 tablespoons oregano
2 tablespoons sugar
1 tablespoon black pepper
½ cup vinegar

1½ cups olive oil
1 cup grated Parmesan cheese
2 heads iceberg lettuce, chopped
Green peppers, chopped
Black olives, chopped

Combine all ingredients; refrigerate. Simple as that!!! Serves 12.

Best of Friends

Spicy Mayonnaise

¼ cup olive oil (good quality)
1 egg
3 medium cloves garlic, crushed
1 teaspoon Dijon mustard
1 teaspoon salt

Few dashes cayenne pepper
1 cup safflower oil, divided
3 tablespoons raw, unpasteurized,
  full-strength apple cider vinegar

Combine first 6 ingredients in blender container and mix well on medium speed. Drizzle ½ cup oil very slowly into blender on low speed. Add vinegar; mix well. Add remaining oil, again very slowly at low speed. Yields approximately 1½ cups.

Cape May Fare

VEGETABLES

New Jersey is known as The Garden State for a good reason. Over 150 types of fruits and vegetables are grown there such as tomatoes, blueberries, cranberries, peaches, spinach, bell peppers, asparagus, eggplant and lettuce.

Glazed Asparagus

The simple but elegant glaze is also good with snowpeas.

**16 stalks fresh asparagus, rinsed
  and peeled, if desired
2 tablespoons soy sauce**

**2 tablespoons lemon juice
2 tablespoons butter or margarine**

Break white parts off asparagus. Place in rapidly boiling water and cook until tender but crisp, about 5–7 minutes. Remove from heat and drain. Before serving, combine soy sauce, lemon juice, and butter in a large skillet. Over medium heat, reduce by half or until sauce becomes syrupy. Add asparagus and warm for one minute, shaking asparagus until well coated. Serve immediately. Serves 4.

Of Tide & Thyme

Roasted Asparagus

**1 pound fresh asparagus
¼ cup balsamic vinegar**

**Fresh ground pepper
Grated Parmesan cheese**

Wash and break off tough ends of asparagus. Lay in ovenproof dish long enough to accommodate whole stalk. They may overlap. Sprinkle with balsamic vinegar and pepper. Roast in high heat for exactly 8 minutes. Remove from oven and sprinkle with Parmesan cheese. Serve hot or cold.

Recipes from the Skipjack Martha Lewis

Belgian Onion Pie

½ cup (1 stick) butter
3 large Spanish onions, cut into
   half moons and sliced thin
3 tablespoons flour
¼ cup hot light cream
¼ cup hot milk
2 large eggs, beaten

⅛ teaspoon nutmeg
2 tablespoons grated Parmesan
   and Romano mix
¼ teaspoon salt
⅛ teaspoon pepper
1 baked (9-inch) pie shell

Preheat oven to 400°. Heat butter until foamy in a large frying pan. Add onions and sauté until limp. Cover and cook for 5 minutes. Mix in flour; then add cream and milk. Remove from heat and cool slightly. Add eggs, nutmeg, Parmesan and Romano cheese mix, salt and pepper. Pour into a baked pie shell. Bake for 30–40 minutes, until brown and center is set. Yields 10 servings.

Food Fabulous Food

Gourmet Smothered Onions Amandine

⅓ cup butter
1 cup whole or slivered almonds
1 tablespoon brown sugar
1 teaspoon salt

Dash each of cayenne pepper,
   nutmeg, and ground cloves
3 dozen very small onions (frozen
   ones do well)

Melt butter in a casserole on top of stove and add everything except the onions. Stir until well blended. Add onions and stir until they are well coated. Cover and bake in a moderate oven (350°) about an hour, stirring 3 or 4 times. Makes 5 servings.

Cooking Along the Susquehanna

Meme's Creamed Carrots

2 teaspoons butter
½ small yellow onion, chopped
2 teaspoons flour
6 large carrots, scraped and cut
   julienne style

1 cup chicken broth
Salt and pepper to taste
2 teaspoons finely chopped fresh
   parsley

Melt butter in saucepan; add onion and sauté 2 minutes. Add flour and mix together well (a roux). Add carrots and chicken broth and simmer until tender. Add salt and pepper to taste. Add parsley just before serving. Serves 6.

A Taste of Tradition

Carrot Soufflé

A sweet carrot dish.

2 cups diced carrots, cooked and
   drained
⅓ cup sugar
¼ cup butter

1 teaspoon vanilla extract
2 eggs
½ cup milk

Blend ingredients in a blender until thick and smooth. Pour into a buttered soufflé dish. Bake in a preheated 450° oven for 30 minutes. Serve immediately. Yields 4 servings.

Capital Celebrations

Antrim 1844's
Herbed Mashed Potatoes

2 pounds Yukon potatoes, well
  scrubbed
2 tablespoons kosher salt
¼ cup diced garlic

¼ cup fresh herbs, chopped
¼ cup butter
¼ cup heavy cream
Salt and pepper to taste

Cover potatoes with cold water and salt. Bring to a boil and simmer until tender. Drain. When potatoes are slightly cooled but still hot, peel and place in a bowl with garlic, herbs, and butter. Mash to desired consistency. Stir in cream and season with salt and pepper. Serves 4.

Maryland's Historic Restaurants and their Recipes

Executive Potatoes

1 (2-pound) package frozen hash
  brown potatoes
1 teaspoon salt
1 teaspoon pepper
1 can cream of chicken soup

1 small onion, chopped
½ cup melted butter
1 pint sour cream
2 cups grated Cheddar cheese
1½ cups crushed cornflakes

Put hash browns in 9x13-inch casserole. Sprinkle with salt and pepper. Pour can of soup on potatoes. Sauté chopped onion in butter and pour onto potatoes. Mix well. Spread sour cream on top. Sprinkle grated cheese on top of sour cream. Sprinkle crushed cornflakes on top of cheese. Bake 1 hour and 15 minutes at 300°.

Bread of Life

Seventy square miles make up the District of Columbia. Designed by Major Pierre Charles L'Enfant around 1791, it was the first American city planned for a specific purpose and became the nation's capitol in 1891. The country had been governed from Philadelphia, Pennsylvania, previously. Both Virginia and Maryland donated part of their land for the capital district. The Virginia portion of D.C. was later ceded back to Virginia.

Washington Red Skins

4 pounds red potatoes
1 stick butter, more or less,
   depending on size of baking
   dish

4 cloves garlic, or to taste, minced
1½ teaspoons salt, or to taste
½ teaspoon ground white pepper,
   or to taste

Scrub the potatoes and cut into halves, if large. Steam the potatoes in their skins for 25 minutes or until done (this will depend on size) using a vegetable steamer or just a colander set over water in a big pot. Cool and refrigerate them.

When ready to cook again, roughly chop the potatoes, leaving the skins on. Rub baking dish with about one tablespoon of the butter. Toss potatoes with garlic, salt and pepper, and press into the pan. Melt remaining butter and pour over top. Bake on the top rack of a 350° oven for about an hour, until the potatoes are crisp and golden. Serves 8.

Best of Friends

Sweet Potato Surprise

Our favorite way to eat sweet potatoes at Thanksgiving. Be warned that this recipe makes a lot of sweet potatoes. You might want to halve the ingredients unless you're crazy about left-over sweet potatoes. This dish is not sweet.

4 pounds sweet potatoes or yams
2 green apples or ripe pears,
   sliced
4 bananas, chopped
2 tablespoons butter
2 tablespoons minced fresh ginger
½ teaspoon cinnamon

½ teaspoon allspice
1 teaspoon salt
1½ cups apple juice
½ cup lemon or lime juice
½ cup chopped dried apricots
2 cups chopped pecans

Peel the potatoes and boil until soft. Drain. Sauté apples (or pears) and bananas in butter with ginger, cinnamon, allspice, and salt. Cook slowly, covered, stirring occasionally, for 10–15 minutes. Purée the potatoes with the fruit juices in a food processor. Stir the sautéed fruit into the purée. Stir in the apricots. Heap the mixture into a buttered, 9x13-inch, baking dish or deep casserole. Top with chopped pecans. Bake, uncovered, at 350° for 45 minutes. Makes 16 servings.

Hoboken Cooks

Peanut Butter and Jelly Potatoes

Medium-size sweet potatoes
Milk
Salt and pepper to season

Peanut butter
Jelly

Scrub and bake potatoes in a moderate oven (375°) for 45 minutes. Cut in half; scoop out the centers. Mash with milk and season with salt and pepper. Refill potato skin halfway. Put in a tablespoon each of peanut butter and jelly. Fill with remaining mashed potatoes. Return to oven for 15 minutes.

PB&J USA

Spinach in Phyllo Dough

10 ounces frozen spinach, or
  2 bags fresh
2 breasts of chicken, chopped
  finely
1 small onion, diced
1 cup grated Cheddar cheese

1 tablespoon Parmesan cheese
Salt and pepper to taste
8 pieces phyllo dough (to make 2
  rolls)
¼ cup melted butter

Mix all of the ingredients except phyllo dough and butter. Brush each sheet of phyllo dough with butter, layering a total of 4 sheets at a time. Place spinach-chicken mixture onto center of phyllo dough. Starting at the edge with the mixture, roll up the dough like a jellyroll. Repeat the procedure for second roll. Brush the rolls with remaining butter. With seam-side-down on baking sheet, partially slice diagonally in 1-inch slices. Bake at 400° for 20 minutes, or until golden brown. Serves 16.

Recipe by Mrs. John Foley, daughter-in-law of former
Representative John R. Foley of Maryland
The Congressional Club Cookbook

Ratatouille

1 pound dried onions
½ cup olive oil, divided
1 pound dried green peppers
1 pound dried zucchini
1 pound peeled, dried eggplant

2 (15-ounce) cans diced tomatoes, drained
¼ cup oregano
2 tablespoons basil
¼ cup chopped garlic

Sauté onions in ¼ cup oil about 3 minutes on medium heat. Add green peppers. Sauté about 5 minutes. Remove from heat; drain liquid and set aside.

In same pot, add remaining ¼ cup oil. Sauté zucchini for 5 minutes over medium heat. Stir constantly. Add eggplant. Sauté together for 5 more minutes. Add drained onions and green peppers. Mix in tomatoes and spices and cook over medium-low heat for 10–15 minutes. Serve over eggs, as a side vegetable, with a sprinkle of Parmesan cheese. Serves 12.

Restaurant Recipes from the Shore and More...

Eggplant Parmesan

2 medium eggplants
Olive oil
1½ cups tomato sauce

¼ cup grated Parmesan cheese
½ cup mozzarella cheese
¼ cup Italian-style bread crumbs

Peel and slice the eggplants about ⅛ inch thick. Brush with a light coat of olive oil and broil until browned. Turn and brown the other side. Into an ovenproof casserole, pour a little sauce over the bottom and begin to layer with eggplant, cheeses, bread crumbs, and sauce. Finish with sauce and a little cheese. Bake 350° for 35 minutes. Serve hot or cold. Serves 4–6.

Good Things to Eat

 Two-thirds of the world's eggplant is grown in New Jersey. The state ranks second nationally in blueberry production and sixth in tomato production.

Zucchini Pie

4 eggs, beaten
½ cup oil
1 cup Bisquick Baking Mix
1 medium onion, chopped
½ teaspoon salt
¼ teaspoon pepper

3 cups grated zucchini
1 cup grated sharp cheese
½ cup bread crumbs or wheat germ
2 cut-up slices of bacon (or ¼ cup of bacon bits)

Mix the eggs, oil, Bisquick, onion, salt, pepper, and zucchini; pour into a greased pie pan. Sprinkle cheese on top; next sprinkle bread crumbs, then bacon. Bake at 350° for 45 minutes.

DAPI's Delectable Delights

Squash Pie

1⅓ cups strained squash (any kind)
1 teaspoon salt
1½ cups milk
2 large eggs (or 3 small)
1 cup sugar

1 teaspoon cinnamon
½ teaspoon nutmeg
½ teaspoon ginger
1 tablespoon butter, melted
1 (9-inch) unbaked pie shell

Preheat oven to 400°. Mix all together with an electric mixer. Pour into a 9-inch unbaked pie shell. Bake in a 400° oven for 15 minutes. Turn oven down to 325° and bake until center is firm, or when knife inserted in center comes out clean. Cool and serve cold.

Come, Dine With Us!

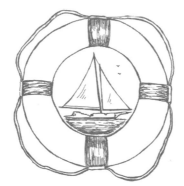

The Penwick House's
Mushroom Turnover

2 sticks butter, softened
4 ounces cream cheese, softened
2 cups all-purpose flour
1 pound fresh mushrooms,
  chopped
2 tablespoons butter

½ teaspoon thyme
½ teaspoon garlic salt
½ teaspoon white pepper
½ teaspoon oregano
½ teaspoon sour cream
1 egg white, beaten

Mix 2 sticks butter and cream cheese together with wooden utensil. Add flour to mixture until completely incorporated. Cover bowl and refrigerate for one hour.

Sauté mushrooms in 2 tablespoons butter until tender. Add thyme, garlic salt, white pepper, and oregano. Remove from heat and add sour cream. Mix well and set aside.

Remove dough from refrigerator and let stand for 45 minutes. Roll out dough into oval shapes. Fill half of each oval with mushroom mixture. Fold dough over and press sides together to seal. Brush egg white over sealed edges. Place turnovers onto a greased flat pan and bake in a preheated 350° oven for 15–25 minutes, until golden brown. Serves 4–6.

Maryland's Historic Restaurants and their Recipes

Italian Tofu with Mushrooms and Peppers

This dish is aromatic and can be eaten on its own or paired with pasta. As a leftover, it can be stuffed in a pita or put on top of a salad.

1 teaspoon olive oil or vegetable oil spray
¼ cup chopped bell pepper
¼ cup chopped onion
1 garlic clove, minced or 1 teaspoon garlic powder
1 cup sliced mushrooms, drained

6 ounces firm tofu, drained and cubed
1 tablespoon vinegar (balsamic tastes best in this recipe)
½ teaspoon dried oregano
½ teaspoon red pepper flakes

In a medium-sized frying pan, heat oil over medium heat. Add pepper, onion, and garlic and sauté for 5 minutes, or until soft. Add mushrooms and tofu, tossing and stirring. Reduce heat to a simmer. Add vinegar, oregano, and red pepper and simmer for 2 minutes. Voila, dinner! Makes 2 servings.

Note: This recipe can be eaten hot or cold and served over mashed or baked potatoes, rice, or pasta. You can purchase frozen chopped bell peppers so that you can measure out only what you need and freeze the rest with no waste. Of course, if you have leftover fresh bell pepper, you can throw it in a salad, in soups, in sandwiches, on cooked veggies, in tofu scrambles, and on top of pizza. The same goes for any extra onions, garlic, or mushrooms.

Total Calories Per Serving: 181; Total Fat of Daily Value 15%; Prot 15g; Fat 10g; Carbo 12g; Cal 158mg; Iron 10mg; Sod 18mg; Dietary Fiber 4g.

Vegan Meals for One and Two

New Jersey boasts being the home to some of the nation's most popular singers and actors. Just to name a few: Frank Sinatra, Paul Simon, Connie Francis, Whitney Houston, Bruce Springsteen, Bette Midler, Dionne Warwick, Jon Bon Jovi, Michael Douglas, Meryl Streep, John Travolta, Danny DeVito, Jack Nicholson, Tom Cruise, Joe Pesci, Bruce Willis, John Forsythe, Jerry Lewis, Eva Marie Saint.

Broccoli Supreme

1 egg, slightly beaten
1 (10-ounce) package frozen
   chopped broccoli, partially
   thawed
1 (8½-ounce) can cream-style corn

1 tablespoon grated onion
¼ teaspoon salt
Dash of pepper
3 tablespoons butter
1 cup herb-seasoned stuffing mix

In a mixing bowl, combine egg, broccoli, cream-style corn, onion, salt and pepper. In a small saucepan, melt butter or margarine. Add stuffing mix, tossing to coat. Stir ¾ cup of the buttered stuffing mix into vegetable mixture. Turn into ungreased 1-quart casserole. Sprinkle with remaining ¼ cup stuffing mix. Bake, uncovered, in a 350° oven for 35–40 minutes. Serves 4–6.

Our Favorite Recipes

Broccoli Rice Bake

2 (10-ounce) packages chopped
   broccoli
1 onion, chopped
1 pat butter
1 cup Minute Rice

1 can cream of mushroom soup
1 (8-ounce) jar Cheez Whiz
1 (6.5-ounce) jar mushrooms
1 (2.8-ounce) can French's French
   Fried Onions

Cook and drain broccoli. Sauté chopped onion in butter. Add Minute Rice; cover, turn off heat and let set 5 minutes. Mix all ingredients, except French fried onions, and put in casserole dish. Bake at 350° for 30 minutes. Top casserole with French fried onions for last 8 minutes of baking.

Our Favorite Recipes–Book Three

Garlicky Green Beans

This dish is delicious enough to set before a king.

1 pound fresh green beans, tips
  removed
2 tablespoons butter
2 tablespoons olive oil
4 garlic cloves, minced
8 sun-dried tomatoes, finely
  chopped

3 tablespoons bread crumbs
3 tablespoons grated Parmesan
  cheese
Salt and pepper

Rinse beans and microwave for 3–5 minutes on full power. Heat butter
and olive oil in skillet. Add garlic and tomatoes and sauté for 3 minutes.
Add beans, bread crumbs, and cheese. Mix and remove from heat.
Season with salt and pepper. Yields 6 servings.

Food Fabulous Food

Green Beans Parmesan

¼ cup vegetable oil
1 small green bell pepper, seeded
  and diced
1 small red bell pepper, seeded
  and diced
¼ cup chopped onion
1 garlic clove, minced

1½ pounds fresh green beans, cut
  into 1-inch pieces
1 teaspoon crumbled dried basil
1 teaspoon salt
¾ cup freshly grated Parmesan
  cheese

Heat oil in heavy medium skillet over medium heat. Add bell peppers,
onion, and garlic and cook until onion is translucent, about 3 minutes.
Add beans, basil, and salt. Cover and steam until tender, about 7 minutes.

Remove from heat. Stir in ½ cup Parmesan. Transfer to serving
dish. Sprinkle with remaining Parmesan. Serve immediately.

Fair Haven Fare

Delaware Succotash

2 thin slices salt pork
1 pint shelled lima beans or
   1 package frozen, thawed
Water
8 ears of fresh corn or frozen,
   thawed

1 large ripe tomato, cubed
1 teaspoon salt
¼ teaspoon pepper
Dash of nutmeg

Lay salt pork in bottom of a saucepan and cover with lima beans. Add enough water to cover and cook over low heat until beans are tender. Cut kernels from fresh corn and combine with beans, cubed tomato, and seasonings. Cover and continue cooking over low heat for 10–15 minutes. Stir frequently. Yields 6 servings.

South Coastal Cuisine

Cora's Skillet Cabbage

2 tablespoons salad oil
3 cups finely shredded cabbage
1 cup chopped celery
1 small green pepper, chopped

1 small onion, chopped
½ teaspoon salt
Dash of pepper

Twenty minutes before serving, using a 10-inch skillet over medium-low heat, place oil in skillet. When hot, stir in all the ingredients until well mixed. Cover pan and cook 5 minutes, stirring occasionally. Serve immediately (vegetables will be crisp). Serves 4.

225 Years in Pennington & Still Cooking

 History students know that Betsy Ross sewed the first American flag, but did you know it was designed by a New Jersey congressman? Francis Hopkinson, a signer of the Declaration of Independence, designed the first American flag, which was adopted by the Continental Congress in 1777. Tradition holds the first time Betsy Ross's famous flag was flown was at the Battle of Cooch's Bridge, Delaware.

4th of July Bean Casserole

Made with bacon and ground beef, this is a tasty side dish for a barbecue, but could be served as a main dish any time of year.

½ pound bacon, diced
½ pound ground beef
1 cup chopped onion
1 (28-ounce) can pork and beans
1 (17-ounce) can lima beans,
 rinsed and drained
1 (16-ounce) can kidney beans,
 rinsed and drained

½ cup barbecue sauce
½ cup ketchup
½ cup sugar
½ cup brown sugar, packed
2 tablespoons prepared mustard
2 tablespoons molasses
1 teaspoon salt
½ teaspoon chili powder

Preheat oven to 350°. In a skillet over medium-high heat, cook bacon, beef, and onion until meat is brown and onion is tender. Remove from heat and drain. Place in a greased casserole dish. Add beans and mix well. In a separate bowl, combine barbecue sauce, ketchup, sugars, mustard, molasses, salt, and chili powder and stir into beef mixture. Cover and bake for 45 minutes. Uncover and bake for 15 minutes longer, or until browned and bubbly. Serves 12 as a side dish. If serving this savory baked casserole as a main course, offer hot corn bread and a green salad to make a full meal.

In the Kitchen with Kendi

Fresh Corn Quiche

3 eggs
1 (¼-inch) slice of onion
1 tablespoon sugar
1 tablespoon all-purpose flour
1 teaspoon salt

3 tablespoons melted butter
1⅓ cups half-and-half, scalded
2 cups uncooked fresh or thawed
  frozen corn
1 (9-inch) pie crust, unbaked

Preheat oven to 375°. In a food processor, combine eggs, onion, sugar, flour, and salt. Add butter and half-and-half and blend. Fold in corn. Turn the mixture into pie crust and bake for 45 minutes, or until slightly puffed up and lightly browned. Cut into wedges and serve immediately. Yields 6–8 servings.

Breakfast at Nine, Tea at Four

Corn Pudding

1 stick margarine
1 large can cream-style corn
2 eggs

4 tablespoons flour
¾ cup sugar (or more to taste)
1 small can evaporated milk

Melt margarine, set aside. In medium-size bowl beat corn, eggs, flour, and sugar; then add margarine. Beat until well blended; add milk. Pour in a deep baking dish. Bake at 350° for one hour.

Bayside Treasures

 With more than 30 acres of beautiful flowers, ferns, lawns and ponds, Leaming's Run in rural Swainton, New Jersey, is the largest annual garden in the United States. It is divided into 25 distinctive gardens, each with a different theme, such as the bamboo garden, shade garden, and colonial farm garden. The garden is named after whaler Thomas Leaming, who built his home—which still stands today—there in 1706.

Tomato Flans

Canned tomatoes can be used here but, oh-boy, is it great made with fresh New Jersey tomatoes! Makes a great side dish.

3 cherry tomatoes, halved	4 eggs
2 tablespoons (¼ stick) butter	½ cup whipping cream
1 tablespoon olive oil	¼ cup grated Parmesan cheese
1 cup minced onion	¼ cup grated Gruyère cheese
1 pound tomatoes, peeled, seeded	Salt
and chopped	Freshly ground pepper

Generously butter 6 (½-cup) custard cups or ramekins. Place 1 cherry tomato half, skin-side-down, in each cup. Melt butter with oil in heavy large skillet over medium-low heat. Add onion and cook until translucent, stirring occasionally, about 10 minutes. Increase heat to high. Add tomatoes and cook until all liquid evaporates, stirring frequently. Cool slightly.

Preheat oven to 375°. Beat eggs and cream to blend. Stir in cheeses and tomato mixture. Season with salt and pepper. Carefully spoon mixture into prepared cups. Arrange cups in roasting pan. Pour enough water into pan to come halfway up sides of cups. Bake until tester inserted in centers comes out clean, 30–35 minutes. Let stand 10 minutes. Run knife around edge of cups to loosen flans. Invert onto plates and serve immediately. Makes 6 servings.

Why Not for Breakfast?

Curried Fruit

1 (29-ounce) can peach slices
1 (29-ounce) can pear slices
1 (20-ounce) can pineapple chunks
1 (20-ounce) can apricot halves

⅓ cup butter
¾ cup brown sugar
4 teaspoons curry powder

Drain fruit. Arrange in a 3-quart ovenproof dish. Melt butter and add brown sugar and curry powder. Stir to blend. Pour over fruit and stir to cover fruit evenly. May be made ahead to this point and refrigerated overnight. In fact, it benefits from being made in advance and letting the flavors marry. Bake one hour at 325°. Serves 12.

Note: This recipe is very flexible. Use fruits you like best: if you like pineapple, for example, use two cans instead of one. Canned cherries (not pie filling) are very pleasant, or you can use maraschino cherries if you like them, though they "bleed" their color onto the other fruit if it is allowed to sit overnight. You can use fresh fruit in this recipe, but it is not necessary, and in fact quite a bit more work, and the fresh advantage is lost in the baking process.

The Queen Victoria® Cookbook

PASTA, RICE, ETC.

The Concord Point Lighthouse in Havre de Grace, Maryland, is the oldest continuously operated lighthouse on the East Coast.

Crabmeat Lasagna

1 pound lasagna noodles
2 cups crabmeat
2 cans seafood bisque
2 cups ricotta cheese
2 cups mozzarella cheese,
  shredded

1 (8-ounce) package cream cheese
1 medium onion, chopped
1 egg, slightly beaten
2 teaspoons basil
2 teaspoons dill weed
2 tomatoes, chopped

Cook noodles according to package directions. Drain and cover with cold water. Mix crabmeat and soup over low heat. Combine cheeses, onion, egg, basil, and dill weed in a separate bowl.

In a buttered lasagna pan, place one layer of noodles, then half the cheese mixture, then noodles, half crabmeat mixture, noodles, cheese, and top with crabmeat mixture to which tomatoes have been added. Bake at 350° for 30 minutes, or until bubbly. Serves 6–8.

Flavors of Cape Henlopen

Lasagna and Spinach Roll Ups

1 (16-ounce) box lasagna noodles
1 (1-pound) container cottage
  cheese
1 (1-pound) container ricotta cheese
¼ cup grated Parmesan cheese
2 eggs, beaten
1 (15-ounce) can spinach, drained
  well
1 teaspoon pesto, jar or homemade

¼ teaspoon ground nutmeg
1 teaspoon dried oregano
1 teaspoon garlic powder
1 teaspoon dried basil
1 teaspoon salt
¼ teaspoon black pepper
2 large cans spaghetti sauce, or
  homemade
1 cup shredded mozzarella cheese

Cook lasagna noodles according to directions on package; drain, rinse, and cool. In a large bowl, mix cottage cheese, ricotta cheese, Parmesan cheese, and beaten eggs. Now add spinach, pesto, nutmeg, oregano, garlic powder, basil, salt and pepper, and mix well. Take one whole noodle and put ¼ cup cheese mixture at one end and roll up like a log; continue to do this with all noodles. Place them in a baking dish, in one layer. Pour spaghetti sauce over them and bake for 40 minutes, covered, so it does not dry out. Then remove cover and sprinkle mozzarella cheese over the top and bake for 5 more minutes.

A Taste of Tradition

Seafood Lasagna

8 lasagna noodles
1 cup chopped onion
2 tablespoons butter or margarine
1 (8-ounce) package cream cheese, softened
1½ cups cream-style cottage cheese
1 beaten egg
2 teaspoons dried basil, crushed
½ teaspoon salt
⅛ teaspoon pepper
2 cans condensed cream of mushroom soup
⅓ cup milk
⅓ cup dry white wine
1 pound shelled shrimp, cooked and halved
1 (7½-ounce) can crabmeat, drained
¼ cup grated Parmesan cheese
½ cup shredded sharp American cheese

Cook lasagna noodles according to directions; drain. Arrange 4 noodles in bottom of greased 9x13x2-inch baking dish. Cook onion in butter or margarine until tender. Blend in cream cheese. Stir in cottage cheese, egg, basil, salt, and pepper; spread half atop noodles. Combine soup, milk, and wine. Stir in shrimp and crab; spread half over cottage cheese layer. Repeat layers, beginning with remaining noodles. Sprinkle with Parmesan cheese. Bake, uncovered, in 350° oven for 45 minutes. Top with American cheese. Bake 2–3 minutes more. Let stand 15 minutes before serving. Makes 12 servings.

A Taste of GBMC

Gourmet Carrot and Olive Lasagna

A very special lasagna—everyone asks for this recipe.

1 onion, chopped
2 tablespoons oil
2 cloves garlic, crushed
½ pound fresh mushrooms, sliced
½ cup black olives, sliced
½ cup carrots, shredded
1 (15-ounce) can tomato sauce
1 (6-ounce) can tomato paste

1 tablespoon crushed oregano
9 lasagna noodles, cooked
  according to package directions
1 pound cottage cheese
1 (10-ounce) package frozen
  spinach, thawed
12–16 ounces mozzarella cheese,
  shredded

Preheat oven to 350°. Spray Pam or grease a 9x13-inch lasagna pan.

In a medium skillet, sauté onion in oil until soft. Stir in garlic. Add mushrooms, olives, and carrots. Mix well. Add tomato sauce, paste, and oregano. Bring to a simmer; cook a few minutes longer for flavors to blend. Set sauce aside.

Place 3 cooked noodles at the bottom of the pan. Add ½ of the cottage cheese, then ½ of the spinach. Pour on ⅓ sauce mixture, and ⅓ mozzarella. Repeat with another layer of noodles, remaining cottage cheese, remaining spinach, and another ⅓ of the sauce and cheese. Finish with another layer of noodles, remaining sauce, and remaining cheese. Bake, uncovered, for 30–40 minutes, or until cheese is bubbly and top is lightly browned.

Simple Pleasures

Chicken Pecan Fettuccine

This is a mouth-watering combination of ingredients.

1 pound chicken breasts, skinned
   and boned
¾ cup butter, divided
3 cups sliced fresh mushrooms
1 cup sliced green onions
¾ teaspoon salt, divided
½ teaspoon freshly ground black
   pepper, divided
½ teaspoon garlic powder, divided

10 ounces fresh fettuccine
1 egg yolk
⅔ cup half-and-half
2 tablespoons freshly chopped
   parsley
½ cup freshly grated Parmesan
   cheese
1 cup chopped pecans, toasted

Cut chicken into ¾-inch pieces. Melt ¼ cup butter in a large skillet. Sauté chicken until lightly browned. Remove chicken from skillet and set aside. To drippings in skillet, add mushrooms, green onions, ½ teaspoon salt, ¼ teaspoon pepper, and ¼ teaspoon garlic powder. Sauté until mushrooms are tender. Return chicken to skillet and simmer for 20 minutes, or until chicken is done. Cook fettuccine in boiling salted water until al dente. Drain well.

Melt remaining ½ cup butter and combine with egg yolk, half-and-half, parsley, and remaining salt, pepper, and garlic powder. Stir butter sauce into fettuccine. Sprinkle with cheese, tossing until well mixed. Add chicken and mushroom mixture; toss until combined. To serve, arrange fettuccine on a warm platter and sprinkle with toasted pecans. Yields 6 servings.

A Matter of Taste

Since more than 100 Revolutionary War battles took place in New Jersey, it is often referred to as "The Crossroads of the Revolution."

Rigatoni Combination

⅓ pound rigatoni shells,
  macaroni, or other pasta
1 large onion, chopped
1 clove garlic, minced
½ large green pepper, chopped
2 teaspoons olive oil

1 (8-ounce) can tomato sauce
1 (16-ounce) can kidney beans,
  drained
1 teaspoon soy sauce or tamari
½ teaspoon chili powder
Pepper and salt to taste

Cook pasta according to package directions. Sauté onion, garlic, and green pepper in oil for 5 minutes in a large pot. Stir in tomato sauce, kidney beans, soy sauce or tamari, and seasonings. Simmer several minutes to heat through. Drain pasta when done, and stir into sauce. Serve as is, or add hot sauce, if desired. Serves 6.

Total Calories Per Serving: 181; Fat 2g; Total Fat of Daily Value 3%; Prot 8g; Iron 3mg; Carbo 33g; Cal 36mg; Dietary fiber 6g.

Meatless Meals for Working People

Pasta in Paradise

This dish is colorful, with an unexpected secret ingredient. (Pssst...it's the mango.)

4 ounces uncooked vermicelli,
  rice noodles, or spaghetti
¼ cup red or yellow bell pepper
  strips (about 1 medium pepper)
1 cup chopped ripe papaya
  (about 1 small papaya)
½ cup chopped ripe mango
  (about 1 half mango or look
  for frozen cubes)

1 cup chopped ripe tomato
  (about 1 medium tomato)
2 tablespoons chopped fresh
  cilantro, or flat leaf parsley
2 teaspoons olive oil
¼ teaspoon cinnamon
½ teaspoon white pepper
2 tablespoons chopped peanuts

Cook pasta according to package directions. Rinse, drain, and set aside to cool. In a large bowl, combine pepper, papaya, mango, tomatoes, cilantro, oil, cinnamon, and white pepper, and toss to mix. Add pasta and toss to mix. Top with peanuts. Makes 2 servings.

Total Calories Per Serving (using rice noodles and cilantro): 376; Total Fat of Daily Value 15%; Prot 7g; Fat 10g; Carbo 68g; Cal 44mg; Iron 2mg; Sod 19mg; Dietary Fiber 4g.

Vegan Meals for One and Two

Pasta Pasquale

4 large cloves garlic, minced
⅓ cup olive oil
1 medium onion, finely chopped
½ pound sweet Italian sausage
½ pound hot Italian sausage
⅓ cup cognac
2 (35-ounce) cans Italian plum
  tomatoes, drained

1 teaspoon freshly ground pepper
½ teaspoon fennel seed
2 pounds rigatoni (or other pasta)
1 cup heavy cream (optional)
Grated Parmesan cheese, to taste

In fry pan, sauté garlic in olive oil until lightly browned. Add onion; sauté until translucent. Remove sausages from casing, crush with fork, add to fry pan. Sauté until brown and well cooked. Add cognac and allow to boil off. Crush tomatoes by hand or very lightly in blender. Place in saucepan with ingredients from fry pan; add pepper and fennel. Simmer for approximately 1½ hours, stirring occasionally. This can be prepared ahead several days, if refrigerated.

Cook pasta according to package directions. Reheat tomato sauce (do not boil). Add cream; mix well. In large bowl, toss cooked pasta, some sauce, and grated cheese. Place in individual dishes with additional sauce, freshly grated pepper, and grated cheese. Serves 6–8.

Cooking Through the Years

Pasta Primavera

¼ cup olive oil
5 cloves garlic, minced
2 green onions, chopped
1 red pepper, sliced
1 yellow pepper, sliced
1 bunch broccoli, cut florets
1 small zucchini, sliced
1 small yellow squash, sliced

Salt and pepper to taste
1 cup chicken broth
1 cup frozen peas
1 pound pencil point pasta
1 cup chopped fresh basil
½ cup Parmesan cheese
2 tablespoons pine nuts or
  walnuts, toasted

Heat oil in large skillet over high heat. Add garlic and green onions; cook 30 seconds. Add red and yellow peppers and cook 2–3 minutes, stirring. Add broccoli, zucchini, squash, and salt and pepper; cook 5 minutes. Add chicken broth and peas; cover and cook until vegetables are tender, but not overcooked, about 5 minutes. Meanwhile, cook pasta according to package directions; drain. Toss with vegetables, basil, and cheese in large serving dish. Sprinkle with pine nuts. Serve with additional Parmesan cheese.

Our Favorite Recipes–Book Three

Skillet Macaroni

2 cups uncooked macaroni
1 cup leftover meats (chicken,
  beef, etc.)

1 (10-ounce) can chicken gravy
1 can milk
Salt and pepper to taste

Cook macaroni according to package instructions. Spray skillet with a cooking spray and lightly brown the leftover meat. Empty can of chicken gravy into skillet. Fill can with milk. Stir mixture together. Add cooked macaroni. Sprinkle with salt and pepper to individual taste. Continue to cook and stir until the macaroni is coated with the gravy mixture.

Variation: You can use cream of chicken soup instead of gravy. Also add leftover vegetables.

A Taste of Heaven

Creamy Macaroni and Cheese

1 (8-ounce) box elbow macaroni
¼ cup butter or margarine
¼ cup flour
½ teaspoon salt
¼ teaspoon pepper
¼ teaspoon dry mustard
¼ teaspoon Worcestershire sauce
2 cups milk
3 cups shredded Cheddar cheese,
   divided
1 cup buttered bread crumbs

Cook macaroni as directed on the box. Drain and reserve. Preheat oven to 350°. Heat butter in a 3-quart saucepan over low heat until melted. Using a whisk, stir in flour, salt, pepper, mustard, and Worcestershire sauce. Cook over low heat, stirring constantly, until mixture is smooth and bubbly. Remove from heat. Stir in milk. Heat to boiling, stirring constantly. Boil and stir for 1 minute. Add 2½ cups cheese; cook on low, stirring constantly, until melted. Stir in macaroni gently. Pour into an ungreased 2-quart casserole dish. Top with buttered crumbs, mixed with remaining ½ cup cheese. Bake uncovered 20–30 minutes or until bubbly.

Country Chic's Home Cookin

Boscaiola Sauce

2 ounces olive oil
½ onion, finely chopped
3½ ounces parma ham or
   prosciutto, julienned
8 ounces mushrooms, julienned
3 ounces dry white wine
Freshly grated pepper
1 cup heavy cream
1 cup tomato sauce

Heat oil in a deep skillet over moderately high heat and sauté onion until golden. Add ham and cook for about 2 minutes; add mushrooms. Cook until water has evaporated. Moisten with dry white wine and reduce by half. Lower heat and add pepper, heavy cream, and tomato sauce. Simmer for a few minutes to thicken. Serve over your favorite pasta with grated cheese.

La Cucina Casalinga

Mango/Tomato/Date Sauce

This sauce is visually beautiful when served.

**2 ripe mangos, peeled, pitted, and
 chopped**
**1 (14.5-ounce) can whole tomatoes,
 chopped (undrained)**

**5 ounces pitted dates (about 16),
 chopped**

Place all the ingredients in a medium-size pot. Cook for 10 minutes over medium-high heat. Serve sauce over cooked pasta, baked potatoes, or a cooked grain. Serves 6.

Total calories per ½ cup: 124; Fat <1g; Total Fat of Daily Value: <1%; Prot 1g; Iron 1mg; Carbo 32g; Cal 32mg; Dietary fiber 4g; Sod 114mg.

Conveniently Vegan

Maryland Risotto

¾ cup olive oil, divided
4 cloves garlic, chopped
1 cup diced onion
3 cups Arborio rice
1 cup dry white wine
**3 cups diced canned or fresh
 tomatoes**

Pinch saffron threads
1 pound small shrimp, peeled
**1 pound lump crabmeat, shells
 removed**
Salt and pepper to taste
Grated Parmesan cheese

Bring 12 cups of water to a boil; then cover and simmer. Heat 6 tablespoons olive oil in a large sauté pan. Add garlic and onion. Add rice and stir until coated, about 2–3 minutes. Add wine and tomatoes; cook until liquid is absorbed. Gradually add 1 cup of the hot water and then add saffron. As water is absorbed, continue to add hot water, 1 cup at a time, stirring constantly.

In a separate skillet, heat remaining 6 tablespoons oil. Add shrimp; cook until opaque, about 5–6 minutes. Add crabmeat; toss to combine. Add to rice and mix well. Add additional hot water if risotto is too tacky. Serve in bowls and season with salt and pepper and Parmesan cheese. Serves 8 as entrée.

Recipe from Executive Chef Michael Cajigao, Phillips by the Sea, Ocean City, Maryland
Coastal Cuisine

Risotto Agli Asparagi
(Risotto with Asparagus)

4 tablespoons olive oil
½ medium onion, finely chopped
2 garlic cloves, minced
1 cup (225 g) Arborio rice
½ cup (1.2 dl) dry white wine
½ pound (450 g) asparagus, cut
  into 1-inch pieces

4–5 cups (1 l) chicken broth,
  divided
4 tablespoons fresh, grated
  Parmesan cheese

Heat olive oil in a large saucepan; add onion and garlic; cook until tender. Add rice to saucepan and fry in oil and vegetable mixture for 2–3 minutes. Pour in white wine and stir until absorbed. Add asparagus and about ½ cup chicken broth, stirring well. When broth is absorbed, add another ½ cup, continuing to stir and adding broth until rice is cooked, about 20–25 minutes. When rice is just about ready, stir in Parmesan cheese and serve immediately.

Let's Cook Swiss

Carrot Brown Rice

A flavorful and colorful rice.

2⅓ cups chicken broth
1 cup brown rice
½ pound carrots, peeled and
  chopped or julienned

2 medium onions, sliced
1 tablespoon butter
½ teaspoon salt

Bring broth to a boil. Add rice, carrots, onions, butter, and salt; stir. Cover tightly and cook over low heat until all liquid is absorbed, about 50 minutes.

Of Tide & Thyme

Rice-Broccoli Casserole

½ cup diced celery
½ cup chopped onion
½ stick butter or margarine
2 cups cooked rice

1 cup cream of chicken soup
1 small jar Cheez Whiz
1 (10-ounce) package frozen
  chopped broccoli

Sauté celery and onion in butter. Add all the other ingredients in greased casserole. Bake at 350° for 45 minutes. Makes 6 servings.

Atlantic Highlands

Mushroom Bacon Pizza

1 large (10 ounce) Italian bread
  shell
4 ounces shredded mozzarella
  cheese

1¾ cups Mushroom Bacon
  Sauté, well drained
½ cup sliced plum tomatoes

Place bread shell (scooped-out round loaf) on pizza pan or baking tray. Sprinkle with cheese. Spoon well-drained Mushroom Bacon Sauté over cheese. Top with sliced plum tomatoes. Bake in preheated oven at 450° until hot and cheese is melted, about 10 minutes. Makes 4 servings.

MUSHROOM BACON SAUTÉ:
12 ounces bacon (about 12 slices)
1½ pounds fresh white
  mushrooms, sliced
1 cup chopped onion
1 small clove garlic, minced

2 teaspoons crushed oregano
  leaves
1 teaspoon salt
½ teaspoon ground black pepper

In large skillet over medium heat, cook bacon until crisp, about 5 minutes. Transfer to a paper towel, crumble, and set aside. Pour off all but 4 tablespoons bacon fat. Add mushrooms, onion, and garlic. Cook, stirring in crumbled bacon, oregano, salt and pepper. Use half the mixture to make one pizza, and refrigerate the rest. It can be frozen. Makes 3½ cups.

225 Years in Pennington & Still Cooking

MEATS

Originally gray, which was the color of the sandstone it was built out of, the White House in Washington, D.C., was painted white to cover smoke stains caused by having been burned during the War of 1812.

Beef Burgundy

2 pounds beef cubes
4 tablespoons A-1 Steak Sauce
1 package onion soup mix

1 cup red wine
1 can cream of celery soup

Preheat oven to 300°. Mix all ingredients in ovenproof dish. Cook 3 hours. Serves 4.

A Taste of GBMC

Uncle Bill's Beef Roast

1 (3-pound) roast of beef, your
  choice
4 cloves garlic, 3 sliced, 1 chopped
2 tablespoons vegetable oil
½ cup chopped onion
2 tablespoons flour

1 or 2 cans cream of celery soup
1–2 cans water
6 small whole onions
6–8 carrots, peeled
6 small potatoes
Salt and pepper to taste

Use a sharp pointed knife to stick into roast about every 2 inches, then stick in a slice of garlic deep enough to go below surface of roast. Brown roast on all sides in a heavy skillet or Dutch oven in oil. Add chopped garlic and chopped onion; cook until brown. Mix flour with enough water to mix smoothly, with no lumps; add to garlic and onion. Add soup and one can of water per can of soup. Add whole onions, carrots, potatoes, salt and pepper to taste. Cover and cook over very low heat until done. Check during cooking time; add additional water, if needed.

Barineau-Williams Family Cookbook Vol. II

Made of approximately 36,000 granite and marble blocks stacked without metal supports, the Washington Monument is Washington, D.C.'s tallest structure and is the world's tallest freestanding masonry structure. It is 555 feet and 5⅛ inches tall. By government mandate, it will always be the tallest structure in Washington, D.C.

Sauerbraten and Potato Dumplings

This recipe has been handed down for several generations.

SAUERBRATEN (SOUR BEEF):

1 pound beef cubes
Salt and pepper to taste
1 heaping tablespoon pickling
   spices
1½ cups white vinegar

2–4 medium onions, sliced
3 cups water
2 tablespoons sugar
12 gingersnaps

Put beef in pot and season with salt and pepper. Put pickling spices in cheese cloth bag and tie with string. Add spice bag, vinegar, and onions, and boil for ½ hour. Add water and sugar and simmer 2–3 hours. When liquid boils down, add more liquid (3 parts water to 1 part vinegar). When meat is tender, remove the spice bag. Mix the ginger-snaps with a little water until smooth. Add this to the meat mixture and simmer until hot. This makes 6–8 servings.

POTATO DUMPLINGS:

6 medium-sized potatoes
2 eggs
¾ cup flour

½ cup bread crumbs
¼ teaspoon ground nutmeg
2 teaspoons salt

Boil potatoes in their jackets. Drain and allow to cool. Skin and press through ricer. Add other ingredients and mix well. Form into balls, about the size of a golf ball, and place on paper towels to absorb moisture. When ready to cook, bring about 3 cups water to a boil. Add a few dumplings at a time. When they rise to the top, allow to cook for 3 minutes. Remove to warmed plate. Continue until all dumplings are cooked. Serve with the sour beef.

Variation: You can use instant potatoes made just with water (about 3 cups) and allowed to cool before mixing with other ingredients.

Favorite Recipes Home-Style

Corned Beef with Cabbage, Potatoes, Carrots, and Onions

How can you tell when your corned beef is done? Insert a metal or wooden skewer into the thickest part of the brisket. If it slides out easily, it's done. If not, it needs to continue cooking a bit longer. A warning for first-time cooks: the corned beef brisket will shrink by about half during cooking.

1 (4- to 6-pound) corned beef brisket, with seasonings packet

3 medium onions, peeled and quartered

4 large carrots, peeled and cut into thirds

4–6 russet potatoes, peeled and halved (or small red new potatoes, scrubbed)

1 large or 2 small heads cabbage, cut into wedges and cored

Salt and freshly ground pepper, to taste

Fresh grated horseradish and Dijon-style mustard (as condiments)

Place beef in a stockpot or Dutch oven. Add seasonings packet and enough cold water to cover by about 1 inch. Bring to a boil over medium-high heat, skimming and discarding any foam that rises to the surface. Cover and lower heat to a very low simmer, and cook for 2–3 hours, checking periodically to make sure there is enough liquid in the pot (if not, add more water). During the last 30 minutes of cooking, add onions, carrots, and potatoes to pot; cover and simmer for about 15 minutes. Add cabbage, arranging it on top of the meat and other vegetables; cover and simmer until all vegetables are tender, approximately 15–20 minutes longer.

Using a slotted spoon, remove cabbage from pot and arrange on a large platter. Remove other vegetables and arrange. Using strong tongs, remove corned beef brisket and place in center of platter. Slice beef across grain into ¼-inch slices. Moisten the vegetables and meat with a ladle of broth before serving. Pass horseradish and mustard alongside. Serves 6.

Note: If you simmer corned beef brisket slowly, the final product is tender and juicy. If you boil it too hard or too long, it's tough and stringy.

In the Kitchen with Kendi

Peppered Chutney Roast Beef

1 (3- to 4-pound) beef tenderloin
¾ cup unsweetened pineapple
  juice
½ cup steak sauce
⅓ cup Worcestershire sauce
⅓ cup port wine
¼ cup lemon juice

2 teaspoons seasoned salt
2 teaspoons cracked pepper
1 teaspoon lemon pepper
  seasoning
1 teaspoon dry mustard
3 slices bacon
⅓ cup Major Grey's Chutney

Advance preparation: Place tenderloin in a large ziploc bag. In a small bowl, combine pineapple juice, steak sauce, Worcestershire sauce, wine, lemon juice, seasoned salt, pepper, lemon pepper, and dry mustard. Pour over meat in plastic bag. Seal and refrigerate overnight, turning meat occasionally. (Don't lose any sleep over this. Just turn once before bed and once in the morning.)

Preheat oven to 425°. Drain tenderloin, reserving marinade. Rub beef with additional cracked pepper and place in shallow roasting pan. Arrange bacon slices over tenderloin. Roast uncovered for 30–40 minutes. Baste tenderloin with marinade twice during roasting. Spoon chutney over tenderloin. Bake 5–10 minutes more until meat thermometer registers 140°. Let stand 15 minutes before slicing. Yields 12 servings.

Food Fabulous Food

Teriyaki Steak

½ cup soy sauce
1 clove garlic, minced, or ⅛
    teaspoon instant minced garlic
2 tablespoons brown sugar
½ teaspoon ground ginger

2 tablespoons Worcestershire
    sauce
1 tablespoon lemon juice
1 (1½ –2 pound) flank steak

Combine all ingredients, except steak. Add steak to marinade, coating well. Cover and refrigerate 6–24 hours, turning occasionally. Remove steak from marinade. Broil or grill about 5 minutes each side, or to liking. Cut across grain in thin slices. Makes delicious sandwiches cold.

Bread of Life

Steak and Onion Pie

1 cup onion, sliced
¼ cup shortening
1 pound round steak, cut into
    small pieces
¼ cup flour
2 teaspoons salt
½ teaspoon paprika

Dash of ginger
Dash of allspice
2½ cups boiling water
2 cups raw potatoes, diced
⅛ teaspoon pepper
Dough for 1 pie crust

Cook onion slowly in shortening until yellow. Remove onion; set aside. Roll meat in mixture of flour, seasonings, and spices. Brown in hot shortening. Add boiling water; simmer, covered, until meat is tender, about one hour. Add potatoes and cook for 10 minutes longer.

Roll pie dough into circle, about ¼-inch thick. Make several openings for steam to escape. Pour meat and potatoes into greased 8-inch casserole. Cover with reserved onion. Fit pastry over top and seal edges. Bake in a 450° oven for 25–30 minutes. Serves 6.

Our Favorite Recipes

Steak Diane

6 filet mignon steaks, 1 inch thick   1 teaspoon vegetable oil
1 teaspoon butter

Pound steaks to ½-inch thick. Melt butter and oil in sauté pan on medium-high heat, but do not burn butter. Add steaks and brown on one side until blood comes on top; then turn and cook for one minute longer (will be rare). You may cook for one more minute if you want medium rare, but do not over cook because they can dry out.

SAUCE:
2 teaspoons butter   4 teaspoons fresh parsley
6 shallots, minced   1 teaspoon Worcestershire sauce
6 fresh mushrooms, sliced   Salt and pepper to taste
4 teaspoons minced fresh chives   2 ounces brandy

Melt butter in saucepan and add shallots, mushrooms, chives, and parsley. When shallots soften, add Worcestershire sauce, salt and pepper. Now add sauce to meat and simmer 2 minutes. Add brandy and touch with lighted match. Serves 6.

A Taste of Tradition

Cranberry-Orange Relish

Very easy to prepare, this tart relish makes a great accompaniment to turkey and beef dishes. Make it at least a couple of days ahead of time to properly chill the mixture and allow flavors to blend. The relish will keep for several months, if well covered, in the fridge.

1 orange, peeled and chopped   1 teaspoon allspice
  (reserve peel for zest)   2 sticks cinnamon
1½ cups sugar   1 (12-ounce) bag cranberries
¾ cup water   1 tablespoon orange zest
1 teaspoon cloves

Place all ingredients, except cranberries and orange zest, in a small saucepan and bring to a boil. Cook about 3 minutes until syrupy and well blended. Add cranberries and cook about 5 minutes longer, or until berries begin to pop. Remove from heat and stir in orange zest. Let cool, then place in fridge to chill.

Simple Pleasures

Veal and Peppers

2 pounds veal cubes
1 tablespoon paprika
Vegetable cooking spray
1 cup chopped onions
2 medium tomatoes, chopped

1 cup crushed tomatoes
2 medium green peppers, chopped
2 medium red peppers, sliced
2 cups cooked noodles

Sprinkle veal with paprika, and brown in vegetable cooking spray. Add onions and sauté until golden. Add tomatoes and peppers. Cover and simmer one hour. Serve with noodles. Serves 4.

Sealed with a Knish

Veau Guillaume Tell
(Veal Roast with Apples)

2 pounds (1 kg) boneless loin of
  veal
Oil for roasting
1 cup (23 cl) dry white wine,
  divided
Salt, pepper, nutmeg, and paprika
  to taste

3 fluid ounces (1 dl) heavy cream
2 tablespoons Calvados (apple
  brandy)
2 apples

Sauté meat on all sides in a frying pan on high heat for 7 minutes. Put into ovenproof glass plate and cover loosely with aluminum foil. Put in preheated 175° oven (80° C) for 3 hours. (Or roast it the way you are used to.) Deglaze roasting pan with half of the white wine, simmer with salt, pepper, nutmeg, and paprika. Add cream and Calvados. Peel and slice apples, cook in rest of white wine until tender. Serve sauce over sliced veal roast and decorate with apple slices.

Let's Cook Swiss

Calves' Liver with Herbs

A favorite from the Winterthur archives.

LIVER:

1 (¼-inch) slice calves' liver per person
1 cup milk
½ cup flour
½ cup clarified butter
Salt and pepper to taste
Bacon
Watercress

Moisten liver slices with milk, dredge them with flour, and place in a saucepan with hot clarified butter. Cook over moderately hot flame. When browned on one side, turn over, and cook a few more minutes until browned. Season with salt and pepper. Liver should not be cooked too much, as it becomes tough. When cooked, arrange the slices on a hot serving dish and pour the Sauce over them. Garnish with crisp bacon and watercress.

SAUCE:

½ cup butter
1 teaspoon chopped parsley
1 teaspoon chopped tarragon
Juice of 1 lemon

Toss the butter in the pan until soft. Add parsley, tarragon, and lemon juice, and mix well together. Correct the seasoning and pour the Sauce over the liver. Serve very hot. Serves 12.

Winterthur's Culinary Collection

Moussaka

2 onions, chopped
Vegetable cooking spray
3 pounds ground beef
½ teaspoon garlic powder
1 (16-ounce) can tomatoes

1 (6-ounce) can tomato paste
1 teaspoon cinnamon
4 large eggplants, sliced
Flour
¼ cup bread crumbs

Sauté onions in vegetable cooking spray. Add the beef, and brown, stirring to keep it crumbled. Stir in garlic, tomatoes with juice, tomato paste, and cinnamon. Simmer for one hour. Dust the eggplant slices in flour; brown in vegetable cooking spray. Grease a baking dish with vegetable cooking spray and sprinkle with bread crumbs. Alternate layers of eggplant and meat in the dish, ending with eggplant. Refrigerate while preparing Moussaka Sauce. Pour Sauce over the Moussaka. Bake for one hour at 350°. Serve hot. Serves 8–10.

MOUSSAKA SAUCE:

4 tablespoons margarine
¾ cup flour

1 quart non-dairy creamer
6 eggs, beaten

Melt margarine. Stir in flour and brown slightly. Add non-dairy creamer slowly, stirring constantly. When thick, gradually add beaten eggs. Remove from heat immediately and pour over the Moussaka before baking.

Sealed with a Knish

Stuffed Cabbage, II

Hungarians call this recipe "krakacs." Traditionally it's served with wide egg noodles.

1 pound ground chuck	1 carrot
¼ cup raw rice	1 head cabbage
1 egg	1 cup lemon juice
¼ teaspoon salt	2 cups brown sugar
1 onion	4 cups tomato sauce

Combine the beef, raw rice, and egg, mixing well. Add salt. Grate onion and carrot, and add to beef mixture, mixing well.

Cut out the stem of the cabbage. Put it in a large pot and cover with boiling water. Let it set for 2–3 minutes. Pull off as many leaves as possible. Then put it back in the hot water, let it set, and pull off some more leaves. Continue until the remaining leaves are too small to use. Cut out the tough center stems of the leaves. Put a tablespoon or so of meat filling in the center of each leaf, and roll it up. Place the leaves, seam-side-down, closely together in the pot.

Combine the lemon juice, sugar, and tomato sauce, and pour over the stuffed cabbage rolls. Cover pot tightly. Cook over moderate heat about 30 minutes. Reduce heat and simmer another 40 minutes. Or, you can simmer for 20 minutes and then bake at 350° for 20 minutes to brown the tops. Makes 8 servings.

Hoboken Cooks

Black-Iron Skillet One Dish Meal

1 pound hamburger (or ½ pound ground beef and ½ pound ground turkey)	1 green pepper, chopped
	1 (1-pound) can stewed tomatoes
1½ pounds zucchini squash, thinly sliced	Seasoned bread crumbs
	⅛–¼ pound (2–4 ounces) grated cheese
1 medium onion, sliced	

In skillet that can go in the oven, brown meat. Top with 4 layers of vegetables and cover. Simmer 10 minutes. Uncover and top with bread crumbs, then cheese. Put skillet in oven and bake at 350° for 25 minutes.

225 Years in Pennington & Still Cooking

Meat Loaf Supreme

½ cup chopped onion
½ cup chopped green pepper
½ cup chopped celery
2 teaspoons bacon drippings
1½ pounds ground beef
½ pound pork sausage

½ cup bread crumbs
½ cup ketchup
¼ cup milk
½ teaspoon salt
1 egg
3 slices bacon

Sauté onion, green pepper, and celery in bacon drippings and a little water until tender. Mix ground beef, pork sausage, bread crumbs, ketchup, milk, salt, and egg together. Add this mixture to sautéed vegetables. Shape and place in pan. Place bacon strips on top. Bake 45 minutes at 350°.

A Taste of Heaven

Peppy Stuffed Peppers

4 green peppers
1 pound ground beef
2 cups cooked rice (⅔ cup raw)
¼ cup chopped onion

1½ teaspoons salt
⅛ teaspoon pepper
2 (8-ounce) cans tomato sauce,
   divided

Cut peppers in half lengthwise. Remove seeds and wash. Combine beef, cooked rice, onion, salt, pepper, and ½ can tomato sauce. Pile mixture into pepper halves. Pour remaining tomato sauce over each pepper. Cover tightly, bake in 350° oven for 1¼ hours or until peppers are tender, basting occasionally. Makes 4–8 servings.

Jaycee Cookin'

The first organized baseball game was played at Elysian Field in Hoboken, New Jersey, on June 19, 1846. The New York Nine beat the New Jersey Knickerbockers by a score of 23-1.

Pizza Burgers

1 pound ground beef	2 tablespoons oil
1 egg	1 (15-ounce) can tomato sauce
½ cup Italian bread crumbs	½ teaspoon oregano
Salt and pepper to taste	6 slices mozzarella cheese

Mix the ground beef, egg, bread crumbs, salt and pepper in a large bowl to make the burgers. Shape into 6 even-sized burgers. Heat a large skillet over medium-high heat. Add the oil and brown the burgers on both sides. Remove to a plate and set aside. Reduce heat and pour off excess fat into a cup (discard fat when cooled). Add the tomato sauce, a little water rinsed in the can, and oregano. Bring to a boil, stirring well. Reduce heat and simmer. Add the burgers, cover, and cook for 15 minutes. Just before serving, place a slice of mozzarella cheese on each burger, replace cover, and melt cheese. Turn off heat and serve with cooked fusilli pasta and green beans. Serves 4–6.

Good Things to Eat

Popover Pizza

1 pound ground beef	½ teaspoon pepper
1 (15-ounce) can tomato sauce	2 cups Cheddar cheese, shredded
½ cup chopped green pepper	¾ cup water
1 cup plus 2 tablespoons Bisquick Baking Mix, divided	¼ cup butter or margarine
1 tablespoon parsley	4 eggs
	¼ cup chopped green onions

Brown ground beef in a 10-inch skillet. Stir in tomato sauce, green pepper, 2 tablespoons Bisquick, parsley, and pepper. Heat to boiling. Boil and stir 1 minute. Pour into ungreased 9x13-inch pan. Sprinkle with cheese. Heat water and margarine to boiling in a 3-quart saucepan. Add 1 cup Bisquick all at once. Stir vigorously over low heat until mixture forms a ball, about 1½ minutes. Remove from heat. Beat in eggs, one at a time; continue beating until smooth. Spread over beef mixture. Sprinkle with onions. Bake in 400° oven for about 25–30 minutes, until puffy and golden brown. Serve immediately. Serves 6.

What's Cookin'

Mexican Sandwiches

3 pounds ground beef
1 onion, chopped
3 tablespoons oil
1 (10- to 12-ounce) package
  longhorn cheese, grated

1 (15-ounce) can tomato sauce
1 (4-ounce) can salsa
1 (4-ounce) can chopped ripe
  olives
2 dozen sandwich rolls

Brown ground beef and onion together in vegetable oil; drain off grease. Add cheese, tomato sauce, salsa, and olives, and mix well. Pinch some bread out of the center of the roll and fill with beef mixture. Wrap each roll in foil and bake at 350° for 30 minutes.

A Taste of Heaven

Hungry Jack Beef and Bean Round-Up

1½ pounds ground beef
¼ cup chopped onions
1 cup barbecue sauce
1 tablespoon brown sugar
1 (16-ounce) can baked beans with
  brown sugar

1 (10-ounce) can Hungry Jack
  biscuits
½ cup (2 ounces) shredded
  Cheddar cheese

Heat oven to 375°. Brown ground beef and onions in skillet. Drain. Stir in barbecue sauce, brown sugar, and beans. Heat until bubbly. Pour into 1½- to 2½-quart casserole. Separate biscuit dough into biscuits. Cut in half, crosswise. Place biscuits, cut-side-down, over hot meat mixture in spoke fashion around edge of casserole. Sprinkle cheese over biscuits. Bake 22–27 minutes, or until biscuits are golden brown. Serves 6.

A Cookbook of Treasures

Barbeque Sauce

Don't mistake this Barbeque Sauce for the bottled version in the supermarket. This recipe is 30-plus years old and quite unique.

1 egg, well beaten
½ cup corn oil
1 cup cider vinegar
2 teaspoons salt
1½ teaspoons poultry seasoning
¼ teaspoon pepper

Combine all ingredients in a bowl and mix well. Generously brush onto chicken or pork during the last 10–20 minutes of cooking on the grill.

Collected Recipes

Crock Pot Ribs

They will melt in your mouth.

¾–1 cup vinegar
½ cup ketchup
2 tablespoons sugar
2 tablespoons Worcestershire
  sauce
1 garlic clove, minced
1 teaspoon dry mustard
1 teaspoon paprika
½–1 teaspoon salt
⅛ teaspoon pepper
2 pounds pork spareribs
1 tablespoon vegetable oil

Combine first nine ingredients in a slow cooker. Cut ribs into serving-size pieces. Brown in skillet in the oil. Add browned ribs to slow cooker and cook on low 4–6 hours, or until tender.

Country Chic's Home Cookin

Maryland Pork Chops

8 pork chops
2 tablespoons oil
½ teaspoon salt
½ teaspoon sage
4 tart apples, cored and sliced in
  rings

½ cup brown sugar
2 tablespoons flour
1 cup hot water
1 tablespoon cider vinegar
½ cup seedless raisins

Brown pork chops in oil in skillet. Sprinkle with salt and sage. Place in a baking dish. Top with apple rings; sprinkle with sugar. Blend flour into oil in skillet; stir until brown; add water and vinegar. Cook until thickened. Add raisins and pour over pork chops. Bake at 350° for 1 hour. Makes 6–8 servings.

Come, Dine With Us!

Pork Chops in Applesauce Gravy

2 pounds pork chops
1 tablespoon oil
1 (¾-ounce) envelope brown
  gravy mix
1½ cups applesauce

½ cup water
1 tablespoon honey
2 teaspoons lemon juice
1 teaspoon Worcestershire sauce
¼ teaspoon ginger

In large, heavy skillet, brown chops in oil. Drain off excess fat. Combine gravy mix, applesauce, water, honey, lemon juice, Worcestershire sauce, and ginger. Pour over pork. Cover tightly and simmer 50–60 minutes, or until pork is tender. Stir gravy once or twice during cooking period.

The Great Gourmet

Glazed Pork Tenderloin

¼ cup oil
3 tablespoons soy sauce
2 tablespoons apricot jam
1 teaspoon rosemary
1 teaspoon minced garlic
¼ cup strained orange juice

2 tablespoons grated orange rind
1 teaspoon Dijon-style mustard
1 (3- to 4-pound) whole pork
  tenderloin
¼ cup red wine vinegar

Combine oil, soy sauce, jam, rosemary, garlic, orange juice, orange rind, and mustard in a food processor fitted with a steel blade. Whirl until ingredients have blended and thickened slightly. Transfer to a glass or enamel bowl large enough to contain tenderloin and coat meat in the marinade. Cover with plastic wrap and refrigerate 24–48 hours. Turn tenderloin several times to recoat with marinade. Bring to room temperature 2 hours before final preparation.

Preheat oven to 450°. Remove tenderloin from marinade and place in a roasting pan; reserve marinade. Roast 20 minutes per pound. Transfer to a heated platter. Over medium heat, deglaze roasting pan with vinegar, scraping up any particles clinging to pan. Add reserved marinade and stir constantly until very hot. Cut tenderloin into ½-inch slices and serve with sauce.

Note: Doubling recipe is fine, but do not double vinegar.

In the Komondor Kitchen

Marinated Pork Tenderloin with Creamy Mustard Sauce

Savory tenderloin grand for Spring entertaining and excellent served with spinach salad. A dash of ginger added to the marinade can create a delightful oriental touch.

¼ cup soy sauce	2½ tablespoons brown sugar
¼ cup bourbon	1 (2-pound) pork tenderloin

In a 11x7-inch baking dish, combine first 3 ingredients, then add the tenderloin. Cover and refrigerate for 2 hours or more, turning the meat at least twice. Remove meat from marinade and place on a rack in a roasting pan. Reserve the marinade for basting, and bake for 45 minutes at 325°, basting the meat occasionally with marinade.

MUSTARD SAUCE:

⅔ cup sour cream (non-fat)	2 tablespoons dry mustard
⅔ cup light mayonnaise	3 green onions, finely chopped

Combine all ingredients in a small mixing bowl, cover and chill. Serve pork either warm or cold with Mustard Sauce on side. Serves 6 as an entrée.

Of Tide & Thyme

Sautéed Medallion of Pork Tenderloin

½ pound dark, sweet, pitted
   cherries
1 cup beef broth
¼ cup orange juice
2 tablespoons brown sugar
1 tablespoon granulated sugar
1 tablespoon lemon juice
2–3 dashes ginger
4 tablespoons butter, softened

2 ounces sun-dried cherries
2½ pounds pork tenderloin,
   cut and trimmed into 2-ounce
   medallions
1 cup flour
½ cup vegetable oil
Cherry brandy
Salt
Pepper

In blender, combine pitted cherries and beef broth. On medium speed, purée until smooth. Pour puréed cherries into a saucepan. Add orange juice, brown sugar, sugar, lemon juice, and ginger. Bring to a boil, reduce heat, and let simmer 5–6 minutes. Remove from heat, and whisk in softened butter until smooth. Add dried cherries.

Dust pork medallions with flour and sauté in a large pan with hot oil. Brown evenly on both sides. Discard oil and deglaze pan with a glug of cherry brandy. Reduce brandy by one-third. Add cherry sauce, salt and pepper to taste. Continue to cook for about 3–4 minutes. Remove from heat and serve. Yields 6 servings.

Note: For ease of preparation, substitute for fresh cherries 1 (16-ounce) can of dark, sweet, pitted cherries, drained.

Food Fabulous Food

The Naval School was founded in 1845 with seven teachers and 50 midshipmen at Fort Severn, Annapolis, Maryland. Renamed the United States Naval Academy in 1850, it is now a National Historic Landmark. "The Yard," as they call the campus, is now 338 acres and the Brigade of Midshipmen is 400 strong.

Pork Tenderloin with Stilton and Port

This dramatic sauce may also accompany a beef tenderloin.

2 pork tenderloins, approximately
  1 pound each
2 tablespoons vegetable oil
2 cups port wine

1 cup chicken stock
1 cup heavy cream
6–8 ounces Stilton cheese

Heat oil in large skillet. Add pork and brown on all sides. Transfer pork to covered roasting pan. Deglaze skillet with port and reduce by half. Add chicken stock and bring to a boil. Pour over pork and bake at 450° until done, approximately 15 minutes. Remove pork and keep warm. Reduce liquid by half and slowly stir in cream. Cook over medium heat until sauce thickens. Add Stilton and stir to blend. Spoon sauce over sliced tenderloin. Serves 6–8.

Capital Classics

Ham and Turkey Pie

1 medium onion, sliced
3 carrots, pared and sliced
¾ teaspoon thyme
¼ teaspoon basil
½ pound mushrooms, sliced
3 tablespoons oil
1 teaspoon salt
¼ teaspoon pepper

3 tablespoons flour
½ cup chicken broth
¾ cup white wine
3 cups turkey, diced
Pastry for 2-crust pie
¼ pound ham, sliced
1 egg, slightly beaten

Sauté onion, carrots, thyme, basil, and mushrooms in oil for about 10 minutes, or until golden. Remove from heat and mix in salt, pepper, and flour. Stir in broth and wine; return to heat and bring to boil, stirring. Simmer for 5 minutes; stir in turkey. Roll out and fit pastry in 9-inch pie pan. Line with slices of ham. Roll out remaining pastry; after filling pie with turkey mixture, put in place. Fold edges to seal well and make several gashes for steam vents. Brush with half the beaten egg. Bake in preheated 375° oven for 25 minutes; brush with remaining egg and bake an additional 25 minutes. Serve warm or cold. Serves 8.

Mid-Day Magic

Easter Meat Pie
(Pizza Cianne)

½ pound prosciutto
½ pound baked ham
½ pound salami
½ pound sausage
1 pound mozzarella

1 pound farmer's cheese
½ cup grated cheese
2 dozen eggs (hard-boil 1 dozen)
Black pepper
Pizza Cianne Crust

Cut meat into small pieces; do the same with the cheeses and mix all ingredients together with chopped, hard-boiled eggs. Mix in the raw eggs. Put ½ Pizza Cianne Crust into pan; add meat and cheese mixture. Cover with remaining crust; bake at 350° until top is golden brown.

PIZZA CIANNE CRUST:

4 pounds flour
1 pound shortening (Crisco)

Black pepper to taste
1 quart lukewarm water

Mix flour, shortening, and pepper; add water. Knead into dough.

La Cucina Casalinga

Roast Leg of Lamb with Artichokes

1 (5- to 6-pound) leg of lamb,
  trimmed of fat
2 garlic cloves, sliced
2 tablespoons olive oil
½ teaspoon thyme
1 teaspoon oregano

Pinch sea salt and pepper, to taste
3 cups boiling water
¼ cup lemon juice
2 packages frozen artichokes,
  rinsed and defrosted

Preheat oven to 400°. Make small slits into the leg of lamb and insert garlic slices. Mix oil with thyme, oregano, salt and pepper, and rub all over roast. Place in a roasting pan, and cook in the oven for 30 minutes. Reduce heat to 350° and continue baking for 1½ hours. Add water and lemon juice, basting roast with juices. Add artichokes; bake for another ½ hour or until lamb is done and artichokes are tender. Let the lamb rest for 10 minutes before serving. Serves 6–8.

Dr. John's Healing Psoriasis Cookbook...Plus!

POULTRY

Editors Moseley and McKee tour Princeton, one of the world's most respected institutes of higher learning. First founded in Elizabeth, New Jersey, in 1746, the Ivy League college moved to Newark and then to Princeton in 1756.

Karen's Chicken Chalupas

2 cans cream of chicken soup
1 pint sour cream
1 small can diced green chiles
1 bunch green onions, chopped
1 small can sliced black olives
   (optional)

¾ pound grated Jack cheese
4 large chicken breasts, cooked
   and cut into pieces
1 dozen flour tortillas
¾ pound grated Cheddar cheese

In large bowl, mix soup, sour cream, chiles, green onions, olives, and Jack cheese. Remove 2 cups of mixture and set aside.

Add chicken to above mixture. Put ½ cup into each tortilla and roll up. Place in large casserole or 9x13x2-inch pan. Pour the reserved 2 cups of mixture over top of rolled tortillas; cover with grated Cheddar cheese. Bake at 350° until hot and bubbly (for approximately 35–45 minutes). Can be made ahead and frozen. Makes 4–6 servings.

Fair Haven Fare

Salsa Chicken

6 boneless, skinless chicken breasts
1 (16-ounce) jar salsa

1 can cream of mushroom soup
1 cup shredded Cheddar cheese

Preheat oven to 350°. Place clean, dry chicken breasts in baking dish. Mix salsa with soup and pour over chicken. Bake 30–40 minutes. Sprinkle cheese over chicken during last 10 minutes of baking. Serves 6.

South Coastal Cuisine

The first residents of New Jersey were the Lenni Lenape Indians 10,000 years before European explorers arrive. Henry Hudson established a Dutch colony called New Netherland in New Jersey in 1609 when it was know as "the northeast territory." It later became New Jersey after the Isle of Jersey in the English Channel.

Chicken and Spinach Enchilada Casserole

This is a great entrée for a casual dinner party.

2 pounds boneless chicken breasts
4 tablespoons (½ stick) unsalted butter
1 large onion, chopped
1 (10-ounce) box frozen chopped spinach, thawed and drained
3 cups sour cream
1 teaspoon ground cumin

1 (4-ounce) can chopped green chiles (or more to taste)
¼ cup milk
Salt and freshly ground pepper to taste
12 flour tortillas
8 ounces shredded Monterey Jack cheese

Place chicken breasts in a skillet and add water to just cover. Poach on medium-low heat until cooked through, approximately 15–20 minutes. Remove from water and cool. Shred or cut into bite-sized pieces and place in a mixing bowl.

Preheat oven to 350°. Grease a 9x13-inch baking dish. In a small skillet, melt the butter and sauté the onion until tender, about 5 minutes. In a large bowl, combine cooked onion, spinach, sour cream, cumin, chiles, and milk. Season with salt and pepper. Add half the sauce to the shredded chicken and mix well. Layer 3 tortillas in bottom of casserole dish. Cover with ⅓ of the chicken mixture. Repeat process 3 times, ending with a layer of tortillas. Cover casserole with remaining sauce, spreading evenly with a spatula. Top with grated cheese. Bake casserole approximately 40 minutes, or until heated through and bubbly and cheese begins to brown. Serve hot. Serves 6–8.

In the Kitchen with Kendi

Make Ahead Chicken Casserole

1 (6¼-ounce) package Uncle Ben's
   Long Grain and Wild Rice
4 whole chicken breasts, cooked
   and torn from bone
2 cans mushroom soup
½ soup can water
1 cup chopped celery

1 cup chopped bell pepper
¾ cup mayonnaise
1 medium onion, chopped
1 can sliced water chestnuts,
   drained
1 large package slivered almonds

Prepare rice as directed on package. Spread evenly over bottom of large (9x13x2-inch) ovenproof baking dish. Place pieces of chicken breast over top of rice. Blend remaining ingredients, except almonds, and pour over chicken and rice. Refrigerate overnight. Remove from refrigerator and top with almonds; cover with foil and bake at 350° for 1½ hours. Sprinkle with paprika before serving.

Our Favorite Recipes

Best Ever Chicken

4 whole skinless, boneless,
   chicken breasts
½ pound sliced mushrooms, or
   more, if desired
1 (14½-ounce) can crushed
   tomatoes (can use stewed)

½ cup Italian Dressing or Russian
   Dressing
1 package dry onion soup mix
1 bay leaf

Place chicken breasts in a baking dish; top with sliced mushrooms. Add tomatoes. Mix dressing with onion soup mix and pour over. Toss in bay leaf. Bake, uncovered, one hour at 350°, basting frequently. Serve with rice or noodles. If too much liquid, drain some prior to serving. Remove bay leaf before serving. Serves 4–6.

Where There's a Will...

Baked Chicken Reuben

4 boned, skinless chicken breasts
¼ teaspoon salt
⅛ teaspoon pepper
1 small can sauerkraut, drained
Low-fat Russian or Thousand
   Island dressing

4 slices fat-free Swiss cheese
1 tablespoon chopped parsley
Chopped chives

Preheat oven to 325°. Coat a small glass or ceramic baking dish with vegetable oil cooking spray. Arrange chicken pieces in the dish and sprinkle with salt and pepper. Cover the chicken with sauerkraut. Pour desired amount of dressing evenly over all and top with cheese and parsley. Cover with foil and bake one hour, or until fork tender. Sprinkle with chopped chives to serve. Serves 4.

Two grams of fat per serving.

Bountiful Blessings

Chicken Breast Diane

4 large boneless chicken breast
   halves, or 8 small breasts
½ teaspoon salt
¼ teaspoon black pepper
2 tablespoons olive or salad oil,
   divided
2 tablespoons butter or margarine,
   divided

3 tablespoons chopped fresh
   chives or green onions
Juice of ½ lime or lemon
2 tablespoons of brandy or cognac
   (optional)
3 tablespoons chopped parsley
2 teaspoons Dijon-style mustard
¼ cup chicken broth

Place chicken breast halves between sheets of waxed paper or plastic wrap. Pound slightly with mallet. Sprinkle with salt and black pepper. Heat 1 tablespoon each of oil and butter in large skillet. Cook chicken over high heat for 4 minutes on each side until done. Do not overcook or they will be dry. Transfer to warm serving platter. Add chives or green onions, lime or lemon juice and brandy or cognac, if used, parsley, and mustard to pan. Cook 15 seconds, whisking constantly. Whisk in broth. Stir until sauce is smooth. Whisk in remaining butter and oil. Pour sauce over chicken and serve immediately.

DAPI's Delectable Delights

Chicken Pillows

6 chicken breast halves
2 tablespoons fresh lemon juice
3 tablespoons virgin olive oil,
   divided
2 carrots
1 small yellow summer squash
6 thin asparagus spears (optional)
6 scallions

6 slices mozzarella cheese
½ cup fresh bread crumbs
1 clove garlic, minced
⅛ teaspoon salt
2 tablespoons minced mixed fresh
   herbs, such as basil, parsley,
   chives

Skin and bone the chicken breasts to obtain long, triangular filets; pound lightly. Marinate the breasts in the lemon juice and one tablespoon of the oil for one hour at room temperature, turning occasionally.

Meanwhile, prepare the vegetables. Trim the carrots to 5 inches in length and cut into ¼-inch-wide strips. Blanch in boiling water for 3 minutes. Also trim the squash to the same size and blanch for 30 seconds. Trim the asparagus spears and scallions to 5-inch lengths and blanch for one minute. Remove the breasts from the marinade and place them smooth-side-down on a work surface. Reserve the marinade. Place one slice of cheese on each breast. Place one strip of each vegetable across the top. Roll up the breasts in loose packages and fasten with wooden picks. Arrange the chicken pillows in a baking dish. Brush them with the marinade and cover the dish with foil. This preparation may be done ahead of time, and the dish may be refrigerated until it is to be cooked.

Bake the chicken at 375° until it feels firm but springy to the touch, about 20 minutes in a preheated oven. While the breasts are baking, heat the remaining 2 tablespoons of oil in a small skillet and lightly brown the bread crumbs. Add garlic, salt, and mixed herbs. Remove the pillows from the oven and sprinkle them with bread crumb mixture. Broil until golden, about 2–3 minutes. Remove picks and arrange the pillows on a warmed platter. Serves 6.

225 Years in Pennington & Still Cooking

Mary Jane's Chicken Cordon Bleu

8 slices Swiss or muenster
  cheese
8 slices tavern ham or deli sliced
  ham

8 boneless, skinless chicken
  breasts
Milk
Bread crumbs

Preheat oven to low 275°. Place a slice of cheese on work surface; top with slice of ham, then a chicken breast. Roll up with cheese on outside. Dip in milk, then into bread crumbs. Place in 9x13-inch baking dish that has been sprayed with cooking spray. Continue with remaining cheese, ham, and chicken. Bake, uncovered, at 275° for 1½–2 hours. They will get nice and golden brown when done.

Our Favorite Recipes–Book Three

Cream Cheese and Spinach Stuffed Chicken Rolls

6 boneless chicken breast halves
1 (8-ounce) package cream cheese,
  softened
½ cup chopped cooked spinach
1 clove garlic, minced
⅛ teaspoon nutmeg

Salt and pepper to taste
1 large egg, beaten with
  1 tablespoon water
½ cup unseasoned bread crumbs
3 tablespoons margarine, melted

Heat oven to 375°. Flatten chicken between sheets of plastic wrap to uniform ¼-inch thickness. In large bowl, beat cream cheese with spinach, garlic, nutmeg, salt and pepper. Spoon equal amount of mixture across narrow end of each breast. Roll jellyroll-style. Dip in egg, then in crumbs; shake off excess. In baking dish, arrange chicken in single layer, seam-side-down; drizzle with melted margarine. Bake 25–30 minutes or until golden brown. Makes 6 servings.

Atlantic Highlands

Oven Chicken Nuggets

4 chicken breasts, boned
¼ cup grated Parmesan cheese
4 tablespoons grated Cheddar
  cheese
½ cup bread crumbs

1 teaspoon thyme
1 teaspoon salt
1 teaspoon basil
⅛ teaspoon pepper
½ cup melted butter or margarine

Skin chicken breasts; cut into 1-inch squares. Combine Parmesan cheese, Cheddar cheese, bread crumbs, thyme, salt, basil, and pepper; blend well. Dip chicken pieces into butter; roll in crumb mixture. Arrange chicken in single layer on foil-lined baking sheets. Bake at 400° for 10 minutes.

What's Cookin'

Garlic Chicken Bites

2 boneless, skinless chicken
  breasts (1 pound), cut into
  bite-sized strips
½ cup extra virgin olive oil
4 cloves garlic, minced

¼ teaspoon black pepper
½ cup finely ground bread
  crumbs
¼ teaspoon cayenne

Marinate chicken strips in olive oil, garlic, and pepper for 30 minutes. Drain off excess marinade. Preheat oven to 475°. Mix bread crumbs with cayenne. Dip both sides of chicken strips in mixture. Arrange strips in one layer on a baking sheet. Bake for 15 minutes. Turn and bake 5 minutes more until browned.

The Glen Afton Cookbook

Chicken a la Bethany

4–6 chicken breasts
1 egg, beaten
Flour for dredging
Butter
Salt and pepper to taste
1 can chicken broth

¼ cup vinegar
1 cup sugar
1 red pepper, sliced
1 green pepper, sliced
1 onion, sliced
1 can crushed pineapple

Lightly dip chicken breasts in egg and then in flour. Sauté in buttered skillet. Add salt and pepper to taste. In a separate saucepan, mix chicken broth, vinegar, and sugar. Add sliced peppers, onion, and pineapple. Simmer until vegetables are cooked.

To thicken sauce, mix small amount of hot water with 2 tablespoons flour; stir until smooth and add to sauce. Serve chicken topped with sauce. Accompany with rice.

South Coastal Cuisine

Country Chicken

2 sweet or hot sausage links, sliced
2 red potatoes, diced
6 tablespoons extra virgin olive
    oil, divided
2 boneless, skinless chicken
    breasts
2 tablespoons flour for coating

2 shallots, chopped
2 cloves garlic, pressed
3 ounces white wine
1 (7-ounce) jar roasted red
    peppers, drained
3 teaspoons sweet basil

In a small skillet (or sauté pan) brown sausage and potatoes in 1 tablespoon olive oil, turning frequently to avoid burning. Remove potatoes and sausage from pan and allow to drain on paper towels. Heat remainder of olive oil in a large skillet. While oil is heating, slice each chicken breast lengthwise into 4 pieces; coat with flour. Sauté chicken in olive oil for 2 minutes. Add shallots and garlic and continue to sauté until chicken is lightly browned. Reduce heat. Add wine, sausage, potatoes, roasted red peppers, and basil, cooking for 5 minutes more.

Collected Recipes

Main Street Chicken

SUN-DRIED TOMATO PESTO:
½ cup sun-dried tomatoes
¾ cup fresh parsley
8–10 large black olives, pitted
1 tablespoon red wine vinegar
1 garlic clove, peeled
2 shallots
Salt to taste
1 tablespoon black pepper, or
   to taste
2 tablespoons olive oil

In a food processor, combine the tomatoes, parsley, black olives, red wine vinegar, garlic, and shallots. Process until ingredients are combined and smooth. Season to taste with salt and black pepper. Add the olive oil. Store at room temperature or in the refrigerator until needed.

CHICKEN:
6 whole boneless, skinless
   chicken breasts
1 small eggplant, skinned and
   sliced into 12 rounds, floured,
   pan-fried in olive oil
½ pound fresh spinach, lightly
   sautéed, drained
3 red peppers, halved, roasted
Salt and pepper to taste
Olive oil
White wine to taste

Remove the cartilage from the center of the chicken breasts so you have 12 halves. Lightly pound the chicken halves. Put 6 breast halves on a baking sheet. Distribute the eggplant, spinach, and roasted red peppers in even layers on the chicken breast halves. Place the remaining chicken breast halves on top to form "sandwiches." Season to taste with salt and pepper. Pour an ample amount of olive oil and wine over them. Bake at 425° for 15–20 minutes. Meanwhile, prepare the sauce.

SAUCE:
½ cup white wine
⅓ cup white wine vinegar
3 tablespoons shallots
2 tablespoons heavy cream
8 ounces (2 sticks) butter
1 scallion, thinly sliced
Salt and white pepper to taste

In a saucepan over medium-high heat, reduce the white wine, white wine vinegar, and shallots until there is only ¾ tablespoon left. Add the heavy cream and reduce again until ¾ tablespoon is left. Lower the heat and whisk in the butter, a little at a time, until it is emulsified. Add the scallion and season with salt and white pepper. Place each chicken breast on a serving plate. Top with the Sun-Dried Tomato Pesto and spoon the Sauce around the chicken. Serves 6.

Cooking Secrets

Chicken Cacciatore

3 large cans whole tomatoes
Salt to taste
Pepper to taste
Basil to taste
Garlic powder to taste
Oregano to taste
3 medium onions, sliced
1 whole frying chicken, cut up

In a saucepot, put whole tomatoes (squeezed, leaving small chunks). Add seasonings; let simmer for about 1 hour. Sauté onions lightly in frying pan. Add to sauce. Fry each piece of chicken halfway. Lay pieces of chicken in casserole dish. Pour on sauce. Cover and bake in oven for about 30 minutes. Serve with spaghetti.

Out of the Frying Pan Into the Fire!!!

Pollo Alla Romana
(Chicken Roman Style)

4 chicken quarters
Well seasoned flour
1½ ounces butter
3 tablespoons olive oil, divided
3 ounces freshly chopped onion
2 ounces cooked ham, cut in strips
4 tablespoons dry white wine
3–4 spikes rosemary
12 ounces ripe tomatoes, peeled
  and chopped, or 1 (14-ounce)
  can peeled tomatoes
2 green peppers, halved and
  seeded

Coat chicken joints with seasoned flour. Heat butter and 1 tablespoon oil in a shallow pan with a lid and fry chicken joints until golden brown on both sides, about 12 minutes. Remove joints from pan. Add onion; fry gently for 3–4 minutes then return chicken and add ham, wine, and rosemary. Cook until wine is absorbed, then add tomatoes. Cover pan and simmer gently for 30 minutes. Meanwhile, cut prepared peppers into ½-inch-wide strips and fry gently in the remaining oil for 10 minutes. Add to chicken. Continue cooking until chicken is tender, about 45 minutes. Check the seasoning and serve.

La Cucina Casalinga

Italian Chicken
(Savory Chicken Italiano)

2½ pounds frying chicken
Salt and pepper
3 tablespoons cooking oil
2 cups spaghetti sauce
1 (10¾-ounce) can chicken broth
1 tablespoon parsley
1 teaspoon garlic powder
¼ cup shredded mozzarella

Cut up chicken; sprinkle chicken pieces with salt and pepper. Then brown chicken in oil in frying pan. After it is browned, drain off fat. Add spaghetti sauce, chicken broth, parsley, and garlic powder. Simmer, covered, for 40 minutes. After it has finished cooking, top with shredded mozzarella cheese. Makes 4 servings.

A Taste of Heaven

Gorgonzola Chicken

1 (2–3 pound) roasting chicken
5 or 6 ounces gorgonzola or
  Roquefort cheese
½ cup cold water
2 tablespoons cognac, divided
½ cup heavy cream

Set oven to 350°. Wash chicken inside and out with cold water and pat dry with paper towels. Very gently run your fingers just under the skin, insert and flatten pieces of cheese. You will probably have ½–1 ounce left. Bake chicken in a shallow roasting pan, uncovered, about 1 hour and 15 minutes, or until juices from breast or thigh run clear. Place on a warm plate. Deglaze roasting pan with water, scraping up brown bits. Place in a small saucepan and boil down by half, over high heat, stirring and skimming off fat. Add 1 tablespoon cognac, pour in any juices accumulated on the plate, and boil down. Add the second tablespoon cognac and the cream and stir. Taste. You may want, at this point, to whisk in a bit more cheese. Carve chicken and pass the sauce. Especially good with boiled new potatoes.

Slices of cold roasted chicken are also very good the next day tossed in a salad with greens and thinly sliced onions, the leftover cheese, and a vinaigrette or oil and vinegar dressing.

In the Komondor Kitchen

Chicken and Chips

1½ cups chopped celery	1 cup shredded sharp Cheddar
1½ cups sliced, fresh mushrooms	cheese
3 tablespoons butter	1 cup sour cream
3 cups chopped, cooked chicken	1 cup mayonnaise
1 (10-ounce) can cream of chicken	½ teaspoon salt
soup	½ cup slivered almonds
½ cup milk	1½ cups crushed potato chips

Sauté celery and mushrooms in butter in skillet until tender. Combine with chicken, soup, milk, Cheddar cheese, sour cream, mayonnaise, and salt in large bowl and mix well.

Spoon mixture into a 9x13-inch baking dish. Sprinkle with almonds and potato chips. Bake at 375° for 30–35 minutes or until hot and bubbly. Yields 6–8 servings.

Beyond Peanut Butter and Jelly

Company Chicken Casserole

2 tablespoons butter	2 cups medium cooked noodles
2 tablespoons flour	2 cups chopped, cooked chicken
¼ teaspoon prepared mustard	1 package frozen broccoli spears,
1 teaspoon salt	cooked
¼ teaspoon black pepper	⅓ cup slivered almonds
2 cups milk	
1 cup Velveeta or grated American	
cheese	

Melt butter and stir in the flour, mustard, salt, pepper, and milk. Cook and stir until thickened. Remove from heat and stir in the cheese; set aside. Arrange layers of noodles, chicken, and broccoli (cut into 1-inch pieces, reserving flowerettes) in a 2-quart casserole dish. Pour cheese sauce over layered ingredients; arrange broccoli flowerettes on top, and sprinkle with the almonds. Bake 20 minutes at 350°. Can be made ahead.

A Cookbook of Treasures

Hot Chicken

2 cups cooked, diced chicken
1 cup Uncle Ben's Long Grain &
   Wild Rice
1 cup water chestnuts
2 tablespoons onion
½ cup mayonnaise

2 cups French-style green beans,
   drained
1 can cream of celery soup
2 tablespoons pimento
Salt and pepper to taste

Mix all ingredients. Bake in large, greased baking dish in 350° oven for about 50 minutes. Serve hot.

What's Cookin'

Chicken and Almond Crepes

2 tablespoons butter
2 tablespoons minced onion
2 tablespoons flour
1½ cups half-and-half
1½–2 cups finely chopped chicken

¼ cup sherry
12–16 crepes
¼ cup grated Parmesan cheese
¼ cup grated Swiss cheese
¼ cup sliced almonds

Melt butter in medium skillet. Add onion and sauté. Blend in flour gradually. Stir in half-and-half and cook until thickened. Remove half of this sauce. Stirring constantly, add chicken and sherry to remaining half of the sauce. Spread a heaping teaspoonful on each crepe. Roll up and place in greased 9x13-inch baking pan or shallow casserole dish. Cover with remaining sauce. Sprinkle with cheeses and almonds. Bake at 450° for 10–15 minutes or until brown. Makes 6–8 servings.

Atlantic Highlands

 On display at the Delaware History Museum in Wilmington is the world's largest frying pan; 10 feet in diameter. The frying pan, built in 1950 for use at the Delmarva Chicken Festival, holds 180 gallons of oil and 800 chicken quarters.

Roasted Wild Duck

1 wild duck
½ medium apple, cut in half
  and seeded

½ medium onion, sliced
4 strips bacon

Clean and dry wild duck. Place apple and onion in cavity of duck. Place bacon strips over breast. Wrap tightly in aluminum foil with shiny side of foil to meat. Place in baking pan. Roast in a 325° oven until tender, 3–4 hours. Makes 3–4 servings.

Come, Dine With Us!

Roast Duck
with Sage and Onion Stuffing

3 tablespoons butter
½ cup finely chopped onion
2 cups finely shredded bread
1 teaspoon salt
½ teaspoon sage

¼ teaspoon freshly ground pepper
1 tablespoon chopped parsley
¼ cup applejack (apple brandy)
1 (4–5 pound) duck

Melt butter in a large skillet, then sauté the onions until just translucent. Add the shredded bread, salt, sage, and pepper; toss. Stir in parsley and applejack, then correct the seasoning, if necessary. Cover until needed.

Wash and prepare the duck for roasting as you would a large chicken. Tie the legs together and slip the wings under the back. Place on a rack in the roasting pan and rub with salt. Roast for 30 minutes at 425°. Remove from oven and, wearing disposable gloves, pour out any fat accumulated in the cavity. Insert the stuffing and lace the cavity shut, loosely. Prick the skin in many places with a fork and continue roasting at 325° for about 2 hours, or until skin is nicely browned and crisp. Serve with sweet potatoes and baked apples. A Medoc or Cabernet Sauvignon will do nicely for wine.

Conducting in the Kitchen

Cornish Hens

Pretty arranged on a platter with lettuce leaves and peach halves filled with cranberry sauce.

½ cup raisins
3 tablespoons cooking sherry
6 tablespoons butter, divided
1 cup sliced celery
1 cup chopped onion
2 tablespoons parsley flakes

3 cups cooked rice
3 tablespoons orange juice
½ teaspoon salt
3 (1-pound) Cornish game hens
Salt and pepper, as desired

Marinate raisins in sherry for 15 minutes. Melt 3 tablespoons butter in skillet. Add celery, onion, and parsley, and cook until tender. Add rice, orange juice, salt, and marinated raisins; toss lightly. Sprinkle hens inside and out with salt and pepper, as desired. Rub with remaining 3 tablespoons of melted butter.

Fill cavity of each hen with ½ cup stuffing. Place in baking pan and bake in a 350° oven for 1¼–1½ hours, or until golden brown and tender, brushing occasionally with pan drippings. Spoon remaining dressing into greased baking pan. Cover and place in oven during the last 30 minutes of baking time. Makes 5 servings.

Our Favorite Recipes

Crock Pot Stuffing

Neck and giblets from turkey
2 (16-ounce) packages herbed-
   seasoned stuffing cubes
2 sticks butter or margarine
4 stalks celery, finely chopped

1 medium onion, finely chopped
1¼ teaspoons ground sage
Salt and pepper to taste
1 large carton or 2 small cans
   Swanson's chicken broth

Wash neck and giblets and put in a saucepan with water and some salt and pepper; cook until done. Strain the broth and add enough water to make 5 cups of broth. Set aside. You can cut up the giblets and put in the stuffing if you like.

In a very large bowl, empty both bags of stuffing mix (I use Pepperidge Farm cubed, herbed stuffing mix). Melt butter in a large frying pan and sauté celery and onion until tender. Add the sautéed celery, onions and butter, strained broth, sage, and a little salt and pepper to stuffing mix. Mix gently. It should be fairly wet. Spray a large crock pot with non-stick spray. Put mixture in crock pot. Pour ½ cup or so of the chicken broth over the stuffing. Cook on high for half an hour, then turn to low for 4–6 hours. Pour chicken broth over the stuffing whenever it looks like it's drying out. You can tell when it is done. It's golden, moist, and tastes great.

This is an excellent, moist, well seasoned stuffing; doesn't take up valuable oven space during the holidays. This serves a crowd, so cut recipe in half for just a few people.

Country Chic's Home Cookin

Turkey and Leek Shepherd's Pie

This is a great recipe for using up Thanksgiving leftovers.

2 teaspoons olive oil
2 large leeks (white and light
   green parts only), washed and
   thinly sliced
1½ cups thinly sliced carrots
   (2–3 carrots)
1 tablespoon minced garlic
⅓ cup dry white wine
3 tablespoons flour
2 teaspoons fresh sage or ½
   teaspoon dried rubbed sage

2 cups chicken broth or leftover
   gravy
2 cups diced cooked turkey or
   chicken
1 cup frozen peas
Salt and pepper to taste
3 cups mashed potatoes (leftover
   or frozen)
1 large egg, beaten
1 tablespoon olive oil

Heat 2 teaspoons oil over medium heat. Add leeks and carrots and cook, stirring until the leeks soften, about 7 minutes. Add garlic and cook, stirring 1 minute more. Pour in wine and stir until most liquid is evaporated; add flour and sage, stirring constantly until flour starts to turn light brown, about 2 minutes. Stir in broth, bring to simmer; stir constantly, until sauce thickens and carrots are barely tender about 5 minutes. Add turkey and peas, salt and pepper. Transfer to a deep 10-inch pan or 2-quart dish. Mix potatoes with egg and 1 tablespoon oil. Spread potato mixture over turkey mixture. Set on baking sheet and bake 25–30 minutes at 425°, until the potatoes and filling are heated through and the top is golden brown. Serves 6.

Around the Table

SEAFOOD

Thomas Point Shoal Lighthouse, Maryland, is a fine example of the unique "screwpile" design. It is the last structure of this type left on its original site, and was the last staffed lighthouse in Chesapeake Bay.

Maryland Crab Cakes

1 pound crabmeat, picked
2 egg whites, beaten
½ cup bread crumbs
1 teaspoon Worcestershire sauce
1 tablespoon parsley

1 tablespoon baking powder
1 teaspoon mayonnaise
1 teaspoon Old Bay Seasoning
Vegetable cooking spray

Thoroughly mix all ingredients together in a medium bowl. Shape into patties or cakes. Spray a nonstick skillet or griddle with vegetable spray. Cook each side over medium heat until golden brown. Serves 4.

Barineau-Williams Family Cookbook Vol. II

Eastern Shore Crab Cakes

This is an old receipt from the Eastern Shore of Maryland.

1 pound crabmeat
Salt and pepper to taste
1 egg
¼ pound butter
1 tablespoon lemon juice

1 hard-boiled egg
1 tablespoon Worcestershire sauce
Bread crumbs (from 2–3 slices
   bread)

Put crabmeat in a bowl and season to taste with salt and pepper. Add slightly beaten egg, melted butter, lemon juice, cut up hard-boiled egg, and Worcestershire sauce. Then add just enough soft bread crumbs to make it into cakes (2 or 3 slices of bread). Fry the cakes a golden brown.

Maryland's Way

There are a number of different types of crabmeat to choose from when preparing recipes. . . "Lump" is the largest pieces of meat from the crab's body; it is the most expensive form of crabmeat. "Backfin" is white body meat in lump and large flakes and is best for dishes where appearance is important. "Special," flakes of white body meat other than lump, is good for casseroles and crabcakes. "Claw" is small, brownish meat from the claws; as the least expensive type of crab meat, it is good for appetizers, soups, and dips.

Best Maryland Crab Cakes

Best tasting crab cakes ever!

4 slices white bread with crusts
   trimmed, or ½ cup dry bread
   crumbs, or 6 saltines, crumbled
½ teaspoon dry mustard
½ teaspoon Chesapeake-style
   seafood seasoning
¼ teaspoon Ac'cent

1 egg, beaten
½ cup mayonnaise
½ teaspoon lemon juice
½ teaspoon Worcestershire sauce
1 pound crabmeat, shell and
   cartilage removed

Mix bread crumbs, mustard, seafood seasoning, and Ac'cent together
and set aside.

In another bowl, gently fold together egg, mayonnaise, lemon juice,
Worcestershire sauce, and bread crumb mixture. Add crabmeat, and
shape into individual cakes. Refrigerate for at least 2 hours to avoid
breaking apart when cooked.

Place under broiler and broil until brown, or fry in oil until brown
and drain on paper towels before serving. Serves 4–6.

Of Tide & Thyme

Kinkead's Crab Cakes

MUSTARD SAUCE:

¾ cup mayonnaise
1 tablespoon red wine vinegar
½ teaspoon Old Bay Seasoning
½ teaspoon chili powder
2 tablespoons Dijon mustard

2 tablespoons honey
1 tablespoon chopped fresh
 parsley
Pepper to taste

Combine first 7 ingredients in a mixing bowl. Season with pepper. Set aside. Yields 1 cup.

CORN AND CHERRY TOMATO RELISH:

24 cherry tomatoes, halved
4 ears corn, shucked and blanched
3 green onions, chopped
1 small onion, finely diced
1 teaspoon sugar

1 tablespoon chopped fresh
 parsley
¼ cup red wine vinegar
Salt and pepper to taste

Combine first 7 ingredients in a mixing bowl. Season with salt and pepper and set aside. Yields 2 cups.

CRAB CAKES:

1 small red pepper, finely chopped
¼ cup finely chopped onion
1 large shallot, minced
1 clove garlic, minced
3 tablespoons peanut oil
3 pounds jumbo lump crabmeat,
 cleaned
1 egg, beaten

⅛ teaspoon cayenne
4 dashes Tabasco
Salt and pepper to taste
3 cups bread crumbs
4 tablespoons butter
Mustard Sauce
Corn and Cherry Tomato Relish

Sauté red pepper, onion, shallot, and garlic in peanut oil over high heat in a skillet. Set aside to cool. Gently combine red pepper mixture, crabmeat, egg, cayenne, and Tabasco in a mixing bowl. Season with salt and pepper. Form into 6 crab cake patties. Dredge crab cakes in bread crumbs. Refrigerate for 1 hour. Sauté crab cakes in butter in a large skillet until golden on each side. Serve with Mustard Sauce and Corn and Cherry Tomato Relish on the side. Yields 6 crab cakes.

Note: Can also be used as an appetizer by forming crab mixture into 12 small crab cakes.

Capital Celebrations

Mushroom Crab Cakes

1 pound backfin, backfin-lump,
  or lump crabmeat
2 ounces shiitake mushrooms,
  stems removed
2 ounces portobello mushrooms,
  gills removed
2 ounces domestic mushrooms,
  gills removed
¼ cup minced onion
1 tablespoon olive oil

1½ tablespoons white wine
1½ tablespoons minced garlic
1 tablespoon minced fresh basil
1 egg, beaten
⅜ cup mayonnaise
1 tablespoon Old Bay Seasoning
½–1 cup unseasoned bread
  crumbs
2 tablespoons butter

Thoroughly clean crabmeat of any shells. Set aside. Finely chop all mushrooms. Sauté mushrooms and onion in olive oil until onions are translucent. Add wine, garlic, and basil. Cook until most of the liquid evaporates. Allow mixture to cool.

When room temperature, add crabmeat, egg, mayonnaise, Old Bay, and ½ cup bread crumbs. Use hands to mix together thoroughly. (Mixture should be firm, but not dry.) Continue to add bread crumbs until mixture reaches desired consistency. Fashion mixture into 8 cakes.

Melt butter in shallow fry pan or on griddle. Gently fry cakes at a moderate temperature until cakes are golden. Serves 2 as an entreé, 8 as an appetizer.

Recipe from Chef/Partner David Graham, Van Scoy's Bistro, Cape May, New Jersey

Coastal Cuisine

Crab Enchiladas in Sour Cream Sauce

SOUR CREAM SAUCE:

¼ teaspoon minced garlic
½ teaspoon salt
1 cup sour cream
2 tablespoons chopped onion
2 tablespoons chopped cilantro
2 tablespoons chopped green
  chiles

Mash garlic with salt. Combine all ingredients and add more chiles if you prefer sauce to be hotter.

ENCHILADAS:

6 corn tortillas
1 tablespoon vegetable oil
1½ cups crabmeat
6 tablespoons minced onion
1 small can salsa con tomatillos
1 cup shredded Jack cheese
Sour Cream Sauce

Heat tortillas, one at a time, in hot oil until soft. Place ¼ cup crabmeat in center of each tortilla and sprinkle with 1 tablespoon onion. Spread with a little tomatillo sauce (in Mexican food or International section at the market). Roll up and place seam-side-down in an 8x11-inch baking dish. Cover with remaining salsa. Sprinkle with cheese. Bake at 400° for 15 minutes, or until hot, and cheese is melted. Serve with Sour Cream Sauce. Serves 4–6.

Cooking with the Allenhurst Garden Club

Soft Shell Crabs

Clean crabs; remove eyes and sandbag, the "dead man's fingers" under the points, and the "apron" on the lower back shell. Dry well; salt and pepper them, and sprinkle lightly with flour. Fry in deep hot fat. They will brown quickly. Dry out on brown or absorbent paper. Serve with lemon wedges or tartar sauce.

Maryland's Way

Stewed Crabmeat and Dumplings

4 slices of salt pork or bacon
2 medium potatoes, diced
1 medium onion, diced
¼ teaspoon salt

Dash black pepper
2 cups water
1 pound crabmeat, special
10 Dumplings

Fry salt pork in the bottom of a 4-quart pot. Remove the pork, leaving the grease on the bottom of the pot. Add the potatoes, onion, salt, pepper, and 2 cups of water to the pot and cook over medium heat for 5 minutes. Add crabmeat atop the vegetables. Do not stir. Bring to a boil. Make 10 small, circular pancakes, about 3 inches in diameter, from Dumpling dough (below), and drop one at a time into the boiling crab stew. Reduce heat to simmer and cook for 15 minutes, or until the dumplings are no longer doughy. Serve with a tossed salad.

DUMPLINGS:
1 cup flour
¾ teaspoon salt

1 teaspoon baking powder
¼–⅓ cup water

Sift flour, salt, and baking powder. Add water slowly and knead to form a dough. Sprinkle flour on waxed paper, and roll out dough to ¼-inch thickness. Cut out dumplings with a knife or cookie cutter in the shape and size desired, and cook as directed. Serves 6–8.

Mrs. Kitching's Smith Island Cookbook

Snow Hill Inn's Crab Quiche

1 sheet puff pastry
5 eggs, beaten
1 cup heavy cream
8 ounces sharp Cheddar cheese,
   grated

6 ounces Swiss cheese, grated
½ teaspoon seafood seasoning
1 teaspoon chopped cilantro
¾ pound crabmeat

Fit puff pastry into a large pie pan. Combine eggs, cream, and cheeses. Add seasonings and stir in crabmeat. Pour into pastry shell and bake at 375° for 45 minutes, or until a knife inserted in center comes out clean. Serves 8.

Recipe from Snow Hill Inn, Snow Hill, Maryland
Maryland's Historic Restaurants and their Recipes

Crab Quiche

6 ounces crabmeat
1 cup shredded sharp American
   cheese
1 (3-ounce) package cream cheese,
   cut into ¼-inch cubes
¼ cup sliced green onion
1 (2-ounce) jar chopped pimento

2 cups milk
Dash of nutmeg
1 cup buttermilk biscuit baking
   mix
4 eggs
¾ teaspoon salt

Heat oven to 400°. Grease 10-inch pie plate. Mix crabmeat, cheeses, onion, and pimento in pie plate. Beat remaining ingredients until smooth (about 15 seconds in blender on high or 1 minute with hand beater in bowl). Pour into pie plate. Bake about 35–40 minutes, until knife inserted in center comes out clean. Cool 5 minutes before serving. Serves 8.

Cape May Fare

 The olive-green and white "blue crab"—named for its vivid blue claws—is abundant in estuaries and coastal habitats of the Western Atlantic. The blue crab is a crustacean, like its cousins, the shrimp and the crayfish, and has ten legs. It walks sideways using the three middle pairs, uses its front pincer claws for defending itself and securing food, but earns its scientific name from the remaining pair. *Callinectes,* in Greek, means "beautiful swimmer," and its hind legs, shaped like paddles, make the crab a remarkable swimmer.

Crab Strata Casserole

2 cups milk
1 tablespoon finely chopped onion
1 cup finely chopped celery
1 tablespoon prepared mustard
Dash of Worcestershire sauce
⅔ cup mayonnaise

1 pound crabmeat
4 eggs
½ teaspoon salt
Dash of pepper
12 slices bread (remove crusts)
½ pound grated sharp cheese

Heat milk to boiling point, then set aside to cool. In a large bowl, mix onion, celery, mustard, Worcestershire sauce, and mayonnaise. Add crabmeat and gently toss until coated. In another bowl, beat eggs with salt and pepper; add slowly to milk.

In a greased 2½-quart casserole, break 6 slices of bread into small pieces; pour crab mixture on top. Break the remaining 6 slices of bread over the crab layer. Slowly pour egg and milk over all and cover; chill overnight in refrigerator. Scatter grated cheese on top before placing casserole in pan of water and baking at 325° for 1 hour. Serves 12.

Steppingstone Cookery

Crab and Smithfield Ham

1 pound lump or backfin crabmeat
½ cup butter or margarine
¼ cup finely chopped green
  pepper

¼ teaspoon salt
⅛ teaspoon pepper
1½ teaspoons Old Bay Seasoning
4 thin slices Smithfield ham

Remove cartilage from crabmeat. Melt butter in skillet. Add green pepper and sauté a few minutes. Add crabmeat, salt, pepper, and Old Bay. Sauté briefly until crabmeat is just heated through. Cover crab with ham slices. Cover skillet and simmer for 2–3 minutes until edges of ham curls and flavors are well blended. Serve as is or on toast.

More Favorites from the Melting Pot

Crab Casserole

½ jar pimento cheese or cheese
  whip
1 pound backfin crabmeat
3 eggs, beaten
1 cup butter
1 teaspoon salt
1½ cups evaporated milk

1 tablespoon parsley
Pepper to taste
½ teaspoon Worcestershire sauce
½ teaspoon prepared mustard
1 tablespoon minced green pepper
½ cup buttered crumbs

Combine cheese, crabmeat, eggs, butter, salt, milk, parsley, pepper, Worcestershire, mustard, and green pepper. Put into a deep buttered baking dish or casserole dish. Sprinkle with the crumbs and bake at 375° until piping hot and delicately brown. Serves 4.

DAPI's Delectable Delights

Imperial Crab Casserole

1 pound crabmeat
2 tablespoons chopped onion
2 tablespoons chopped green
  pepper
2 tablespoons flour
½ cup milk

½ teaspoon salt
Dash of pepper
¼ teaspoon Worcestershire sauce
1 teaspoon lemon juice
2 tablespoons margarine, melted
2 hard-boiled eggs, chopped

Check crabmeat for pieces of shell and remove. Sauté onion and green pepper until tender; blend in flour and add milk gradually, stirring. Cook until thick, stirring. Add seasonings, Worcestershire, lemon juice, and margarine. Stir some of hot mixture into eggs to prevent curdling and add to remaining sauce. Add crabmeat; put in a greased casserole (or may use individual ramekins or cleaned crab shells). Bake in 350° oven for 25–30 minutes, or until top is browned.

Bread of Life

Maryland's Finest Crab Imperial

1 (1-pound) can fresh backfin
   lump crabmeat
¼ teaspoon salt
Dash of pepper
1 tablespoon chopped pimento
1 tablespoon chopped green
   pepper

1 whole egg, beaten
1 cup heavy mayonnaise (or
   Miracle Whip)
½ teaspoon Worcestershire sauce
Dash of paprika

Remove all shell from lump crabmeat so as not to break up the lumps. Place crabmeat in bowl and add salt and pepper. Sprinkle with pimento and chopped green pepper. In another bowl, beat egg and fold in mayonnaise with Worcestershire sauce. Place enough of this dressing mixture in the crabmeat to allow it to stick together. Pack the crabmeat mixture lightly in a crab shell for baking or in a shallow pan. Bake at 350° for 30 minutes. Remove from oven and sprinkle top with paprika.

A Family Tradition

Talbot County Crab Imperial

2 pounds crabmeat
2 eggs
1 stick butter
¼–½ cup mayonnaise

1 teaspoon yellow mustard
1 or 2 slices bread
2 tablespoons Old Bay Seasoning
Salt and pepper to taste

Thoroughly pick through the crabmeat to remove all shell. Set aside. Beat eggs with fork or whisk until foamy. Melt butter and add. Beat for one minute more. Add remaining ingredients, beating mixture after each addition. Mix with crabmeat in buttered baking dish. Sprinkle a little more Old Bay on the top. Bake at 350° for about 45 minutes. Allow to cool 5 minutes before serving.

A Taste of GBMC

Shrimp and Crab au Gratin

2 tablespoons butter or margarine
3 tablespoons all-purpose flour
1 tablespoon chicken flavored
   gravy base
2 cups milk
5 ounces (1¼ cups) shredded
   processed American cheese,
   divided
Yellow food coloring

8 ounces fresh or frozen cooked
   lump crabmeat, or 1 (7½-ounce)
   can crabmeat, drained and
   cartilage removed
8 ounces fresh or frozen shelled
   shrimp, cooked
Paprika
Toast points

Melt butter in saucepan; blend in flour and chicken base. Add milk. Cook and stir until thickened and bubbly. Add 1 cup of the cheese; stir to melt. Tint with a few drops of yellow food coloring. Cut crabmeat into pieces; add crab and shrimp to creamed mixture. Pour into 4 (8-ounce) casserole dishes; top with remaining cheese and sprinkle with paprika. Bake at 350° until hot, 10–15 minutes. Serve with toast points. Makes 4 servings.

A Second Helping

Shrimp and Basil

½ cup olive oil
1 pound shrimp
4 large tomatoes, coarsely
 chopped (or canned)
½ cup chopped fresh basil
⅓ cup sliced pitted olives

3 large cloves garlic, minced
2 tablespoons minced shallots
Salt and pepper to taste
1 pound fettuccini, cooked
Grated Romano cheese

Heat oil in heavy skillet over medium-high heat. Add shrimp, tomatoes, basil, olives, garlic, and shallots. Season with salt and pepper. Cook until shrimp turn pink, stirring frequently, about 3 minutes. Put cooked pasta in bowl. Pour sauce over pasta and toss. Sprinkle with Romano cheese.

Gardeners in the Kitchen

Sam's Spicy Grilled Shrimp

½ cup light olive oil
5 teaspoons Cajun seasoning mix
¼ cup oriental sesame oil
¼ cup fresh lemon juice
2 tablespoons minced fresh ginger

2 teaspoons dry mustard
2 teaspoons Tabasco sauce
3 pounds large, uncooked shrimp,
 peeled and deveined (tails
 intact)

Whisk together all but shrimp in a large bowl. Add shrimp to the mix, stir to coat. Let stand for only 30 minutes, no more, no less. Start grill 10 minutes before putting the shrimp on. Use grill basket or skewers. Grill 2–3 minutes on each side.

Bountiful Blessings

The Sandcastle Stadium in Atlantic City, New Jersey, is host to the minor league baseball team, Atlantic City Surf. The Surf captured the inaugural Atlantic League championship title in 1998.

Shrimp with Feta

A one dish meal with a Mediterranean flair.

SAUCE:

¼ cup olive oil
¼ cup chopped green onions
4 large tomatoes, peeled, seeded, and diced
⅓ cup dry white wine, such as French Muscadet

1 clove garlic, minced
⅛ teaspoon oregano
½ cup chopped fresh parsley
Salt
Freshly ground black pepper

In a heavy skillet, heat oil and sauté the onions over medium heat until soft. Add remaining sauce ingredients and simmer, uncovered, until the sauce thickens, about 20 minutes. Stir occasionally and make sure the sauce does not boil.

SHRIMP:

¼ cup olive oil
2½ pounds fresh shrimp, shelled and deveined
2 tablespoons lemon juice
Salt
Freshly ground black pepper

4 tomatoes, peeled and sliced
¼ pound feta cheese, crumbled
Chopped fresh parsley, for garnish
Chopped pitted black olives, for garnish

Preheat oven to 425°. In a large heavy skillet, heat oil and sauté shrimp until they are just pink, about one minute or less. Toss shrimp with lemon juice. Spread sauce evenly on the bottom of a shallow casserole dish. Layer shrimp on top of sauce. Season with salt and pepper. Place sliced tomatoes on top of shrimp. Sprinkle feta cheese on top of tomatoes. Bake at 425° for 15 minutes or until cheese is somewhat melted.

Serve on a bed of angel hair pasta and garnish with a sprinkling of chopped parsley and olives. Yields 4 servings.

A Matter of Taste

Greek Style Shrimp

5 tablespoons olive oil, divided
1 teaspoon chopped garlic
2 cups peeled, cubed tomatoes
 (fresh or canned)
½ cup dry white wine
Salt and pepper to taste
¼ cup chopped fresh basil

1 teaspoon dried oregano
1½ pounds shrimp, peeled and
 deveined
⅛–¼ teaspoon hot red pepper
 flakes
½ pound crumbled feta

Heat 2 tablespoons oil in skillet; add garlic. Cook briefly, then add tomatoes. Cook about 1 minute and then add wine, salt, pepper, basil, and oregano. Cook over moderate heat about 10 minutes.

Heat the remaining 3 tablespoons oil in large skillet and add shrimp. Cook quickly about 1 minute, just until shrimp turn red. Sprinkle with red pepper flakes.

Preheat oven to 400°. Spoon shrimp and any pan juices into small baking dish. Sprinkle with crumbled feta cheese and spoon tomato sauce over. Place in oven; bake 10 minutes till piping hot. Serve over pasta.

Steppingstone Cookery

Grilled Shrimp with Thai Peanut Butter Spread & Apricot Marmalade

THAI PEANUT SPREAD:

1 (1-inch) piece of fresh ginger, chopped
3 cloves garlic, chopped
1 teaspoon curry paste
1 cup chunky peanut butter
3 tablespoons sugar
3 teaspoons Thai fish sauce
¾ cup coconut milk

Combine all ingredients in food processor and process until smooth; set aside.

APRICOT MARMALADE GLAZE:

1 cup apricot marmalade
1 cup cider vinegar
½ teaspoon black pepper
½ teaspoon ground coriander
1 star anise
2 teaspoons minced ginger
2 tablespoons chopped cilantro

Combine all ingredients in saucepan; bring to a boil. Simmer until syrupy and strain; set aside.

1 pound medium shrimp
3 tablespoons olive oil, divided
Salt and pepper to season
4 (6-inch) tortillas
Thai Peanut Spread
Apricot Marmalade Glaze

Toss shrimp with 2 tablespoons oil and salt and pepper. Grill 2–3 minutes on each side. Lightly rub each tortilla with remaining oil. Place on grill 30 seconds on each side. Spread with Thai Peanut Spread. Lay 5–6 shrimp on tortillas. Place a tablespoon of Apricot Marmalade Glaze on shrimp. Roll up and serve. Serves 4.

PB&J USA

Shrimp and Scallops Gruyère

Delicious—worth the time spent in preparation. Sauce may be made ahead and shrimp and scallops added on the serving day.

¾ cup plus 2 tablespoons butter, divided
¾ cup flour
3 cups milk
12 ounces Gruyère cheese
¼ teaspoon garlic powder
3 teaspoons salt, divided
Pepper to taste

¼ teaspoon dry mustard
2 teaspoons tomato paste
3 teaspoons lemon juice, divided
1 pound raw scallops
1 pound shrimp, cooked and cleaned
½ pound mushrooms, sliced
3 tablespoons diced green pepper

Make a cream sauce in the top of a double boiler with ¾ cup butter, flour, and milk. Cut the cheese into small pieces and add to the sauce. Stir until cheese melts. Add garlic powder, 2½ teaspoons salt, pepper, mustard, tomato paste, and 2 teaspoons of the lemon juice.

Poach scallops for 10 minutes in water to which the remaining 1 teaspoon lemon juice and ½ teaspoon salt have been added. If cream sauce is too thick, add a little scallop broth. Drain scallops and add scallops and shrimp to the sauce. Sauté the mushrooms in the remaining 2 tablespoons butter. Add to the sauce. Heat for 15 minutes. Sauté green pepper in a little butter and add to sauce. Put all in chafing dish. Serve with rice or patty shells. Serves 8–10.

Winterthur's Culinary Collection

Tarragon Scallops

1 pound fresh scallops
¼ cup milk
¼ cup flour
Fresh ground pepper
6 tablespoons vegetable oil
4 tablespoons butter

Juice of ½ lemon
3 tablespoons finely chopped
  tarragon
2 tablespoons finely chopped
  parsley

Put scallops in a bowl and add milk. Let scallops soak in milk for a few minutes. Put flour on a plate. Season flour with pepper. Lightly dredge scallops in flour, shaking off the excess. Sauté scallops in oil in a skillet until browned. Remove scallops from skillet and set aside. Discard oil from skillet. Add butter to skillet, then add lemon juice, tarragon, and parsley. Cook until butter begins to bubble. Return scallops to skillet and heat through. Serve over cooked pasta or rice. Serves 2.

Lambertville Community Cookbook

Sautéed Scallops
with Angel Hair Pasta

A tasty combination!

2 pounds sea scallops, quartered
2 tablespoons butter or margarine
¼ cup white wine
2 tablespoons lemon juice
2 tablespoons chopped chives

2 cloves garlic, pressed
⅛ teaspoon white pepper
1 pound angel hair pasta, cooked
Fresh parsley sprigs, for garnish

Rinse scallops in cold water and drain. Coat a large skillet with cooking spray. Add scallops and butter; cook over high heat 5–8 minutes, stirring constantly. Remove scallops using a slotted spoon; set aside. Add wine, lemon juice, chives, garlic, and pepper to skillet. Cook over medium heat 5 minutes, stirring occasionally. To serve, spoon sauce over pasta; spoon scallops over sauce. Garnish with parsley sprigs.

South Coastal Cuisine

Oyster Fritters

1 cup flour
1 teaspoon baking powder
1 teaspoon salt
¼ teaspoon pepper
2 eggs

1 cup milk
1 quart oysters
Oil
Tartar or seafood sauce

Combine flour, baking powder, salt and pepper in a bowl. In another bowl, beat together eggs and milk. Stir in dry ingredients. Stir oysters into the batter. Pour about 1 inch of oil into a skillet. Heat until bubbly. Using a large spoon, drop about 3 oysters into oil. Fry until golden brown on each side. Remove and put on paper towels. Keep warm in a 200° oven. Serve with tartar or seafood sauce.

Chesapeake's Bounty

Oysters Maryland

1 pint select oysters
8 toast points
4 thin slices cooked Maryland
   country-cured ham

2 cups cream sauce (butter, flour,
   milk)
Chopped parsley

Heat oysters in their own liquor until plump. Place toast points in flat ovenproof dish; over this put thin slices of ham. Place oysters on ham, cover with hot cream sauce and place in moderate oven, 350°, until bubbly and hot. Sprinkle with chopped parsley and serve. Serves 4.

Maryland's Way

 It is believed that Francis Scott Key, a Maryland lawyer, wrote America's national anthem on September 14, 1814, while watching the bombardment of Fort McHenry in Baltimore Harbor. Congress adopted his song, "The Star-Spangled Banner," as the national anthem of the United States in 1931.

Wicomico Pan Fried Oysters

2 (12-ounce) cans fresh shucked
  oysters
2 eggs, beaten
2 tablespoons milk
1 teaspoon salt

Dash of pepper
1½ cups dry bread crumbs
1½ cups flour
Lemon wedges
Tartar sauce

Drain oysters. Combine eggs, milk, and seasonings. Combine crumbs and flour. Roll oysters in crumb mixture. Dip in egg mixture and roll again in crumb mixture. Fry in hot fat on moderate heat until brown on one side. Turn carefully and brown the other side. Cooking time is approximately 5 minutes. Drain on paper towels. Serve with lemon wedges and tartar sauce. Serves 6.

Note: For a quick tartar sauce, combine 1 cup mayonnaise and pickle relish; thoroughly mix. Chill.

A Family Tradition

Oyster-Macaroni Bake

1 small package elbow macaroni
  or spaghetti, cooked and
  drained
1 quart oysters
Chopped parsley

Salt and pepper to taste
1 cup light cream
Butter
Bread crumbs

Butter 2-quart casserole. Beginning with macaroni, alternate layers of macaroni, oysters, parsley, and seasonings. When casserole is full, pour cream over all. Top with well-buttered bread crumbs. Bake in 350° oven for about ½ hour. Serves 8.

My Favorite Maryland Recipes

Salmon Croquettes

1 pound salmon fillets
¾ teaspoon seasoned salt, divided
¼ plus ⅛ teaspoon freshly
    ground pepper, divided
1 large potato, peeled and cut into
    1-inch chunks
1 tablespoon milk
1 tablespoon butter
½ cup finely chopped onion
⅓ cup seeded and finely chopped
    green pepper
1 large egg, lightly beaten
½ cup dried bread crumbs
½ cup vegetable oil
Lemon wedges

Season salmon with ½ teaspoon salt and ⅛ teaspoon pepper. Place in large skillet and add enough cold water to barely cover. Simmer until salmon looks opaque when flaked in center, about 10 minutes. Transfer salmon to plate.

Boil potato in salted water until done. Drain well. Add milk and butter to potato and mash. Cool completely. Remove skin and bones from salmon. Place salmon in bowl and add mashed potato, onion, green pepper, and egg. Season with remaining ¼ teaspoon salt and ¼ teaspoon pepper.

Place bread crumbs in shallow dish. Using about ⅓ cup for each, form salmon mixture into 8 patties. Coat with crumbs, shaking off excess. Heat oil in skillet over medium-high heat. Add croquettes and cook until underside is golden brown, about 3 minutes. Turn and cook other side about 3 more minutes. Drain on paper towel briefly. Serve hot with lemon wedges.

DAPI's Delectable Delights

Salmon with Vinaigrette

4 salmon fillets, skins removed,
1-inch thick
Salt and pepper to taste
¼ cup dry white wine
3 tablespoons fresh lemon juice
1 garlic clove, minced
1 tablespoon finely chopped fresh
basil

1 teaspoon finely chopped fresh
tarragon
¼ cup extra virgin olive oil
2 large plum tomatoes, peeled,
seeded, diced
1 medium leek, white and tender
green portions, sliced into thin
julienne strips

Place fillets in a non-reactive baking dish and season with salt and pepper. Pour white wine over and cover. Let marinate at room temperature for 30 minutes.

In a small bowl, combine juice, garlic, basil, and tarragon. Whisk in olive oil in a thin, steady stream. Stir in tomatoes and season with salt and pepper. Preheat oven to 450°. Prepare parchment paper squares and place a thin layer of leeks on paper; top with salmon fillet and spoon tomato mixture on top. Fold parchment paper over to enclose and, starting at one end, crimp paper with tiny folds to seal. Bake for about 12 minutes. Serves 4.

Where There's a Will...

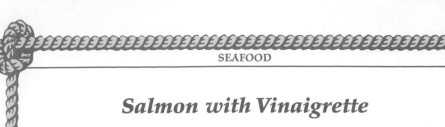

The Smithsonian Institution in Washington, D.C., was established in 1846 with funds bequeathed to the United States by James Smithson. The Institution is as an independent trust instrumentality of the United States, holding more than 140 million artifacts and specimens in its trust for "the increase and diffusion of knowledge." The Institution is also a center for research dedicated to public education, national service, and scholarship in the arts, sciences, and history. The Smithsonian is composed of sixteen museums and galleries and the National Zoo, and numerous research facilities in the United States and abroad.

Grilled Salmon with Gazpacho Salsa

A spicy salmon entrée.

1 cucumber, peeled, seeded, and
   finely chopped
1 red pepper, chopped
1 medium red onion, chopped
2 large tomatoes, skinned, seeded,
   and chopped
3 tablespoons red wine vinegar

1 tablespoon Worcestershire sauce
1 teaspoon Tabasco
1 teaspoon salt
¼ cup plus 2 tablespoons olive
   oil, divided
4 salmon steaks, 1 inch thick

Combine cucumber, red pepper, onion, tomatoes, vinegar, Worcestershire sauce, Tabasco, salt, and ¼ cup olive oil. Place ⅓ of mixture in blender or food processor and purée. Stir purée into remaining vegetables and cover. Set aside for 1 hour.

Rub salmon steaks with remaining 2 tablespoons olive oil and grill over hot coals until steaks are crisp, brown, and just cooked through, about 4 minutes each side.

Cut each steak in half lengthwise and place on serving dish. Place spoonful of salsa over each steak. Serve remaining salsa separately. Serves 4.

Capital Classics

Pesto-Crusted Salmon
with Roasted Tomato Oil

1 cup fresh basil leaves
2–3 cloves garlic, minced
2 tablespoons Parmesan cheese
3 tablespoons roasted pecans

Extra virgin olive oil
Plain bread crumbs
4 (6- to 8-ounce) salmon fillets
Salt and pepper to taste

In food processor, blend basil, garlic, Parmesan cheese, and pecans to form dry paste. Add enough olive oil to produce a runny paste. Scrape into bowl and add bread crumbs until crust has a slightly moist crumb texture. Set aside.

Preheat oven to 375°. Season salmon with salt and pepper. Apply a thin (about ⅛-inch) coat of crust to meat side of each fillet. Place salmon in baking dish, pesto-side-up, and drizzle with olive oil. Bake until desired doneness, about 8–10 minutes per inch of thickness of fish. Place fillets on plates. Drizzle with tomato oil. Serves 4.

ROASTED TOMATO OIL:
3 ripe plum tomatoes, halved and
  seeded
Salt and pepper to taste

2 cloves garlic, minced
1 cup extra virgin olive oil

Roast tomatoes in a 400° oven until dry and starting to char. Let cool a bit. Place in blender with remaining ingredients and purée.

Recipe from owner Larry Boylan, The Inn at Sugar Hill, Mays Landing, New Jersey

Coastal Cuisine

Maryland Rockfish Stuffed and Baked

BREAD STUFFING:

¾ cup chopped celery
¼ cup chopped onion
¼ cup melted fat (or oil)
1 quart soft bread cubes

2 tablespoons milk (or water)
1 teaspoon salt
Dash of pepper
1 teaspoon poultry seasoning

Cook celery and onion in fat until tender. Combine all ingredients and mix thoroughly. Stuff fish.

3–4 pounds dressed rockfish
2 teaspoons salt
Bread Stuffing

2 tablespoons melted fat (or oil)
Paprika

Clean, wash, and dry fish. Sprinkle inside and out with salt. Stuff fish loosely with Bread Stuffing. Close opening with skewers. Place fish in a well-greased baking pan. Brush with fat and sprinkle with paprika. Bake for 40–60 minutes, or until fish flakes easily when tested with a fork. Baste occasionally with fat. Remove skewers. Serves 6.

A Family Tradition

Rockfish Chesapeake

1 pound rockfish fillets
¼ teaspoon Worcestershire sauce
½ teaspoon lemon juice

½ teaspoon seafood seasoning
1 teaspoon white wine
2 tablespoons mayonnaise

Heat oven to 450°. Place fillets on foil-lined baking dish. Mix remaining ingredients. Spread mayonnaise mixture thinly and evenly over the fillets. Bake at 450° for 6–8 minutes. Fish is done when it flakes. Makes 4 servings.

More Favorites from the Melting Pot

Boiled Rockfish with Sauce

SAUCE:

1½–2 cups white sauce
1 teaspoon lemon juice, or to taste
Dash red pepper
¼ cup capers

½ teaspoon Worcestershire sauce
   (optional)
¾ teaspoon salt and pepper

Mix all ingredients together and set aside.

1 (2- or 3-pound) rockfish, cleaned
1 onion slice
2 whole cloves
1 carrot
1 bay leaf

2 peppercorns
4 hard-boiled eggs, sliced
Lemon wedges, for garnish
Parsley, for garnish

Place cleaned rockfish in cheese cloth, tie closed, and drop in boiling salted water to which has been added a slice of onion, 2 whole cloves, carrot, bay leaf, and 2 peppercorns. Boil 6–10 minutes per pound. Lift out of water carefully and place on large platter before removing cheesecloth.

Pour Sauce over fish and garnish with slices of hard-boiled eggs, lemon wedges, and parsley. Another garnish to use with rock is to render 6–8 slices of bacon which have been diced into small pieces, and pour the hot bacon grease and rendered bacon over the boiled rockfish. This recipe serves 4.

A Cook's Tour of the Eastern Shore

Tilapia Veracruz

4 (6- to 8-ounce) Tilapia or other
  firm whitefish fillets
Olive oil plus 1 tablespoon,
  divided
Lemon or lime juice plus
  3 tablespoons, divided
Salt and pepper
Dried oregano
1 small green pepper, seeded and
  chopped
1 large onion, chopped

3 cloves garlic, minced
4 tablespoons water
1 (4-ounce) can diced green chiles
¼ cup sliced pimento-stuffed
  green olives
1 teaspoon ground cinnamon
¼ teaspoon ground white pepper
1 (14½-ounce) can stewed
  tomatoes
1 tablespoon drained capers

Rinse fish, pat dry, and arrange on lightly oiled 9x13-inch baking dish.
Brush with olive oil and lemon or lime juice, salt and pepper, and sprinkle with oregano. Refrigerate while making sauce.

Heat 1 tablespoon oil in nonstick frying pan over medium-high heat.
Add green pepper, onion, garlic, and water; cook, stirring often, until
vegetables are tender-crisp (about 3–5 minutes). Add chiles, olives, 3
tablespoons lemon or lime juice, cinnamon, and white pepper; cook for
1 minute. Add tomatoes to pan and bring mixture to a boil. Boil, uncovered, stirring often, until sauce is slightly thickened (about 5 minutes).
Remove fish fillets from the refrigerator. Pour sauce over fish. Bake in
a 350° oven until fish is just opaque but still moist in the thickest part
(about 10–15 minutes); cut to test .

To serve, transfer fish and sauce to individual serving plates and
sprinkle with capers. Serves 4.

Restaurant Recipes from the Shore and More...

More than half of the Atlantic coast's breeding population of great blue herons nests in Chesapeake Bay. The bay, the nation's largest estuary, and surrounding areas pro-vide both the ideal food and habitat necessary for great blue heron survival. As a result, the great blue heron is rivaled only by the blue crab as the symbol of Chesapeake Bay wildlife.

Baked Fish a la Dee

This preparation is ideal for many different types of fish.

1¾ pounds fish
4 tablespoons olive oil, divided
Juice of 2 lemons
4 cloves garlic, chopped, divided
Salt and black pepper to taste
1 tablespoon dry basil
2 celery stalks, diced

2 carrots, shredded
½ yellow onion, chopped
½ cup dry white wine (you may
    add ½ cup water with wine for
    more sauce)
Lemon slices, for garnish

Wash fish, pat dry with paper towel, and cut into 4 equal portions. Using a pastry brush, coat shallow roasting pan or oven-wear dish with olive oil. Place fish in pan and coat lightly with olive oil, using pastry brush. Pour lemon juice over fish. Then sprinkle fish with ½ the chopped garlic. Add salt and pepper and set preparation aside.

In a non-stick pan, add remaining oil, garlic, and basil and sauté for 3–4 minutes with celery, carrots, and onion. Add wine; cook for 1½ minutes (to burn off alcohol). Remove from heat. Spoon vegetables and liquid on top of fish and place slice of lemon on each portion. Place preparation in a preheated 350° oven for 25 minutes or until fish is tender. Serves 4.

Dr. John's Healing Psoriasis Cookbook...Plus!

Harrison's Chesapeake House's Broiled Sea Trout

⅔ cup butter
2 teaspoons lemon juice
Salt and pepper to taste
1 medium onion, sliced

2 strips bacon, cut in half
2 sea trout fillets
2 dashes paprika

Melt butter and simmer with lemon juice, salt and pepper. Place 3 slices of onion and 2 half-strips of bacon on each fillet. Pour lemon butter over trout and cook under broiler until lightly browned. Sprinkle with paprika and serve immediately. Serves 2.

Recipe from Harrison's Chesapeake House, Tilghman Island, Maryland
Maryland's Historic Restaurants and their Recipes

Chesapeake Broiled Shad

2 pounds boned shad fillets
¼ cup melted fat (or oil)
2 tablespoons lemon juice
1 tablespoon grated onion
1½ teaspoons salt
1 teaspoon paprika
¼ teaspoon crushed thyme
Dash of pepper
Chopped parsley
Lemon wedges

Cut fillets into serving-size portions. Combine remaining ingredients, except parsley and lemon wedges. Place fish, skin-side-up, on a well-greased broiler pan. Brush with sauce. Broil about 3 inches from source of heat for 5 minutes. Turn carefully and brush other side with sauce. Broil 5–7 minutes longer or until fish is lightly browned and flakes easily when tested with a fork. Sprinkle with parsley and garnish with lemon wedges. Serves 6.

A Family Tradition

Baked Flounder Fillets with Vegetables

2 tablespoons olive oil
1 small fennel bulb, cut into fine
   2-inch long strips
2 leeks, white part only, cleaned
   and cut into fine 2-inch long
   strips
1 carrot, cut into fine 2-inch long
   strips
1 zucchini, cut into fine 2-inch
   long strips
1 garlic clove, finely minced
¼ teaspoon tarragon
Dash sea salt and pepper to taste
4 fillets of flounder, about ¾
   pound each
4 tablespoons fresh lemon juice

Preheat oven to 400°. Cut 4 large sheets of heavy duty aluminum foil large enough to accommodate the fish.

   Heat olive oil in a large skillet and sauté the vegetables and garlic for 5 minutes, stirring often. Add tarragon and cook a few minutes more to soften vegetables. Season with salt and pepper. Spread vegetables evenly over the 4 fish fillets. Sprinkle 1 tablespoon lemon juice over each fish. Enclose fish in the foil and crimp the edges together well. Place the foil package of fish on a baking sheet and bake for 20 minutes, or until fish is cooked through. Serves 4.

Dr. John's Healing Psoriasis Cookbook...Plus!

Flounder Creole

1 green pepper, cut in strips	¼ teaspoon basil
3 onions, sliced	¼ teaspoon chili powder
1 teaspoon garlic powder	⅛ teaspoon ground cloves
1 (16-ounce) can stewed tomatoes	Pepper to taste
3 ounces tomato paste	1 pound flounder fillets
1 chicken bouillon cube	4 ounces partially cooked okra
¼ cup water	Cooked rice

In a saucepan combine all of the ingredients except the fish, okra, and rice. Bring to a boil; simmer 5 minutes. Add the flounder and okra, cover and simmer 10 minutes. Serve with rice. Makes 4 servings.

Sealed with a Knish

Flounder Roll Ups

1 (9-ounce) package frozen chopped spinach, cooked and well drained	4 large flounder fillets (flounder may be substituted with lemon sole)
2 large cloves garlic, minced	2 teaspoons butter or margarine, melted
Juice of 1 lemon	
1 cup feta cheese, broken into pieces	¼ cup chopped fresh parsley

Preheat oven to 350°. In a bowl, mix cooked spinach with garlic and juice of 1 lemon. Add the feta cheese and mix well. Take each fillet and add mixture (¼ cup) to center of fillet. Roll and secure with toothpick. Place fillets in ovenproof casserole; add butter, sprinkle with parsley. Bake at 350° for 30 minutes.

The Glen Afton Cookbook

Seafood au Gratin

½ lemon, sliced
½ small onion, sliced
3 cups water
1 tablespoon fresh basil
2½ pounds rockfish
1 pound scallops

½ small onion, minced
¼ cup chopped green pepper
2 tablespoons butter
½ pound sliced mushrooms
¼ cup bread crumbs

Boil lemon and onion slices in water. Add basil and cook for 5 minutes. Add rockfish and scallops and poach for 5 minutes. Remove and break apart the fish, reserving the liquid, but discarding the lemon and onion. In a saucepan, sauté the minced onion and pepper in butter, then add mushrooms.

SAUCE:

1 cup butter
1 cup flour
2 cups cream
2 cups fish stock
½ teaspoon dry mustard

½ cup shredded Swiss cheese or
  Gruyère
¼ cup dry white wine or ¼ cup
  sherry
Salt and pepper to taste

Melt butter in a saucepan and slowly add the flour. Then add the cream and stock until thickened. Add the mustard, cheese, wine, salt and pepper. Combine the fish, vegetables, and sauce. Pour into a baking dish. Cover with bread crumbs. Bake for 35 minutes at 350°.

Chesapeake's Bounty

Annapolis Harbor Boil

¾ cup (6 ounces) Chesapeake-style
 seafood seasoning
8 lemons, 4 thinly sliced, 4 wedged
 for condiments
1 large yellow onion, sliced in
 rings and separated
1 large bell pepper (any color)
 sliced lengthwise in ½-inch
 strips
5 pounds red potatoes, scrubbed
 and halved, if necessary, to
 make no larger than 4-inch
 circumference

1½ pounds smoked sausage,
 cut into 3-inch lengths and
 browned
2 pounds medium unshelled
 shrimp, deheaded and rinsed
8 small ears of corn, halved
1 pound drawn butter or
 margarine
1½ cups cocktail sauce

Fill a 5-gallon crab pot ¾ full with hot water; add Chesapeake-style seafood seasoning and the 4 sliced lemons, and bring to a rolling boil. Add onion, pepper, and potatoes and boil for 20 minutes. Add sausage and boil an additional 20 minutes. Add shrimp and corn and allow to boil for 4 minutes, then turn off heat and leave for an additional 5 minutes in the water. Drain the entire mixture and ladle all items into 1 or 2 very large serving bowls. Serve immediately with butter and cocktail sauce. Serves 8–10.

Note: Chesapeake seafood seasoning is a regional specialty used in everything from seafood dishes to poultry and vegetables. The two most famous brands are Old Bay Seasoning and Wye River Seasoning.

Of Tide & Thyme

CAKES

Beneath the United States Naval Academy Chapel in Annapolis, Maryland, is the crypt of John Paul Jones, the Revolutionary War hero who inspired his fellow countrymen with the noted phrase, "I have not yet begun to fight!"

Chocolate Mousse Cake

CRUST:

1 cup chocolate-wafer crumbs (about 18 wafers)

4 tablespoons softened butter

A day ahead, mix chocolate-wafer crumbs and butter. Press into bottom of a 10x3-inch springform pan. Refrigerate while making filling.

FILLING:

¾ cup butter (1½ sticks), cut into small pieces

4½ cups (2¼ [12-ounce] packages) semisweet chocolate pieces

2 cups whipping cream, divided

5 large eggs, separated

2 teaspoons instant coffee powder

⅓ cup orange-flavor liqueur

In a heavy 4-quart saucepan over low heat, heat butter and chocolate pieces just till melted and mixture is smooth, stirring frequently. Remove pan from heat. Stir in ¼ cup of the heavy cream.

In medium bowl with wire whisk, beat egg yolks and instant coffee powder until coffee dissolves. With whisk, beat egg yolk mixture into melted chocolate mixture; slowly beat in orange liqueur. In large bowl with mixer at medium speed, beat remaining heavy cream till stiff peaks form. Fold whipped cream, half at a time, into chocolate mixture. In small bowl with mixer at high speed, beat egg whites till they stand in stiff peaks. With rubber spatula, fold beaten whites, half at a time, into chocolate mixture until blended. Pour mixture over crust in springform pan. Cover and refrigerate overnight.

GLAZE:

1½ cups (¾ [12-ounce] package) semisweet chocolate pieces

2 tablespoons confectioners' sugar

3 tablespoons orange-flavor liqueur

3 tablespoons milk

1 teaspoon instant coffee powder

Next day prepare glaze. In 2-quart saucepan over low heat, heat chocolate, sugar, liqueur, milk, and coffee powder till chocolate melts and mixture is smooth, stirring constantly. Remove from heat and let stand at room temperature to cool slightly till of good spreading consistency.

Remove side of springform pan from cake. Place cake, still on pan bottom, on wire rack over waxed paper. Spread Glaze over top and down side of cake. Refrigerate cake until ready to serve. Makes 24 servings which may be topped with additional whipped cream, if desired.

Gardeners in the Kitchen

Chocoholics Dream

True chocoholics will experience Nirvana when tasting this fabulous cake.

CAKE:

½ cup strong brewed coffee
8 ounces semisweet chocolate, cut
   into pieces

1 cup granulated sugar
1 cup unsalted butter
4 eggs

Preheat oven to 350°. Grease a 9x5x3-inch loaf pan. Line with parchment, and grease parchment well. In a small saucepan, combine coffee, chocolate, sugar, and butter. Cook over medium heat until butter and chocolate are melted. Stir occasionally. Remove from heat and stir in eggs. Blend well and pour into prepared pan. Bake at 350° for 55–65 minutes, or until cake cracks around sides and is crisp on top. Remove from oven and cool in pan. Cover with foil and refrigerate overnight or for up to one week.

At serving time, invert chilled cake on an oval serving platter; remove pan and carefully peel off the parchment.

TOPPING:

1 cup whipping cream
¼ cup confectioners' sugar
¼ teaspoon vanilla extract
2 tablespoons shaved semisweet
   chocolate

Fresh raspberries, for garnish
Fresh strawberries, for garnish
Candied violets, for garnish

Whip cream with sugar and vanilla until soft peaks hold their form. Frost the top of the cake with whipped cream mixture. Dust with grated chocolate. Mound berries at either end of the cake on the plate. Place a few berries on top of cake. Stud berry mounds with candied violets and place a few on the top of the cake. Yields 8–10 servings.

A Matter of Taste

A diner is defined as a restaurant resembling a railroad dining car. New Jersey has the most diners in the world and is sometimes referred to as the Diner Capital of the World.

Hungarian Chocolate Cake

There is no flour in this cake—the chocolate, pecans and butter make up for it though! The cake can be made a day ahead, but should be stored in the refrigerator.

1 cup pecans, very finely ground
10 eggs, separated
⅔ cup sugar
10 tablespoons butter

8 ounces bittersweet chocolate, or
German sweet chocolate
¾ cup apricot preserves
⅔ cup pecans, chopped

Grind the pecans in a Mouli grater or nut grinder; the texture should be as fine and fluffy as flour. In a large bowl, mix the egg yolks and sugar. Stir occasionally, but do not beat, to dissolve the sugar while assembling the remaining ingredients.

In the top of a double boiler, place the butter and chocolate. Set over hot water, and heat gently until the mixture is smooth. Stir the melted chocolate mixture into the egg yolk/sugar mixture until blended. Remove 1 cup of the mixture and set aside for cake frosting.

Fold the ground pecans into the mixture remaining in the bowl. Beat the egg whites until stiff, but not dry. Stir ¼ of the egg whites into the nut mixture. Gently fold in the remaining whites. Pour the mixture into a greased, floured, 8-inch springform pan. Bake at 350° for 50–60 minutes, until the center feels springy to the touch.

Set the pan on a rack to cool. Gently ease a spatula around the edge so the cake falls evenly as it cools. When cool, remove the sides of the pan. Transfer the cake to a serving dish. Slice the cake to make 2 layers. Spread apricot preserves over bottom layer, and put second layer back on top. If the top of the cake is a little bumpy, you can flip the top layer over. In any case, it will be covered with the frosting.

If the frosting mixture is not stiff enough to spread, refrigerate it for 20–30 minutes. Using a small spatula, frost the top and sides of the cake. Pat the chopped nuts around the edges. Refrigerate until served. Makes 8–12 servings.

Hoboken Cooks

Decadent Fudge Bundt Cake

1 cup butter or margarine,
  softened
1½ cups sugar
4 eggs
½ teaspoon baking soda
1 cup buttermilk
2½ cups all-purpose flour
1½ cups semisweet chocolate
  mini-morsels, divided

2 (4-ounce) bars sweet baking
  chocolate, melted and cooled
⅓ cup chocolate syrup
2 teaspoons vanilla extract
4 ounces white chocolate, chopped
2 tablespoons plus 2 teaspoons
  shortening, divided

Cream butter in a large mixing bowl; gradually add sugar, beating well at medium speed of an electric mixer. Add eggs, one at a time, beating after each addition. Dissolve soda in buttermilk, stirring well. Add to creamed mixture alternately with flour, beginning and ending with flour. Add 1 cup mini-morsels, melted chocolate, chocolate syrup, and vanilla, stirring just until blended. (Do not overbeat.)

Spoon batter into a heavily greased and floured 10-inch Bundt pan. Bake at 300° for 1 hour and 25–35 minutes, or until cake springs back when touched. Invert cake immediately onto a serving plate and let cool completely.

Combine white chocolate and 2 tablespoons shortening in top of a double boiler; bring water to a boil. Reduce heat to low; cook until mixture is melted and smooth. Remove from heat. Drizzle melted white chocolate mixture over cooled cake. Melt remaining ½ cup mini-morsels and 2 teaspoons shortening in a small saucepan over low heat, stirring until smooth. Remove from heat and let cool; drizzle over white chocolate.

Country Chic's Home Cookin

Three Chocolate Cake

1 (18½-ounce) package devil's
  food cake mix
1 (4⅛-ounce) package instant
  chocolate pudding mix
½ cup brewed coffee

4 large eggs, beaten
1 cup sour cream
½ cup vegetable oil
½ cup dark rum
2 cups semisweet chocolate chips

Preheat oven to 350°. Combine all ingredients, except chocolate chips.
With electric mixer, blend on low speed. Beat on medium speed for one
minute. Scrape sides of bowl, and beat for one minute longer. Fold in
chocolate chips. Pour into a greased and floured Bundt pan. Bake for
55–60 minutes. Turn out of pan and cool.

Flavors of Cape Henlopen

Buttermilk Cake

1 cup butter
3 cups sugar
4 eggs
¼ teaspoon baking soda

3 cups flour
1 cup buttermilk
2 teaspoons vanilla

Preheat oven to 325°. Cream the butter and sugar. Add eggs. Combine
baking soda and flour. Add alternately with the buttermilk. Add vanilla. Bake for 1 hour and 10 minutes at 325° in an angel food cake pan.

The Great Gourmet

Francie's One-Step Pound Cake

2¼ cups unbleached or
  all-purpose flour
2 cups sugar
½ teaspoon salt
½ teaspoon baking soda
1–2 teaspoons grated lemon or
  orange peel, if desired

1 teaspoon vanilla
1 cup butter or margarine,
  softened
1 (8-ounce) carton pineapple, or
  mandarin orange yogurt, or 1
  cup dairy sour cream
3 eggs

Combine ingredients in large mixing bowl. Blend at low speed, then beat 3 minutes at medium speed. Pour into a greased and floured 10-inch Bundt or tube pan. Bake at 325° for 60–70 minutes, or until top of cake springs back when touched lightly in center. Cool cake upright in pan 15 minutes. Remove from pan and cool completely before cutting and serving.

GLAZE TOPPING: (OPTIONAL)
1 cup powdered sugar

1–2 tablespoons fresh or
  concentrated lemon juice

If glazing cake, combine powdered sugar and enough lemon juice to make a drizzling consistency. Glaze cooled cake. Serves 8–10.

Recipe by Mrs. George W. Gekas, wife of Representative from Pennsylvania
The Congressional Club Cookbook

Crusty Cream Cheese Pound Cake

1 cup butter or margarine,
  softened
½ cup shortening
3 cups sugar
1 (8-ounce) cream cheese, softened

3 cups sifted cake flour, or 2¾
  cups all-purpose flour
6 eggs, beaten
1 tablespoon vanilla extract

Cream butter and shortening. Gradually add sugar, beating well at medium speed of mixer. Add cream cheese, beating well until light and fluffy. Alternately add flour and eggs, beginning and ending with flour. Stir in vanilla. Grease and flour 10-inch tube pan. Bake at 325° for 1 hour and 15 minutes.

Restaurant Recipes from the Shore and More...

Cream Cheese Pound Cake

1 (8-ounce) package cream cheese
¾ pound butter
6 eggs

1 teaspoon vanilla
3 cups sugar
3 cups flour

Let cream cheese, butter and eggs come to room temperature. Cream cheese and butter thoroughly. Add eggs, one at a time, and mix well. Add vanilla. Sift flour and sugar together; add a small amount at a time to creamed mixture. Spray a Bundt or tube pan with vegetable pan coating and dust with flour. Spread dough in pan and bake 1½ hours at 325°, or until tester comes out clean. Cool cake 15 minutes in pan before removing. Cut into thin slices and serve plain or with a fruit sauce. Serves 16–20.

The Queen Victoria® Cookbook

Bavarian Apple Torte

Sophisticated and not too sweet.

CRUST:

½ cup butter, softened
⅓ cup sugar

½ teaspoon vanilla
1 cup flour

Cream butter, sugar, and vanilla. Slowly stir in flour until mixture forms soft dough. Press dough onto bottom and 1½ inches up sides of ungreased 9- or 10-inch springform pan.

FILLING:

1 (8-ounce) package cream cheese
¼ cup sugar

1 egg, slightly beaten
½ teaspoon vanilla

Beat cream cheese and sugar. Add egg and vanilla. Blend until smooth. Pour mixture into pan.

TOPPING:

4 cups apples, peeled, cored, and
   sliced
½ teaspoon cinnamon

⅓ cup sugar
½ cup sliced almonds

Combine apples, cinnamon, and sugar. Layer evenly over cream cheese mixture. Sprinkle almonds over top. Bake at 450° for 10 minutes; lower heat to 400° and bake an additional 25 minutes. Cool completely before removing sides of pan. Serve at room temperature or chilled. Serves 8–10.

Capital Classics

Apple Pie Cake

CAKE:

¼ cup softened butter or margarine
1 cup sugar
1 egg
1 cup all-purpose flour
1 teaspoon salt
1 teaspoon ground cinnamon

2 tablespoons hot water
1 teaspoon vanilla
3 cups peeled and diced cooking apples
½ cup chopped pecans
Rum Butter Sauce
Whipped cream (optional)

Cream butter; gradually add sugar, beating well at medium speed of electric mixer. Add egg; beat until blended. Combine flour, salt, and cinnamon; mix well. Add to creamed mixture; beat on low speed until smooth. Stir in water and vanilla. Fold in apples and pecans; spoon into a greased and floured 9-inch pie plate. Bake at 350° for 45 minutes, or until a wooden toothpick inserted in center comes out clean. Serve warm or cold with Rum Butter Sauce and whipped cream. Yields 1 (9-inch) pie.

RUM BUTTER SAUCE:

½ cup brown sugar, firmly packed
¼ cup softened butter or margarine

½ cup sugar
½ cup whipping cream
1 tablespoon rum

Combine first 4 ingredients into a small saucepan; mix well. Bring to a boil and cook 1 minute. Stir in rum. Yields 1¼ cups.

A Cookbook of Treasures

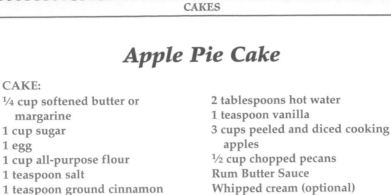

To settle a dispute between the colonies of Pennsylvania and Maryland, a survey was begun in 1762 by British astronomers Charles Mason and Jeremiah Dixon. The Mason-Dixon Line, a straight line between the 39° and 40° parallel, is now used as a regional boundary between North and South.

Jewish Apple Cake

3 cups flour
2 cups sugar
3 teaspoons baking powder
4 eggs, beaten
½ cup orange juice

1 cup Crisco oil
3 teaspoons vanilla
5 apples, peeled, cored, and sliced
2 teaspoons cinnamon, mixed with
    5 tablespoons sugar

Combine the first 7 ingredients. Pour half the batter into a greased tube pan. Layer half the apples and half the cinnamon mixture; repeat layers with remaining batter, apples, and cinnamon mixture. Bake in a 350° oven for 1 hour and 20 minutes. (The cake can be baked 1–2 days before serving because it keeps so well.)

The Happy Cooker 3

Lady Baltimore Cake

1 cup butter
2 cups sugar
1 cup milk
3½ cups flour
1 teaspoon vanilla
2 teaspoons baking powder
8 stiffly beaten egg whites,
    divided

1½ cups powdered sugar
1 cup chopped raisins, soaked
    ten minutes in hot water
1 cup chopped nuts
¾ cup sliced maraschino cherries

Cream butter and sugar. Add milk, flour, vanilla, and baking powder, then fold in 6 beaten egg whites. Bake in 3 layers 20–25 minutes at 400°. Let cool.

    Beat remaining 2 egg whites until very stiff. Add the powdered sugar very gradually, one tablespoon at a time. Add raisins, nuts, and cherries. Spread this filling between layers. Cover cake with Butter Icing.

BUTTER ICING:
½ stick soft butter
2 cups powdered sugar

1 teaspoon vanilla
Milk

Cream butter, sugar and vanilla together; add just enough milk to cream and spread. Cover entire cake.

My Favorite Maryland Recipes

Hummingbird Cake

3 cups all-purpose flour
1 teaspoon baking soda
1 teaspoon cinnamon
2 cups sugar
1 teaspoon salt
3 eggs, beaten

1 cup vegetable oil
1½ teaspoons vanilla
1 (8-ounce) can crushed pineapple
  (undrained)
1 cup chopped pecans
2 cups chopped bananas

Combine first 5 ingredients in a large mixing bowl; add eggs and oil, stirring until dry ingredients are moistened. Do not beat. Stir in vanilla, pineapple, pecans, and bananas. Spoon batter into 3 greased and floured 9-inch round cake pans. Bake at 350° for 25–30 minutes, or until wooden toothpick inserted in center comes out clean. Cool in pans for 10 minutes. Remove and cool completely. Spread frosting of your choice between layers, on top and sides (cream cheese frosting is an excellent choice). Sprinkle pecans on top.

Bayside Treasures

Carrot-Pineapple Cake

I guarantee that this is the moistest carrot cake you'll ever eat.

1 cup shortening
2 cups sugar
3 eggs
3 cups sifted flour
2 teaspoons baking soda

1 teaspoon cinnamon
¼ teaspoon salt
1 cup crushed pineapple
2 cups grated carrots
1 cup pecans (optional)

Cream shortening and sugar. Add eggs, one at a time. Sift flour, soda, cinnamon, and salt together. Add pineapple, grated carrots, and pecans. Bake at 350° for about one hour in a tube pan.

TOPPING:
1 stick butter
1 (8-ounce) package cream cheese,
  softened

1 box powdered sugar
2 teaspoons vanilla
1 cup chopped pecans

Combine butter and cream cheese. Add powdered sugar, mixing until smooth. Add vanilla and nuts. Spread on cake.

Our Favorite Recipes

Old Southern Orange Slice Cake

2 cups sugar
½ pound butter, softened
4 eggs, beaten
3½ cups sifted cake flour (reserve
   1 cup to dredge pecans, dates,
   and candy)
½ teaspoon baking soda
½ cup buttermilk (or ½ cup milk
   and 1 tablespoon vinegar)

1 tablespoon orange juice
2 cups pecans
½ pound dates, cut up
1 pound orange slice candy, cut
   in half
1 can coconut

Cream sugar and butter until light and fluffy. Add eggs. Add flour and baking soda alternately with buttermilk. Add orange juice. Fold in pecans, dates, and candy orange slices that have been dredged in the reserved flour (also add the reserved flour). Fold in coconut. Bake at 250° in a greased and floured tube pan 1½ hours, or until cake tester comes out clean.

GLAZE (OPTIONAL):
½ cup orange juice   ½ cup sugar

Boil until sugar is dissolved.

A Second Helping

Coconut and Nut Cake

2 cups sugar
1 cup oil
4 eggs, beaten
3 cups flour
½ teaspoon baking soda
½ teaspoon baking powder
½ teaspoon salt
1 cup buttermilk
1 cup chopped walnuts, pecans, or
  black walnuts
1 (3½-ounce) can coconut
2 teaspoons coconut flavoring

Combine sugar, oil, and eggs; beat well. Add dry ingredients alternately with buttermilk. Stir in nuts, coconut, and coconut flavoring. Mix well. Pour in greased and lightly floured tube pan. Bake at 350° for 1 hour and 15 minutes, or until toothpick comes out clean and top of cake is lightly browned. Leave cake in pan and pour the syrup over the hot cake. Keep in pan 3–4 hours to absorb the syrup.

SYRUP FOR CAKE:
1 cup sugar
½ cup water
2 tablespoons margarine
1 teaspoon coconut flavoring

Boil sugar, water, and margarine for 5 minutes. Add flavoring; stir well. Pour over cake.

Steppingstone Cookery

Coconut Pecan Cake

2 cups flour
2 cups sugar
1½ cups softened butter
1 cup buttermilk
4 eggs
1 teaspoon baking soda
½ teaspoon salt
1 tablespoon vanilla
2 cups flaked coconut
1 cup chopped pecans

Heat oven to 350°. In large mixing bowl, combine all ingredients, except coconut and pecans. Beat at low speed, scraping bowl often, until all ingredients are moistened. Beat at high speed, scraping bowl often, until smooth (3–4 minutes). Stir in coconut and pecans. Pour into greased and floured 9x13-inch baking pan. Bake for 45–50 minutes, or until center of cake is firm to touch and edges begin to pull away from sides of pan. Cool completely. Frost with browned butter or cream cheese frosting.

More Favorites from the Melting Pot

Carolyn's Coconut Cake

2 cake layers, baked and cooled
   (Duncan Hines Butter Cake is
   good)
¼ cup coconut milk (optional)
2 cups sugar

16 ounces sour cream
1 (12-ounce) package coconut (or
   fresh), divided
1 (8-ounce) container Cool Whip

Split cake layers. Sprinkle layers with coconut milk, if desired. Mix sugar, sour cream, and coconut (save ½ cup for topping). Chill. Keep 1 cup of this mixture for frosting. Spread remaining portion between layers. Combine Cool Whip with reserved 1 cup of frosting mixture. Pile frosting on top and sides of cake and sprinkle with reserved ½ cup coconut. Cover with cake saver and refrigerate 3 days. Yields 12 or more servings.

South Coastal Cuisine

Coconut Cake

1 package Duncan Hines French
   Vanilla Cake Mix
1½ cups milk (skim is fine)
½ cup sugar

1 cup coconut, divided
3½ cups (28 ounces) Cool Whip,
   thawed (fat free works great,
   too)

Prepare cake mix according to package directions for 9x13-inch pan. Cool 15 minutes. Poke holes in cake. Meanwhile, combine milk, sugar, and ½ cup coconut in saucepan. Bring to boil; then reduce heat and simmer for 1 minute. Pour over cooled cake. Cool completely. Fold ½ cup coconut into Cool Whip topping and spread over cake. Sprinkle with additional coconut, if desired. Chill overnight.

To make lower fat cake: Mix with whisk, the cake mix, ¾ cup egg substitute, and 1 cup water. No oil. Bake same as directions.

Our Favorite Recipes–Book Three

Lowfat Rum Cake

CAKE:

1 chocolate Pillsbury Plus Cake
   Mix
½ cup dark rum

½ cup water
¾ Egg Beaters

Spray 2 (9-inch) round cake pans, or 9x13-inch pan, with cooking spray. (If using 9x13-inch pan, leave in pan after baking.) Heat oven to 350°. Using whisk, mix all cake ingredients just until blended. Pour into prepared pans and bake for 20–25 minutes, or until done. Remove from pans. Cool completely. While cake is cooling, make filling.

FILLING:

1 cup skim milk
1 small package instant chocolate
   pudding

¼ cup dark rum
1 small fat-free Cool Whip,
   thawed

Mix milk, pudding mix, and rum. Gently add Cool Whip. Frost cake and refrigerate.

Our Favorite Recipes–Book Three

Strawberry Delight Cake

This is truly a light and refreshing dessert to be served on a hot summer day, or after a heavy meal.

2 small packages strawberry Jell-O
2 cups hot water
2 small packages frozen
   strawberries

2 (8-ounce) containers Cool Whip
1 angel food cake

Dissolve Jell-O in hot water. Add frozen strawberries. When cool, add Cool Whip and stir until smooth. Pinch angel food cake into very small pieces and line the bottom of a 9x13-inch pan with half of the pieces. Spoon half the strawberry/Cool Whip mixture over the cake; repeat layers. Refrigerate until firm, about 2 hours.

—

Barineau-Williams Family Cookbook Vol. II

Strawberry Banana Split Cake

CRUST:

2 cups graham cracker crumbs
¼ cup sugar

½ cup butter or margarine, melted

Combine crumbs, sugar, and butter; press into an ungreased 9x13x2-inch dish. Chill for one hour.

FILLING:

½ cup butter or margarine, softened
2 cups confectioners' sugar
1 tablespoon milk
1 teaspoon vanilla

3 large firm bananas, cut into ¼-inch slices
2 (8-ounce) cans crushed pineapple, drained
2 quarts fresh strawberries, sliced

In a mixing bowl, cream butter, confectioners' sugar, milk, and vanilla. Spread over crust; chill for 30 minutes. Layer with bananas, pineapple, and strawberries.

TOPPING:

2 cups whipping cream
¼ cup confectioners' sugar

1½ cups chopped walnuts

In a small mixing bowl, beat cream until soft peaks form. Add confectioners' sugar; beat until stiff peaks form. Spread over fruit. Sprinkle with nuts. Chill until serving. Serves 8–10.

Barineau-Williams Family Cookbook Vol. II

Blueberry Cake

1½ cups sugar
1 egg
1 cup butter, softened
3 cups flour
1 teaspoon baking soda

½ teaspoon salt
1 teaspoon vanilla
1 cup buttermilk
1½ cups blueberries

Cream sugar, egg, and butter together until fluffy. Sift flour, baking soda, and salt together, and gradually add into the butter mixture along with the vanilla and buttermilk. Beat cake batter until smooth. Stir in berries. Pour into a greased 9x13-inch cake pan. Bake in 350° oven for 45–50 minutes. Serves 8–10.

The Great Gourmet

Cranberry Cake

FROSTING:
5 tablespoons flour
1 cup sugar
1 cup milk

½ cup butter
½ cup cream cheese
1 teaspoon vanilla

Mix flour and sugar in saucepan. Whisk in milk and cook until thickened. Cool. Cream butter and cream cheese until smooth. Beat in flour mixture and vanilla. Chill until cake is cool. Beat occasionally until thick enough to spread.

1½ cups cranberries
¼ cup chopped walnuts
¼ cup water
½ cup butter or shortening
1½ cups sugar
2 eggs, beaten
1 teaspoon red food coloring

Grated rind from 1 orange
2½ cups sifted flour
1 teaspoon baking soda
1 teaspoon salt
3 tablespoons cocoa
1 teaspoon vinegar
1 cup buttermilk

Grease and flour 2 (8-inch) cake pans. Cook cranberries with walnuts in water until skins pop and berries are soft. Cool. Cream butter and sugar; add eggs, food coloring, and orange rind. Sift together flour, baking soda, salt, and cocoa. Add vinegar to buttermilk. Mix sifted ingredients alternately with buttermilk into the egg mixture. Fold in cranberries and walnuts mixture. Bake at 325° for 25–30 minutes. Cool and frost. Serves 10–12.

Cape May Fare

Italian Cheesecake
(Torta De Ricotta)

1 stick butter, melted
1 loaf pound cake, crumbled
3 pounds ricotta cheese
1 dozen eggs

1 cup sugar
2 cups milk
Rind of 1 lemon, grated

Mix butter and pound cake together to form crust on bottom and sides of a 10½-inch springform pan. Mix together ricotta cheese, eggs, sugar, milk, and lemon rind. Pour into springform pan crust. Bake in oven at 375° for 1 hour. Remove and let cool. Refrigerate.

La Cucina Casalinga

Elegant Cheese Cake

CRUST:
1 cup graham cracker crumbs
3 tablespoons margarine, melted

3 tablespoons sugar

Combine crumbs, margarine, and sugar; press into bottom of a 9-inch springform pan. Bake in 325° oven for 10 minutes.

FILLING:
3 (8-ounce) packages cream
    cheese, softened
1⅓ cups sugar
¾ cup flour

3 eggs
1 (13-ounce) can evaporated milk
2 teaspoons vanilla
Cinnamon

Combine softened cream cheese, sugar, and flour. Add eggs, one at a time, beating well after each addition. Blend in milk and vanilla. Pour over crumbs; sprinkle cinnamon on top, and bake in 350° oven for at least one hour. It may take a little longer. The top may crack. Check with a toothpick to see if done. If not, check every 5 minutes. Cool before removing rim of pan. Do not invert. Chill in refrigerator before garnishing and serving. Garnish with cherry pie filling or preserves of any kind.

Favorite Recipes Home-Style

No-Bake Easy Cheesecake

2 packages ladyfingers
2 packages Jell-O No-Bake
    Cheesecake Mix (take out
    crumbs)
1 (8-ounce) package cream cheese,
    softened

3 cups milk
1 (12-ounce) container Cool Whip
1 can blueberry pie filling or
    your favorite fruit topping

Separate ladyfingers and place around sides and on bottom of spring-form pan. Mix cheesecake mix and cream cheese with milk until blended. Add container of Cool Whip and blend for 3 minutes at low speed. Pour mixture into pan. Refrigerate for 2 hours. Top with blueberry pie filling or fruit topping, or serve on side.

The Great Gourmet

Mini Cheesecakes

2 (8-ounce) packages cream
    cheese, softened
½ cup sugar
1 teaspoon vanilla extract
2 eggs

12 vanilla wafers
Cheesecake toppings (such as
    chopped nuts, chocolate chips,
    bite-size fruit, and jam or
    preserves)

Line 12 muffin cups with paper liners. Combine the cream cheese, sugar, and vanilla in a large mixer bowl. Beat at medium speed until creamy. Beat in the eggs. Place one vanilla wafer in each paper-lined muffin cup. Spoon the cream cheese mixture on top of each vanilla wafer, filling the cups ¾ full. Bake at 325° for 25 minutes. Remove to a wire rack to cool. Remove from muffin cups when cool and chill in the refrigerator for 30–60 minutes. Top each cheesecake with desired topping. Serve immediately. Yields 12 mini cheesecakes.

Beyond Peanut Butter and Jelly

Chocolate Arabians

These taste like extra special brownies.

¼ pound unsalted butter
1 cup (3 ounces) semisweet
  chocolate chips
2 large eggs, beaten
1 tablespoon coffee liqueur
½ cup all-purpose flour

¾ cup sugar
1 teaspoon instant espresso
  powder
½ cup (2 ounces) pecans, chopped
24 large pecan halves

In medium saucepan, bring 2 inches of water to a simmer and remove from heat. Cut butter into 1-inch pieces and put into a heat-proof bowl with the chocolate. Set bowl over the hot water and stir until smooth. Cool slightly. Whisk in eggs and liqueur; then stir in flour, sugar, and espresso. Stir ½ cup pecans into batter.

Adjust oven rack to middle position and heat oven to 350°. Line 2 mini-muffin tins (1¾-inch diameter cups) with paper muffin cups. Spoon batter into cups, filling them ¾ full, and placing a pecan half in the center of each cup of batter. Bake until batter is set, and a toothpick inserted into the centers comes out clean, about 20 minutes.

Cool 2–3 minutes in muffin tins, then transfer each piece to a wire rack. (Can store in an airtight container for 3 days or freeze up to one month.) Makes 24 muffins.

Why Not for Breakfast?

Shoo-fly Cupcakes

½ cup mild molasses
1 cup boiling water
1 teaspoon baking soda
2½ cups sifted flour

1 teaspoon salt
½ cup butter
¾ cup sugar

Mix molasses and water with soda and beat until mixture fizzes. Combine flour, salt, butter, and sugar to form crumbs. Reserve ¾ cup for topping. Add crumbs to liquid mixture. Pour batter into paper-lined cupcake tins and top each with about 1 teaspoon per cupcake of reserved crumbs. Bake at 350° for 20 minutes. Makes 18.

Flavors of Cape Henlopen

Black Bottom Cupcakes

1½ cups flour	⅓ cup oil
1 cup sugar	1 cup water
¼ cup cocoa	1 teaspoon vanilla
½ teaspoon salt	1 tablespoon vinegar
1 teaspoon baking soda	

Mix together flour, sugar, cocoa, salt, and baking soda; add oil, water, vanilla, and vinegar; blend well and set aside.

FILLING:

1 (8-ounce) package cream cheese, softened	⅓ cup sugar
	⅛ teaspoon salt
1 egg beaten	1 cup chocolate chips

Beat cream cheese until very soft, add egg, sugar, and salt and beat well; fold in chocolate chips. Put petite cupcake liners into petite cupcake muffin tins. Spoon in chocolate batter to fill half way, and top with 1 teaspoon cream cheese mixture; continue until batters are all used. Bake at 350° for 20 minutes and cool on racks.

A Taste of Tradition

Passover Madelbrot

3 eggs	1 cup oil
1 cup sugar	1 cup chopped walnuts
1½ cups matza cake meal	Fruit preserves
½ teaspoon salt	

Beat eggs and sugar until fluffy. Add dry ingredients and mix together. Add oil; mix, then add nuts. Let stand 20 minutes. Divide dough into 3 parts. Form each part into a rectangular shape and place onto greased cookie sheet. Bake at 350° for 10 minutes.

Remove from oven and, with handle, make an impression through the length of each strip. Fill with any flavor fruit preserves and return to oven for 30 additional minutes. Cool. Slice before serving.

The Happy Cooker 3

COOKIES & CANDIES

In Margate, New Jersey, you can climb inside Lucy, the elephant—a world-famous 65-foot, 100-year-old museum of South Jersey history.

Energy Bars

1 cup quick-cooking rolled oats
½ cup all-purpose flour
½ cup Grape-Nuts Cereal
½ teaspoon ground ginger
1 egg, beaten
⅓ cup applesauce
¼ cup honey
¼ cup brown sugar, packed
2 tablespoons cooking oil
1 (16-ounce) package mixed, dried fruit bits
¼ cup sunflower seeds
¼ cup chopped walnuts

Preheat oven to 325°. Line an 8x8x2-inch baking pan with aluminum foil. Spray foil with nonstick coating. In large mixing bowl, combine oats, flour, Grape-Nuts, and ginger. Add egg, applesauce, honey, brown sugar, and oil. Mix well; stir in fruit, sunflower seeds, and walnuts. Spread mixture in prepared pan. Bake at 325° for 30–35 minutes. Cool; cut. Makes 24 bars.

Flavors of Cape Henlopen

Marble Squares

1 (8-ounce) package cream cheese, softened
2⅓ cups sugar, divided
3 eggs, divided
¾ cup water
½ cup butter
1½ ounces unsweetened baking chocolate
2 cups all-purpose flour
½ cup sour cream
1 teaspoon baking soda
½ teaspoon salt
1 cup (6 ounces) semisweet chocolate chips

In a mixing bowl, beat cream cheese and ⅓ cup sugar until light and fluffy. Beat in 1 egg; set aside. In a saucepan, bring water, butter, and chocolate to a boil, stirring occasionally. Remove from heat. Mix in flour and remaining sugar. Stir in sour cream, baking soda, salt, and remaining 2 eggs until smooth. Pour into a greased and floured 10x15x1-inch baking pan. Dollop cream cheese mixture over the top; cut through batter to create a marbled effect. Sprinkle with chocolate chips. Bake at 375° for 30–35 minutes, or until a toothpick comes out clean. Cool. Yields about 5 dozen squares.

Bountiful Blessings

Raspberry Brownies

24 ounces chocolate chips, divided
¼ cup margarine
11 ounces cream cheese, divided
1½ cups sugar
6 eggs, divided

2 teaspoons vanilla
1½ cups flour
¾ teaspoon baking powder
1 cup heavy cream, divided
⅓ cup raspberry preserves

Heat and stir 12 ounces chocolate chips and margarine until melted and blended; set aside. Beat 8 ounces cream cheese with sugar; beat in 3 eggs. Mix in vanilla, melted chocolate, flour, and baking powder. Pour into greased 9x13-inch pan; set aside.

Heat and stir 6 ounces chocolate chips with ⅔ cup cream until blended; set aside. Beat 3 ounces cream cheese with preserves. Add remaining 3 eggs and melted chocolate; pour over mixture in pan. Bake 50 minutes at 350°. Cool on wire rack. Heat and stir 6 ounces chocolate chips with ⅓ cup cream until blended. Spread over cooled brownies. Chill to set. Store in refrigerator. Makes 2½ dozen.

Sealed with a Knish

White Chocolate Brownies

1 cup unsalted butter
10 ounces white chocolate, broken
   in small pieces
1¼ cups sugar
4 large eggs

1 tablespoon vanilla
2 cups unbleached all-purpose
   flour
½ teaspoon salt
1 cup coarsely chopped pecans

Preheat oven to 325°. Line a 9x11-inch pan with aluminum foil, leaving a little overhang around the edges of the pan; butter the foil. (No aluminum foil necessary if disposable aluminum pan is used.) Heat 1 cup unsalted butter and chocolate, stirring frequently, in a large saucepan over low heat until melted and smooth. Remove from heat.

    Using a wooden spoon, stir sugar into melted chocolate; then stir in eggs and vanilla. (The mixture will look curdled.) Add flour, salt, and chopped pecans, and quickly stir just until mixed. Pour batter into the pan. Bake the brownies until the top is lightly golden but the center is somewhat soft when pressed lightly, 30–35 minutes. Let cool to room temperature. Refrigerate the brownies at least 3 hours. Using the foil, lift the brownies from the pan. Cut into 20–25 squares, although larger portions are usually requested!

Recipe by John Tierney, Representative from Massachusetts
The Congressional Club Cookbook

Chocolate-Pecan Brownies

¾ cup flour
¼ teaspoon baking soda
¾ cup sugar
⅓ cup butter or margarine
2 tablespoons water

1 (12-ounce) package semisweet
  chocolate morsels, divided
1 teaspoon vanilla
2 large eggs
½ cup chopped pecans

Preheat oven to 325°. Grease 9-inch square pan. Mix together flour and baking soda in small bowl. In saucepan, combine sugar, butter, and water. Bring to boil over low heat; remove immediately from heat. Stir in 1 cup chocolate morsels and vanilla until chocolate is melted and mixture is smooth. Pour mixture in bowl. Cool completely. Stir in eggs, 1 at a time. Beat well after each. Gradually stir in flour mixture until smooth. Stir remaining chocolate morsels and nuts into batter. Pour batter into pan. Bake 30–35 minutes (toothpick inserted comes out clean). Place on wire rack to cool. Cut into squares.

Out of the Frying Pan Into the Fire!!!

Knock You Nakeds

1 package German chocolate
  cake mix
1 cup chopped pecans
⅓ cup, plus ½ cup evaporated
  milk, divided

¾ cup melted butter
60 vanilla caramels, 1 (14-ounce)
  package
1 cup semisweet chocolate chips

In a large mixing bowl, combine dry cake mix, pecans, ⅓ cup evaporated milk, and melted butter. Press half of the batter into the bottom of a greased 9x13x2-inch glass baking dish. Bake in a preheated 350° oven for 8 minutes.

In the top of a double boiler, over simmering water, melt caramels with remaining ½ cup evaporated milk. When caramel mixture is mixed well, pour over baked layer. Cover with chocolate morsels. Pour remaining batter on top of morsels. Return to preheated 350° oven and bake 18 minutes. Let cool before cutting into squares.

A Cookbook of Treasures

Scandinavian Almond Bars

1¾ cups all-purpose flour
2 teaspoons baking powder
¼ teaspoon salt
½ cup margarine or butter
1 cup sugar
1 egg
¾ teaspoon almond extract,
    divided

Milk
½ cup sliced almonds, coarsely
    chopped
1 cup sifted powdered sugar
3–4 teaspoons milk

Stir together flour, baking powder, and salt. In a large mixer bowl, beat margarine or butter until softened. Add sugar and beat till fluffy. Add egg and ½ teaspoon almond extract and beat well. Add flour mixture and beat till well mixed.

Divide the dough into fourths. Form each portion into a 12-inch roll. Place 2 of the rolls 4–5 inches apart on an ungreased cookie sheet. Flatten each roll till it is 3 inches wide. Repeat with the remaining rolls. Brush each flattened roll with a little milk and sprinkle with about 2 tablespoons of the chopped almonds.

Bake in a 325° oven for 12–14 minutes, or till edges are lightly browned. While still warm, cut crosswise at a diagonal into 1-inch strips. Cool completely on a wire rack.

Stir together the powdered sugar, ¼ teaspoon almond extract, and enough of the 3–4 teaspoons milk to make a drizzling consistency. Drizzle over the cooled bars. Makes 48.

The Great Gourmet

One of the most famous inventors was Thomas A. Edison, who invented the movie camera and phonograph in his labs in West Orange and Menlo Park, New Jersey. Also, the first incandescent lamp was made by Edison in 1879 in Menlo Park; Roselle, New Jersey, became the first town in the nation to be lighted by electricity in 1883. (The New Jersey town of Edison is named after him.)

Cheesecake Cookies

⅓ cup brown sugar, packed
½ cup chopped walnuts
1 cup flour
⅓ cup melted butter
1 (8-ounce) package cream cheese,
  softened

¼ cup sugar
1 egg
1 tablespoon lemon juice
2 tablespoons cream or milk
1 teaspoon vanilla

Mix brown sugar, chopped nuts, and flour together in a large bowl. Stir in the melted butter and mix until light and crumbly with your hands. Remove 1 cup of the mixture to be used later as a topping. Place remainder in an 8-inch square pan and press firmly. Bake at 350° for about 15 minutes.

Beat cream cheese with ¼ cup sugar until smooth. Beat in egg, lemon juice, milk, and vanilla. Pour this onto the baked crust. Top with reserved crumbs. Return to 350° oven and bake for about 25 minutes. Cool thoroughly, then cut into squares.

Note: May be baked the day before. Cover with plastic wrap and keep refrigerated. (Yes, they can be frozen.)

A Tasting Tour Through the 8th District

Lemon Cheese Bars

1 Pillsbury Plus Yellow Cake
  Mix
2 eggs, divided
⅓ cup oil

1 (8-ounce) package cream cheese,
  softened
⅓ cup sugar
1 teaspoon lemon juice

Mix dry cake mix, 1 egg, and oil until crumbly. Reserve 1 cup. Pat remaining mixture lightly into an ungreased 9x13x2-inch pan. Bake 15 minutes at 350°. Beat cream cheese, sugar, lemon juice, and 1 egg until light and smooth. Spread over the baked layer. Sprinkle with reserved crumb mixture. Bake 15 minutes longer. Cool and cut into bars.

Our Favorite Recipes

Biscotti

1¼ cups sugar
3 eggs
2½ cups flour
2½ teaspoons baking powder
1 cup raisins

¾ cup butter
1 teaspoon vanilla
½ teaspoon salt
1 teaspoon anise seeds
¾ cups chopped hazelnuts

Preheat the oven to 350°. Mix all the ingredients together to form a smooth dough. With floured hands, divide into 3 equal parts and shape each part into a 3x10-inch rectangle, ¾ inch thick. Bake on a lightly greased cookie sheet for 20–25 minutes. Remove from the oven and slice each rectangle diagonally about 1 inch thick. Return the cookies to the oven, which has been turned off. This will dry the biscotti further. Makes 2 dozen.

Good Things to Eat

Almond Biscotti

Delicious with a warm drink; great for dunking!

1¼ cups whole almonds
2¼ cups flour
1½ teaspoons baking powder
¼ teaspoon almond extract
¼ teaspoon nutmeg

2 eggs
¾ cup sugar
¼ teaspoon salt
1½ teaspoons vanilla
¼ pound salted butter, softened

Preheat oven to 350°. Coarsely chop almonds and toast lightly. Let cool. Mix all ingredients well. Batter will be very thick. Divide into 5 logs; shape evenly. Bake for 45 minutes. Remove from oven and slice each log diagonally into strips. Put back in oven for 5–10 minutes until crispy.

Fair Haven Fare

Sour Cream Twists

1 package yeast	¾ cup sour cream
¼ cup warm water	1 whole egg
1 cup shortening	2 egg yolks
3½ cups flour	1 teaspoon vanilla
1 teaspoon salt	1 cup sugar

Dissolve yeast in water. Cut shortening into flour and salt. Stir sour cream, whole eggs, egg yolks, vanilla, and yeast mixture into flour mixture. Mix well. Chill 2 hours.

Roll dough on sugared board. Roll again ¼ inch thick. Cut into strips 1x4 inches. Twist. Bake on ungreased pan at 375° for 15 minutes.

A Second Helping

Vienna Crescents

This Christmas cookie is a favorite at my house.

½ cup sugar	1 teaspoon vanilla
1 cup butter, softened	¼ teaspoon salt
2 cups flour, sifted	Powdered sugar
1¼ cups ground almonds	

Cream sugar and butter until fluffy. Add flour, ¼ cup at a time. Add the almonds, vanilla, and salt. Shape dough into balls and wrap in wax paper. Refrigerate for one hour. Take off 1-inch pieces of chilled dough and roll on flat surface into a strip 1 inch wide and ½ inch thick. Shape into a crescent. Bake on lightly greased cookie sheets at 350° for 15–20 minutes. Cool on sheets a bit, then transfer to cooling racks. When completely cooled, dust with powdered sugar. Makes 4 dozen.

Good Things to Eat

The world's first synthetic fiber, Nylon, was discovered in Wilmington, Delaware, by DuPont researchers, led by Dr. Wallace H. Carothers in the 1930s. Although World War II dampened the initial excitement that surrounded this astonishing creation, the post-war consumer boom saw the explosion of many types of Nylon products. Toothbrushes, women's stockings, lingerie, brushes, shirts, rope, shoe laces, parachutes, and many more products which people use everyday all incorporate the use of Nylon.

Ginger Crinkles

Their aroma spreads throughout the inn when baking, so we often bake them just before serving on chilly afternoons. They go deliciously with apple cider in the autumn.

¾ cup margarine
1 cup brown sugar
1 egg
½ cup molasses
2½ cups flour

2 teaspoons baking soda
1 teaspoon cinnamon
½ teaspoon cloves
2 teaspoons powdered ginger
½ teaspoon salt

Cream margarine and sugar. Add egg and beat well. Mix in remaining ingredients. Chill dough. Form into small balls and roll in granulated sugar. Sprinkle each ball with 2 or 3 drops of water to create crinkled effect. Bake at 375° for 12 minutes. Cool slightly before removing from cookie sheets. Makes about 48 cookies.

The Queen Victoria® Cookbook

Melting Moments Cookies

1 cup all-purpose flour
¾ cup cornstarch
⅛ teaspoon salt

⅓ cup confectioners' sugar
1 cup (2 sticks) butter (no
    substitutes), softened

In medium bowl, stir together flour, cornstarch, salt, and confectioners' sugar. In large mixer bowl, at medium speed, beat butter until smooth. Add flour mixture and beat until well combined. Refrigerate 1 hour. Shape into 1-inch balls. Place 1½ inches apart on ungreased cookie sheet. Flatten with lightly floured fork. Bake at 300° for 15–20 minutes, or until edges are lightly browned. Remove to rack to cool. Store in tins, in layers separated by plastic wrap. Makes 2½ dozen.

Steppingstone Cookery

Festive Cashew Cookies

These cookies make a wonderful gift.

2 cups raw cashews
1 cup rolled oats
1 teaspoon cinnamon
⅓ cup molasses or maple syrup

½ cup water
¼ cup oil
1 teaspoon vanilla extract
Small jar unsweetened jam

Preheat oven to 375°. Grind raw cashews and rolled oats together in food processor for a few minutes. Pour mixture into a large bowl and add remaining ingredients, except jam. Mix all ingredients together.

Form 24 round balls and place on a lightly oiled cookie sheet. With your thumb, form a small well in the center of each ball. Place a small amount of jam in each well.

Bake for 15 minutes at 375°. Allow cookies to cool before removing from cookie sheet. Makes 2 dozen.

Total calories per cookie: 124; Total fat: 12% of daily value; Fat 8g; Prot 2g; Carbo 13g; Cal 20mg; Iron 1mg; Sod 71mg; Fiber 1g.

Simply Vegan

Cherry Winks

2¼ cups sifted flour
1 teaspoon baking powder
½ teaspoon baking soda
½ teaspoon salt
¾ cup softened butter or
    margarine
1 cup sugar
2 eggs
2 tablespoons milk

1 teaspoon vanilla flavoring
1 cup chopped nutmeats
1 cup finely cut, pitted dates
⅓ cup finely cut maraschino
    cherries
⅔ cup cornflake crumbs, or 2½
    cups cornflakes
18 maraschino cherries, cut into
    quarters

Sift together flour, baking powder, soda, and salt. Blend butter and sugar; add eggs and beat well. Stir in milk and vanilla. Add sifted dry ingredients together with nutmeats, dates, and cut cherries; mix well. If using cornflakes, crush into fine crumbs. Shape dough into balls using 1 level tablespoon dough for each. Roll balls in cornflake crumbs and place on greased baking sheets. Top each cookie with ¼ maraschino cherry. Bake in moderate 375° oven about 12 minutes, or until lightly browned. Yields about 6 dozen cookies, 2 inches in diameter.

DAPI's Delectable Delights

Maple Ranger Cookies

½ cup margarine
⅓ cup shortening
1 cup granulated sugar
1 cup brown sugar
2 eggs
1 teaspoon vanilla extract

2 teaspoons maple extract
2¼ cups flour
1 teaspoon baking powder
1 teaspoon baking soda
1 teaspoon salt
3 cups crisp rice cereal

Combine margarine, shortening, sugars, eggs, and flavorings in large bowl and beat well. Stir or sift together dry ingredients and blend in. Add cereal, mixing well. Drop onto greased cookie sheets and bake in preheated 375° oven for 8–12 minutes, or until golden. Cool for a minute before removing from pan. Yields 5 dozen.

Mid-Day Magic

Butter "Fork" Cookies

1 stick margarine
1 stick butter
1¼ cups sugar

1 egg
2½ cups flour
1 teaspoon vanilla

Cream butters and sugar in mixer until light and fluffy (about 15 minutes). Add egg. Mix well. Mix in flour and vanilla until well combined. Drop dough from ½ teaspoon onto cookie sheet. Press down until thin with fork dipped in ice cubes and water. Bake at 350° about 8–10 minutes. Remove from pan after one minute. Cool on rack. Makes about 100 cookies. Store in covered tin can.

More Favorites from the Melting Pot

 Delaware became the first state by ratifying the U.S. Constitution on December 7, 1787. In addition to being called the First State, Delaware is also known as The Diamond State, The Blue Hen State, and Small Wonder.

Italian Cookies

1 (8-ounce) package cream cheese
   (room temperature)
½ pound butter
1 cup sugar
2 teaspoons vanilla or anise
6 cups flour
6 teaspoons baking powder
6 eggs

Cream together cream cheese and butter; add sugar and vanilla.
Combine flour and baking powder. Add eggs and flour alternately.
Either scoop onto cookie sheet, or make small ropes and mound like a
beehive. Bake at 375° for 10–12 minutes.

Out of the Frying Pan Into the Fire!!!

Chocolate Marshmallow Cookies

These cookies will become everyone's favorites.

1¾ cups sifted cake flour
½ teaspoon salt
½ teaspoon baking soda
½ cup unsweetened cocoa
½ cup shortening
1 cup sugar
1 egg
1 teaspoon vanilla
¼ cup milk
18 large marshmallows, halved
36 pecan halves

Sift together cake flour, salt, soda, and cocoa and set aside. In a mixing
bowl, cream shortening and sugar. Add the egg, vanilla, and milk; mix
well. Add dry ingredients and mix well. Drop by heaping teaspoonfuls
about 2 inches apart onto greased cookie sheet. Bake in preheated 350°
oven for 8 minutes. Do not overbake. Remove from oven and top each
cookie with a marshmallow half. Return to oven for 2 minutes. Remove
cookies to wire racks to cool. Meanwhile, make frosting and spread on
each cookie; top with a pecan half. Makes 3 dozen.

FROSTING:

2 cups sifted confectioners' sugar
5 tablespoons unsweetened cocoa
⅛ teaspoon salt
3 tablespoons butter, softened
4–5 tablespoons light cream or
   milk

Beat all ingredients until smooth and of spreading consistency and frost
cookies.

Country Chic's Home Cookin

Lemon Crispies

Great for a children's tea party.

1 box lemon cake mix	1 egg
½ cup butter, melted	1 cup Rice Krispies

Combine cake mix, butter, and egg in a mixing bowl. Gently stir in Rice Krispies. Roll dough into 1½-inch balls. Place 2 inches apart on an ungreased cookie sheet. Bake in a preheated 350° oven for 9 minutes or until edges are golden. Cool on cookie sheet for 1 minute. Remove and cool on a wire rack. Yields 25–30 cookies.

Capital Celebrations

Gobbler Goodies

¼ cup (½ stick) butter or margarine	28 chocolate sandwich cookies
4 cups miniature marshmallows	1½ cups chocolate frosting
6 cups crisp rice cereal	1 (12-ounce) package candy corn

Melt butter in saucepan. Add marshmallows. Cook over low heat until melted, stirring constantly. Stir in the cereal. Remove from heat and let cool for 10 minutes. With buttered hands, form cereal into 28 (1½-inch) balls. Twist apart the sandwich cookies. Spread frosting on each cookie half and use 28 halves as the base for each turkey.

Place each cereal ball on top of a frosted cookie half, pressing to adhere. Press 3 pieces of candy corn in a fan pattern on each remaining cookie half. Press each cookie half into a cereal ball to form a tail. Attach candy corn with frosting to form the turkey's head. Yields 28 Gobbler Goodies.

Beyond Peanut Butter and Jelly

Chocolate Chip Pizza

Fun to make and eat.

½ cup sugar
½ cup dark brown sugar, packed
½ cup butter, softened
1 cup chunky peanut butter
½ teaspoon vanilla extract
1 egg

1½ cups flour
2 cups miniature marshmallows
12 ounces semisweet chocolate
   chips
1 cup chopped pecans

In a mixing bowl, combine sugar, brown sugar, butter, peanut butter, vanilla, and egg with an electric mixer. Add flour. Press dough into disposable 12- or 14-inch aluminum pizza pan, forming a rim around edge. Bake in a preheated 375° oven for 10 minutes. Remove and sprinkle with marshmallows, chocolate chips, and pecans. Bake for an additional 5 minutes, or until marshmallows are golden. Remove from oven, slice, and cool. Yields 10 servings.

Note: During the holiday season, this pizza topped with chopped candied red and green cherries, or red and green M&M's Chocolate Candies makes a nice hostess gift.

Capital Celebrations

Peanut Butter Balls

4 ounces margarine
1 pound confectioners' sugar
2 cups peanut butter
3 cups Rice Krispies

24 ounces chocolate morsels
4 ounces semisweet baking
   chocolate

Blend margarine and sugar. Mix in peanut butter. Add Rice Krispies and mix. Refrigerate. When chilled, form walnut-size balls. Melt chocolate morsels and baking chocolate. Dip peanut butter balls and chill.

In the Komondor Kitchen

Fruit Balls

1 tablespoon butter
2 eggs, slightly beaten
1 cup sugar
½ teaspoon salt
1½ cups chopped cherries,
   apricots, and dates

2 cups Rice Krispies
½ cup chopped nuts
1 teaspoon vanilla
Coconut

Melt 1 tablespoon butter in electric frypan. Add eggs, sugar, salt, cherries, apricots, and dates. Cook over low heat for 10 minutes. Remove from fire and add Rice Krispies, nuts, and vanilla. Roll in coconut.

Bread of Life

Sheila's Fudge

1 stick margarine
1 box confectioners' sugar
2½–3 tablespoons cocoa

¼ cup evaporated milk or a little
   more
2–3 tablespoons peanut butter

Melt margarine on low in saucepan, then put confectioners' sugar in margarine. Add cocoa and evaporated milk. Mix well with mixer, then put on top of stove and cook until hot, but not boiling. Turn stove off; add peanut butter. Stir well; pour in buttered dish.

Bayside Treasures

Three Chocolate Fudge

⅔ cup evaporated milk
1⅔ cups sugar
½ teaspoon salt
2 tablespoons butter
1½ cups miniature marshmallows

½ cup white chocolate chips
½ cup milk chocolate chips
½ cup semisweet chocolate chips
1 teaspoon vanilla

In a 3-quart saucepan, combine milk, sugar, and salt; bring to a boil over medium heat. Cook for 5 minutes, stirring constantly (use a wooden spoon). Remove from heat and add butter, marshmallows, and chocolate chips. Stir until all are melted and blended well. Add vanilla; stir until blended. Spread mixture into a pie plate or pan (nonstick works well). When completely cooled, cut into squares.

Collected Recipes

Mocha Truffles

Serve with after dinner coffee...they're sinfully divine.

12 ounces semisweet chocolate
4 tablespoons unsalted butter, softened
½ cup coffee flavored liqueur

Unsweetened cocoa powder
Sweetened chocolate drink mix powder
Confectioners' sugar

Melt chocolate in the top of a double boiler over simmering water. Remove from heat. With a wooden spoon, beat in the butter. Add liqueur and continue beating. Pour chocolate mixture into a small bowl. Cover and refrigerate until firm, about 2 hours. Roll into balls using a teaspoonful of the mixture for each ball. Roll one third of the balls in cocoa powder. Roll one third of the balls in chocolate drink mix powder. Roll one third of the balls in confectioners' sugar. Refrigerate until serving time. Yields 2½ dozen. These can be frozen up to 4 months.

A Matter of Taste

Caramel Corn

This is a fun recipe to make with children. They love to help shake the bag and use the air popper. It is a simple and inexpensive gift for children to make and give to teachers and friends. Air-popped popcorn works better than popcorn popped in oil.

½ cup (1 stick) butter
1 cup brown sugar, packed
¼ cup light corn syrup

½ teaspoon baking soda
14 cups air-popped popcorn

Combine butter, brown sugar, and corn syrup in a microwave-safe bowl. Microwave on HIGH for 2–3 minutes or until mixture begins to boil; mix well. Stir in the baking soda. Divide popcorn equally among 4 clean paper bags. Pour hot caramel mixture over popcorn. Close bags securely and shake well to coat. Place one bag at a time in the microwave. Microwave on HIGH for 45 seconds. Shake bag vigorously. Spread the popcorn onto waxed paper to cool. Yields 14 cups.

Beyond Peanut Butter and Jelly

PIES & OTHER DESSERTS

Odessa, Delaware, possesses one of the finest preservations of late 18th- and early 19th-century architecture in the region. The center of town is on the National Register of Historic Places and the entire town has been zoned as historic. Shown here is the Corbit-Sharp house.

Peach Pie

CRUST:

4 cups flour
1 tablespoon sugar
2 teaspoons salt
1¾ cups shortening

½ cup ice water
1 tablespoon vinegar
1 egg

Mix flour, sugar, and salt. Add shortening and mix until crumbly. Beat together ice water, vinegar, and egg; cut into mix. Divide into 4 balls. Wrap and refrigerate ½ hour before rolling out. Makes 1–2 crusts.

PIE:

5 pounds peaches
1 teaspoon lemon juice
¼ teaspoon almond extract
½ cup sugar

2 tablespoons flour
½ teaspoon cinnamon
¼ teaspoon salt
Butter

Peel peaches and slice. Pour lemon juice and almond extract over peaches and mix. Mix dry ingredients. Pour over peaches and mix. Put in crust and dot with butter. Bake at 450° for 15 minutes, then 350° for 35–40 minutes.

Recipes from the Skipjack Martha Lewis

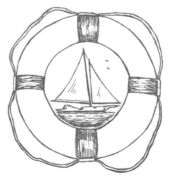

Applesauce Pie

1 (16½-ounce) container
   applesauce or 1 pint homemade
1 cup sugar
4 eggs, separated
½ cup butter, softened
2 tablespoons cornstarch

1 teaspoon vanilla or lemon
   flavoring or ½ teaspoon
   cinnamon
2 cups evaporated milk
½ cup whole milk
2 unbaked 9-inch pie crusts

Put applesauce in a bowl. Add sugar, egg yolks, butter, cornstarch, and your choice of a flavoring and mix until smooth. Add evaporated milk. In separate bowl, beat egg whites until stiff. Fold egg whites into applesauce mixture. Stir whole milk into mixture very slowly. Pour into pie shells. Bake at 400° for 15 minutes; then 350° for 25 minutes. Makes 2 (9-inch) pies.

Mrs. Kitching's Smith Island Cookbook

Sour Cream Apple Pie

FILLING:
2 cups sliced Rome apples
1 (9-inch) pie shell
¾ cup sugar
4 tablespoons flour

1 egg (or substitute), beaten
1 cup sour cream
½ teaspoon vanilla
⅛ teaspoon salt

TOPPING:
⅓ cup sugar
⅓ cup flour

¼ cup butter
1 teaspoon cinnamon

Arrange apples (sliced and peeled) into unbaked pie shell. Mix remaining filling ingredients together and pour over apples. Bake at 350° for one hour. While pie is baking, blend topping ingredients together. Crumble this mixture over top of baked pie. Bake 15 minutes longer. Serve warm.

Note: Can use reduced-fat or fat-free sour cream or plain yogurt.

A Taste of GBMC

Fresh Strawberry Pie

A colorful pie that also makes elegant tarts.

¾ cup sugar
2 tablespoons cornstarch
1½ cups water
¼ cup regular strawberry Jell-O
  (½ of 3-ounce box)

1 (9-inch) baked pastry
1 quart fresh strawberries, washed
  and hulled

Mix sugar and cornstarch in small saucepan. Stir in water. Heat over medium heat until mixture is clear. Add Jell-O and stir well. Let cool. Fill pastry shell with fresh strawberries. Pour sauce over all and let sit until sauce has thickened. Refrigerate. Serves 8.

Of Tide & Thyme

Strawberry Cream Pie

Pastry for 9-inch pie
3 eggs, slightly beaten
6 tablespoons sugar
¼ teaspoon salt
2 cups milk

1 teaspoon vanilla
1 quart strawberries, divided
1 cup sugar
3 tablespoons cornstarch
⅓ cup water

Set oven for 425°. Roll out pastry and line 9-inch pie pan. Trim and flute the edge. Combine the eggs, 6 tablespoons sugar, and salt; then add the milk and vanilla and stir well. Pour mixture into the pastry-lined pie pan. Bake 30 minutes or until a silver knife inserted in the custard an inch from the edge comes out clean. Cool to room temperature.

Wash and hull the strawberries. Reserve half the berries. Put the remaining berries in saucepan and mash them. Add 1 cup sugar and place over low heat. Stir constantly until the mixture comes to a boil. Remove from heat. Blend the cornstarch and water. Stir into berry mixture. Return to heat and cook, stirring constantly, until clear and thickened. Fold in uncooked berries. When cool, spoon mixture over the pie. Chill before serving. Serves 6–8.

A Taste of Catholicism

Heavenly Pineapple Pie

1 (9-inch) pie crust
1 (20-ounce) can crushed
  pineapple with juice
Pineapple juice and water to
  make 1 cup
⅔ cup sugar, divided

1 envelope unflavored gelatin
¼ teaspoon salt
4 large eggs, separated
2 tablespoons lemon juice
½ teaspoon lemon rind

Prepare, bake, and cool pie crust. Drain and save juice from pineapple, pressing out excess juice with back of spoon. Add water to measure 1 cup. Mix ⅓ cup sugar with gelatin and salt in small saucepan. Beat egg yolks with 1 cup pineapple juice. Stir into gelatin-sugar mixture. Cook over very low heat, stirring constantly, about 10 minutes, until mix coats a spoon. Remove from heat. Stir in drained pineapple, lemon juice, and lemon rind. Cool until mix begins to jell. Beat egg whites to soft peaks. Gradually beat in remaining sugar (⅓ cup), beating to a stiff meringue. Gently fold into pineapple mix. Spoon into shell. Chill until firm. Makes 6 generous servings.

Atlantic Highlands

Margarita Pie

½ cup margarine or butter
1¼ cups finely crushed pretzels
¼ cup sugar
1 (14-ounce) can sweetened
  condensed milk

⅓ cup ReaLime lime juice
2–4 tablespoons tequila
2 tablespoons Triple-Sec, or other
  orange-flavored liqueur
1 cup heavy cream, whipped

In a small saucepan, melt butter; stir in pretzel crumbs and sugar. Press crumbs on bottom and sides of a buttered 9-inch pie pan; chill. In a large bowl, combine condensed milk, lime juice, tequila, and Triple-Sec; mix well. Fold in whipped cream. Pour into prepared crust. Freeze or chill until firm (4 hours in freezer, or 2 hours in refrigerator). Garnish each slice with a dollop of whipped cream, an orange twist and a fresh mint sprig.

Cooking with the Allenhurst Garden Club

Grasshopper Pie

32 large marshmallows, or 3 cups
  miniatures
½ cup milk
¼ cup crème de menthe
3 tablespoons white crème de
  cacao
1½ cups chilled whipping
  cream

Few drops green food coloring
  (optional)
Chocolate cookie crust, homemade
  or prepared
Grated semisweet chocolate

Heat marshmallows and milk over medium heat, stirring constantly, just until marshmallows are melted. Refrigerate until thickened. Stir in liqueurs. Beat whipping cream in chilled bowl until stiff. Add food coloring. Fold marshmallow mixture into whipped cream. Pour into crust. Sprinkle with grated semisweet chocolate. Refrigerate at least 3 hours. Serves 6.

Cape May Fare

Chocolate Chip Pie

2 eggs
½ cup flour
½ cup sugar
½ cup brown sugar, packed
1 cup melted butter, cooled
1 (6-ounce) package chocolate chips

1 cup chopped nuts
1 (9-inch) unbaked pie shell
Whipped cream or ice cream
  (optional)

Preheat oven to 325°. In large bowl, beat eggs until foamy. Add flour and sugars and beat until well blended. Blend in melted butter. Stir in chocolate chips and nuts. Pour into pie shell. Bake at 325° for one hour. Remove from oven. Serve warm with whipped cream or ice cream. May be frozen.

What's Cookin'

Fudge Pie

1 cup sugar
1 stick butter, melted
2 eggs

½ cup flour
1 square bitter chocolate, melted
1 teaspoon vanilla

Put sugar in a mixing bowl; add melted butter and beat. Add eggs, one at a time, and beat after each addition. Add flour and beat. Add melted bitter chocolate; beat. Add vanilla and beat again.

Place in a small (8-inch) Pyrex pie plate. Bake at 300° for 25 minutes. When done the top looks a little soft—that is fine. Cool and serve with vanilla ice cream.

In the Komondor Kitchen

Sara's Scrumptious Chocolate Pecan Pie

3 eggs, slightly beaten
1 cup light corn syrup
4 ounces semisweet baker's
  chocolate, melted and cooled
⅓ cup sugar

2 tablespoons butter or margarine,
  melted
1 teaspoon vanilla extract
1½ cups pecan halves
1 (9-inch) deep-dish pie shell

In large bowl, stir eggs, syrup, chocolate, sugar, butter, and vanilla until blended well. Stir in pecans. Pour into pie shell. Bake at 350° for 50–60 minutes, or until knife inserted half-way between edge and center of pie comes out clean.

225 Years in Pennington & Still Cooking

 New Jersey has the highest population density in the U.S. An average 1,030 people per square mile is 13 times the national average; 90% of the people living in New Jersey live in an urban area.

Carrot Walnut Crunch Pie

2 (16-ounce) cans diced carrots,
  drained
2 eggs, beaten
1 (14-ounce) can (1¼ cups)
  sweetened condensed milk
1 tablespoon pumpkin pie spice

Dash of salt
1 unbaked 9-inch pastry shell
½ cup brown sugar, packed
¼ cup margarine or butter, melted
1 cup chopped walnuts

Purée carrots in blender or food processor until smooth. (You should have about 2 cups.) In large mixing bowl, combine eggs, sweetened condensed milk, pie spice, and salt. Add carrots; mix well. Turn into pastry shell. In a small bowl, combine brown sugar and margarine; stir in walnuts. Sprinkle evenly over pie. Cover edge of pie with foil. Bake in a 375° oven for 25 minutes. Remove foil; bake for 20–25 minutes more, or until a knife inserted near center comes out clean. Cool completely on wire rack.

The Great Gourmet

Bal'More Rhubarb Pie

It's best to make this fresh when rhubarb is in season, but this authentic recipe will work as well with frozen rhubarb.

1 pastry shell, with extra pastry
  for top
4 tablespoons flour
1 cup sugar (less, if using
  strawberries)

1 egg, beaten
3–4 cups rhubarb, cut up, or
  combination of rhubarb and
  strawberries (fresh or frozen)

Preheat oven to 425°. Thaw pastry shell, if frozen.

Combine flour and sugar. Add egg, and mix well. Add rhubarb and strawberries (if using). Pour batter into pastry shell, and cover with second shell constructed in a lattice design. Bake at 425° for first 10 minutes. Lower temperature to 350° and continue baking for 35 minutes.

Simple Pleasures

Sweet Potato Custard Pie

1 cup mashed sweet potatoes
1 cup sugar
2½ tablespoons butter, melted
2 eggs, separated

1 teaspoon vanilla
1½ cups scalded milk
1 pinch of nutmeg

Mix potatoes, sugar, and butter; beat well. Add egg yolks, vanilla, milk, and nutmeg; beat total mixture well. Beat egg whites stiff, and add them last; stir well. Pour into a 9-inch pie shell. Bake at 400° for 30 minutes, then reduce heat to 350° for 30 minutes. Test for doneness with a knife.

Come, Dine With Us!

Coconut Pie

1 stick margarine, softened
1 cup sugar
2 eggs
2 tablespoons flour
1 small can coconut

1 teaspoon vanilla
1 (12-ounce) can evaporated milk
1 cup milk
1 unbaked pie shell

Combine margarine and sugar in a bowl. Mix well. Add eggs, flour, coconut, and vanilla, and mix very well. Fold in milk. Stir until well blended and pour into unbaked pie shell. Bake in preheated oven at 350° for one hour.

Bayside Treasures

Pumpkin Pie Dessert Squares

BOTTOM LAYER:

1 box yellow cake mix, divided   1 egg
½ cup melted butter

Grease bottom of 9x12x2-inch pan. Reserve 1 cup cake mix for topping. Combine remaining cake mix, butter, and 1 egg. Press into pan.

FILLING:

1 pound can solid packed   ½ cup brown sugar, firmly packed
   pumpkin   2 eggs, beaten
2½ teaspoons pumpkin pie spice   ⅔ cup milk

Combine all ingredients until smooth. Pour over crust.

TOPPING:

1 cup reserved cake mix   1 teaspoon cinnamon
¼ cup sugar   ¼ cup butter, softened

Combine all ingredients and sprinkle over filling. Bake at 350° for 40–45 minutes; or until knife inserted in center comes out clean. If desired, serve with whipped topping.

A Taste of Catholicism

Charlotte au Chocolat

1 (12-ounce) package semisweet
  chocolate pieces
6 eggs, separated
2 tablespoons sugar
2 cups heavy cream, whipped

4 dozen ladyfingers, split
Whipped cream and chocolate
  candy wafers (for topping;
  optional)

Melt chocolate pieces in top of double boiler. Cool. Beat in egg yolks, one at a time; beat well after each addition. Beat egg whites until frothy. Gradually beat in sugar until stiff peaks form. Beat ¼ of egg white mixture into chocolate. Fold in remaining mixture. Fold in whipped cream. Line bottom and sides of 9-inch springform pan with ladyfingers. Spoon ⅓ chocolate mixture into pan and top with layer of ladyfingers. Repeat layers, ending with chocolate mixture. Garnish with whipped cream and candy wafers, if desired. Chill 4 hours. Cut in thin wedges to serve. Serves 16.

Flavors of Cape Henlopen

Pear-Cranberry Crisp

Enjoy this fall specialty.

4 firm, ripe pears, peeled, cored,
  sliced (2½ pounds)
12 ounces cranberries
⅓ cup sugar
½ teaspoon cinnamon, divided
¾ cup rolled oats

⅔ cup sliced almonds
⅔ cup brown sugar, firmly
  packed
½ cup (1 stick) butter cut into
  ½-inch pieces
1 cup all-purpose flour

Preheat oven to 375°. Toss pears, cranberries, sugar, and ¼ teaspoon cinnamon in 9x9-inch baking dish until blended. Combine oats, almonds, brown sugar, butter, flour, and remaining ¼ teaspoon cinnamon in large bowl or food processor. Blend with fingertips if using bowl; pulse if using food processor until mixture resembles coarse meal. Sprinkle over fruit and pat down lightly. Bake until pears are tender and topping is golden, about 45 minutes. Serve hot or cooled down to warm. Makes 6–8 servings.

Note: Always buy pears 3 days to one week ahead for the best taste.

Why Not for Breakfast?

Apple Cobbler

¾ cup sugar
2 tablespoons flour
½ teaspoon cinnamon
¼ teaspoon salt

5 cups sliced apples
¼ cup water
1 tablespoon butter

Heat oven to 400°. Combine sugar, flour, cinnamon, and salt. Mix with apples; place in ovenproof casserole. Sprinkle with water. Dot with butter. Cover with foil and bake 15 minutes.

CRUST:
1 cup flour
1 tablespoon sugar
1½ teaspoons baking powder

½ teaspoon salt
3 tablespoons shortening
½ cup milk

Sift flour, sugar, baking powder, and salt together. Cut in shortening; stir in milk. Drop by spoonfuls on hot apples. Bake, uncovered, 25–35 minutes. Makes 6 servings.

A Tasting Tour Through the 8th District

Crock Pot Cherry Cobbler

Pull this dish together the night before, so you can turn on the crock pot the minute you walk in the door after work or school.

1 can (about 16 ounces) cherry pie
  filling
1 cup vegan yellow cake mix

⅛ cup softened vegan margarine
¼ cup chopped nuts
Sorbet or soy ice cream, as desired

Pour cherry pie filling into a crock pot, spreading it evenly across the bottom of the crock. In a medium-sized bowl, combine cake mix and margarine until the mixture is crumbly. Sprinkle evenly over cherries. Sprinkle nuts evenly over cake mix.

Set crock pot on LOW, cover, and allow it to cook for 3 hours. Serve hot, right from the crock pot, or serve it over sorbet, if desired. Serves 4.

Note: Any fruit pie filling will do. Refrigerate extra portions of this cobbler and mix it into hot oatmeal, yogurt, or tofu for a breakfast treat.

Total Calories Per Serving (using walnuts–minus frozen dessert): 466; Total Fat of Daily Value 25%; Prot 4g; Fat 16g; Carbo 80g; Cal 35mg; Iron 2mg; Sod 436mg; Dietary Fiber 2g.

Vegan Meals for One and Two

Apple and Almond Tart with Melted Brie

DOUGH:

1½ cups melted butter
½ cup sugar
1 egg, beaten

2¼ cups flour
Pinch of salt

Blend melted butter and sugar together until mixture becomes light and fluffy. Add egg and stir until well combined. Add flour and salt, stirring well. Roll out dough on a floured surface. Place in a greased tart pan.

FILLING:

½ cup + 4 tablespoons melted butter, divided
¾ cup sugar
1 cup almonds, toasted and ground

4 large eggs, beaten
6 tablespoons flour
4 Granny Smith apples
Cinnamon sugar
8 ounces Brie cheese

In a large mixing bowl, combine ½ cup melted butter, sugar, and almonds together until mixture becomes light and fluffy. Add eggs and blend until well combined. Add flour, mixing well.

Fill each tart shell almost to top with the filling. Peel and slice Granny Smith apples, and arrange slices on top of the filling. Brush with 4 tablespoons melted butter and sprinkle with cinnamon sugar.

Bake at 350° until well browned. When just cool enough to handle, unmold and top with a wedge of Brie cheese. Place in a warm oven to melt the Brie slightly. Serve immediately.

Cooking Secrets

Deluxe Apple Tart

CRUST:

1½ cups all-purpose flour
½ teaspoon baking powder
½ teaspoon salt

¼ cup cold butter
¼ cup shortening
3½–4 tablespoons milk

Combine flour, baking powder, and salt; cut in butter and shortening with pastry blender until mixture resembles coarse meal. Sprinkle milk over surface; stir with a fork until ingredients are moistened. Shape into a ball; chill at least an hour. Roll dough to ⅛-inch thickness on a lightly floured surface. Fit pastry into an 11x17x½-inch tart pan or an 11-inch round tart pan with a removable bottom. Set aside.

ALMOND MIXTURE:

½ cup, plus 2 tablespoons
   blanched slivered almonds
½ cup sugar

1 egg
1 tablespoon melted butter

Position knife blade in food processor bowl. Add almonds; process until finely ground. Add sugar, egg and butter; process until well mixed. Spread mixture evenly over the bottom of the pastry; set aside.

FILLING:

2 cups water
2 tablespoons lemon juice
4–5 golden delicious apples
¼ cup sugar
½ teaspoon ground cinnamon

¼ cup butter
½ cup peach preserves
2 tablespoons water
2 tablespoons apricot brandy

Combine water and lemon juice. Peel and core apples; cut into ¼-inch-thick slices. Dip apples in lemon juice mixture; drain well. Arrange apples so slices are overlapping on top of Almond Mixture. Sprinkle with sugar and cinnamon. Dot with butter. Bake at 400° approximately 1 hour.

Combine peach preserves and water; cook over low heat, stirring constantly, until melted. Press through a sieve; add the brandy. After removing tart from oven, carefully brush syrup over tart. Cool. Remove rim of pan before serving. Yields 10–12 servings.

Cooking Along the Susquehanna

Passover Noodle Kugel

1 box Passover noodles
2 apples, pared and sliced
1 (20-ounce) can crushed
  pineapple, drained
1 stick margarine, melted

4 eggs
¾ cup sugar
1 (16-ounce) can mixed fruit,
  drained

Cook and drain noodles.   Mix remaining ingredients with noodles.
Pour into greased 9-inch square pan. Bake at 375° for 50 minutes.

The Happy Cooker 3

Judy's Famous Orange Kugel

Very unique, easy and delicious. Freezes well.

1⅓ cups margarine, softened
1 cup sugar
2 eggs, separated
¼ cup orange juice

1½ teaspoons grated orange rind
4 slices white bread, torn apart
  (enough to make 2 cups)

Cream margarine, sugar, egg yolks, orange juice, and rind.   Mix in
bread pieces. Beat egg whites to soft peaks and fold in. Bake at 350° in
an 8x8-inch pan for ½ hour until lightly browned. Serve hot or cold.

Simple Pleasures

Peach Dumplings

1 cup sugar	1 cup flour
1 tablespoon butter or margarine	2 teaspoons baking powder
2 cups hot water	½ teaspoon salt
2 cups sliced peaches	½ cup milk or cream

Make a syrup with sugar, butter, and hot water. Add peaches and let this come to a boil. Make dumplings by mixing flour, baking powder, and salt into a fairly stiff batter with milk or cream. Drop large spoonfuls of batter into the boiling syrup and peaches. Cover and cook for 20 minutes. Serve while hot. Sauce or milk can be used over dumplings. Serves 4.

Steppingstone Cookery

Lemon Blueberry Bread Pudding

The tart lemon contrasts beautifully with the sweet blueberries.

6 cups French or Italian bread, torn into 1-inch chunks	¾ cup sugar, divided
	Juice and grated rind of 2 lemons
3 cups milk	1½ pints fresh blueberries
4 eggs	1 tablespoon soft sweet butter

In large bowl, soak bread in milk for 20 minutes. Preheat oven to 350°. Beat eggs with all but 2 tablespoons of the sugar. Beat in lemon juice and rind. Pour egg mixture over soaked bread and mix well. Add blueberries and mix. Pour into buttered shallow 3-quart baking dish. Sprinkle remaining sugar over top. Bake about 40 minutes, until top is lightly browned and crusty. Serve warm or cooled.

Lambertville Community Cookbook

 Delaware is 96 miles long and varies from 9 to 35 miles wide; 130 states the size of Delaware would fit into Texas.

Lemon Pudding

2 eggs, separated
1 cup sugar
2 rounded tablespoons flour
¼ cup lemon juice

Grated rind of 1 lemon
1 tablespoon melted butter
1 cup milk

To beaten egg yolks, add sugar and flour mixed; then stir in lemon juice, grated rind, butter, and milk. Lastly, fold in lightly beaten egg whites. Pour into buttered 1-quart ovenproof dish and place in a shallow pan of hot water. Bake for 50 minutes in 350° oven. Serves 4.

Maryland's Way

Lemon Lust

Can be made with any flavor pudding. Especially good made with chocolate.

½ cup (1 stick) butter, softened
1 cup flour
½ cup pecan pieces
1 (8-ounce) package cream cheese, softened
¾ cup confectioners' sugar

1 (12-ounce) container frozen
  whipped topping, thawed
2 (3.4-ounce) packages instant
  lemon pudding mix
3 cups milk

Mix butter, flour, and pecan pieces together and spread in a 9x13-inch baking pan. Bake at 350° for 12–15 minutes, or until lightly browned. Cool thoroughly. Blend together cream cheese, sugar, and 1 cup whipped topping and spread over the cooled crust.

Beat pudding mix and milk until thick, and pour over cheese mixture. Then spread the remaining whipped topping over pudding mixture. Garnish with pecan pieces, shaved chocolate, mint, or strawberries, if desired. Refrigerate until ready to serve.

Where There's a Will...

Fruit Pizza

FILLING:

1 (14-ounce) can sweetened
   condensed milk
½ cup sour cream

¼ cup lemon juice
1 teaspoon vanilla

Mix the milk, sour cream, lemon juice, and vanilla. Refrigerate for at least 30 minutes.

DOUGH:

½ cup (1 stick) softened butter
¼ cup brown sugar
1 cup all-purpose flour

¼ cup quick-cooking rolled oats
¼ cup finely chopped walnuts

Preheat the oven to 375°. Lightly oil a 12-inch pizza pan. Beat the butter and sugar until fluffy. Mix in the flour, rolled oats, and walnuts. Place the dough on the prepared pizza pan and press it into a circle, forming a rim around the edge. Prick with a fork and bake for 10–12 minutes. Cool.

APRICOT GLAZE:

½ cup apricot preserves
2 tablespoons brandy

4 cups thinly sliced fresh fruit
   (such as kiwis, strawberries, and
   bananas)

Melt the apricot preserves in a small saucepan over low heat. Add the brandy and mix. Strain. Spoon the chilled Filling over the cooled crust. Arrange the fruit slices in a circular pattern over the Filling. Brush the Apricot Glaze over the fruit. Cover and refrigerate for 60 minutes. Serve cold; cut into wedges. Yields 8 servings.

Breakfast at Nine, Tea at Four

Fruit Pizza

Here's a beautiful looking dessert that both children and adults will enjoy. You can also substitute several small pita breads for the large pita bread.

1 large (12-inch-wide) pita bread
1 cup unsweetened apple butter
1 kiwi, peeled and sliced
6 large strawberries, sliced

1 apple or pear, peeled, cored, and
  thinly sliced
¼ teaspoon cinnamon

Spread apple butter over pita bread. Arrange slices of fruit on top of apple butter. Sprinkle with cinnamon. Serve as is, or heat in 350° oven for 15 minutes and serve warm.

Conveniently Vegan

Baked Pears with Brie

⅓ cup raisins
¼ cup hazelnuts
2 teaspoons honey

2 ounces peeled Brie cheese
4 pears, peeled, halved and cored
1 cup apple juice or sweet cider

Preheat oven to 350°. Combine raisins and hazelnuts in a food processor or blender and process until finely chopped. With the motor running, add honey and cheese. Continue to process until a soft ball forms. Spoon cheese mixture into cavities of pears and set them in an ovenproof casserole. Pour juice around them and bake until pears are tender, about 35 minutes. Serve hot as a dessert, breakfast, or snack. Serves 4.

Recipe by Mrs. Charles Rangel, wife of Representative from New York
The Congressional Club Cookbook

 Did you know that the Statue of Liberty is actually in New Jersey waters, but under New York City jurisdiction?

Strawberries Bourbonnaise

This deliciously simple recipe is too good to be true. Make it for no reason and it will be something nobody will forget. Make it for a special occasion and it will become a tradition.

2 cups sugar
¼ cup unsalted butter
½ cup heavy cream
½ cup bourbon

1½ quarts strawberries, stemmed
(the fresher the better)
Whipped cream

Use a heavy cast aluminum or black iron skillet and make sure bottom of pan fits burners. Place on medium heat until you feel heat penetrate through bottom of pan to hand held over pan. When pan is hot, immediately add sugar. Stir with long-handled wooden spoon. As sugar starts to melt, stir gently until you have golden-colored syrup. Remove from heat and add butter. When butter is melted, add heavy cream a little at a time . . . very carefully. Stir in bourbon. Let sauce cool down and pour into a glass container. Cover and refrigerate. When cool, this wonderful sauce will be caramelized.

To serve: Place strawberries in individual stemmed glasses. Pour caramel sauce over strawberries. Top with a dollop of whipped cream. Sauce can be kept in refrigerator for several weeks. Yields 8 servings.

Food Fabulous Food

CONTRIBUTING COOKBOOKS

The U.S. Capitol in Washington, D.C., is among the most symbolically important buildings in the nation. It has housed the meeting chambers of the House of Representatives and the Senate for two centuries, and stands today as a monument to the American people and their government.

CATALOG of
CONTRIBUTING COOKBOOKS

All recipes in this book have been selected from the cookbooks shown on the following pages. Individuals who wish to obtain a copy of any particular book may do so by sending a check or money order to the address listed by each cookbook. Please note the postage and handling charges that are required. State residents add tax only when requested. Prices and addresses are subject to change, and the books may sell out and become unavailable. Retailers are invited to call or write to same address for discount information.

AROUND THE TABLE
RECIPES & REFLECTIONS

Mothers' Center of Monmouth County   732-747-7649
P. O. Box 49
Little Silver, NJ 07739

"Fun in the Kitchen," "Bun in the Oven," and "What's for Dinner?" are just some of the creative culinary chapters you'll find in this unique cookbook. Hundreds of recipes with an emphasis on family share these pages with beautiful sketches and quotations, amusing anecdotes and real, tried and true tips.

$ 20.00   Retail price
$ 6.00   Postage and handling
Make check payable to MCMC

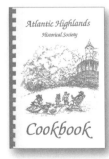

ATLANTIC HIGHLANDS HISTORICAL SOCIETY
COOKBOOK

Atlantic Highlands Historical Society   732-291-1861
P. O. Box 108
Atlantic Highlands, NJ 07716   murray@monmouth.com

Within the pages of this cookbook you'll find a collection of family favorites from the members of the Atlantic Highlands Historical Society. Our mission is to preserve the history of the Atlantic Highlands area.

$ 6.00   Retail price
$ 3.50   Postage and handling
Make check payable to AHHS

BARINEAU-WILLIAMS FAMILY COOKBOOK VOL. II

Barineau-Williams Family
806 Evelyn Court
Tallahassee, FL 32304   gjaillet_56@yahoo.com

This cookbook is a reflection of the Barineau-Williams family, its history and what we believe family to be about: sharing, togetherness and love for one another. Our recipes are diverse, time tested, and there is something for everyone.

$ 10.00   Retail price
$ 3.00   Postage and handling

Make check payable to Barineau-Williams Family Cookbook

BAYSIDE TREASURES

c/o Maxine Landon
Calvary Methodist Church
3159 Marsh Road
Rhodes Point, Smith Island, MD 21824

Bayside Treasures contains 241 recipes in 73 pages. Many recipes including seafood and wild fowl, natural to our area. All of the recipes were contributed by people who live, or have lived, in Rhodes Point. Enjoy!

$ 7.00   Retail price
$ 3.00   Postage and handling

Make check payable to Calvary Methodist Church

BEST OF FRIENDS

Friends School of Baltimore Parents Association
5114 North Charles Street
Baltimore, MD 21210

Established in 1784, Friends School of Baltimore is a prestigious coed Quaker School. To honor the millennium, the Parent's Association collected over 400 recipes from the entire Friends community and bound it into this 223-page cookbook.

$ 12.00   Retail price
$ .60   Tax for Maryland residents
$ 4.00   Postage and handling

Make check payable to Friends School P. A. Cookbook

BEYOND PEANUT BUTTER AND JELLY

International Nanny Association   856-858-0808
900 Haddon Avenue, Suite 438   Fax 856-858-2519
Collingswood, NJ 08108   www.nanny.org

You'll be delighted with the recipes tucked away in this 190-page, bright "grape jelly" with "peanut butter" handprint cookbook by the International Nanny Association. Not only will you find chapters for all categories of foods, but also Make a Wish (birthday theme parties); Festive Holidays (holiday parties) and Move Over, Picasso (crafts).

$ 19.95   Retail price   Visa/MC/Disc accepted
$ 4.95   Postage and handling

Make check payable to International Nanny Association
ISBN 0-9673312-0-X

BOUNTIFUL BLESSINGS

St. John Lutheran Church · 410-859-0020
300 West Maple Road
Linthicum, MD 21090 · threegaps@aol.com

Over 150 pages packed with family favorites make up St. John's latest cookbook. This attractive spiral-bound book lies flat so you won't lose your place. Whether you're in a hurry to fix supper, or have all day to try new recipes, this cookbook is sure to tempt you with dishes that will become your favorites, too.

$ 8.00   Retail price
$ 2.00   Postage and handling

Make check payable to St. John Lutheran Church

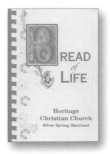

BREAD OF LIFE

Joy Circle of the Christian Women's Fellowship
Heritage Christian Church · 301-384-1510
15250 New Hampshire Avenue
Silver Spring, MD 20905-5361 · heritage_christian@juno.com

Women of the church, friends and relatives contributed recipes for this book, to sell with proceeds to go to the mission projects of our church. It contains 122 pages of recipes plus an index, table of contents, mission statement, prayer of thanksgiving, and a recipe for Preserving Children.

$ 7.00   Retail price
$ .35   Tax for Maryland residents
$ 1.50   Postage and handling

Make check payable to Heritage Christian Church, CWF

BREAKFAST AT NINE, TEA AT FOUR

by Sue H. Carroll
Callawind Publications · 609-884-8690
635 Columbia Avenue
Cape May, NJ 08204

A 200-page collection of more than 150 recipes, this book is the essential companion to Sunday brunch preparation. Most can be done the evening before—freeing the host(ess) for conversation and relaxation. Sue Carroll has owned the famous Mainstay Inn since 1976. A professional cook for 30 years, Sue has become an expert on breakfast, brunch and tea entertaining.

$ 14.95   Retail price · Visa/MC accepted
$ 3.00   Postage and handling

Make check payable to The Mainstay Inn
ISBN 1-896511-08-2

CAPE MAY FARE

Mid-Atlantic Center for the Arts · 609-884-5404
P. O. Box 340 · Fax 609-884-0574
Cape May, NJ 08204

Cape May Fare is a recipe collection from friends and members of the Mid-Atlantic Center for the Arts—a not-for-profit organization committed to promoting the preservation, interpretation and cultural enrichment of Victorian Cape May. Many recipes are from some of Cape May's famous bed & breakfast chefs and humble kitchens. Wipe-clean cover, spiral-bound, 236 pages, and 433 recipes.

$ 10.95   Retail price · Visa/MC/Dis/Amex
$ 3.00   Postage and handling

Make check payable to Mid-Atlantic Center for the Arts
ISBN 0-9663295-1-1

CAPITAL CELEBRATIONS

Junior League of Washington, DC   202-337-2001 ext 38
3039 M Street, NW   Fax 202-342-3148
Washington, DC 20007

Capital Celebrations features more than 200 specially selected, triple-tested recipes from the community and Washington's most renowned chefs. The busy cook can choose from an offering of simple-to-prepare yet elegant international and all-American recipes. 160 pages, 200 recipes.

$ 24.95   Retail price   Visa/MC accepted
$ 1.43   Tax for D.C. residents
$ 3.50   Postage and handling

Make check payable to Junior League of Washington
ISBN 0-9649444-1-3

CAPITAL CLASSICS

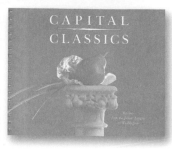

Junior League of Washington, DC   202-337-2001 ext 38
3039 M Street, NW   Fax 202-342-3148
Washington, DC 20007

Capital Classics celebrates the great tradition of entertaining in our nation's capital, where regional styles and international cultures meet. Elegant, but not intricate, triple-tested for home kitchens. Each recipe suits busy lifestyles. 160 pages, 289 recipes.

$ 21.95   Retail price   Visa/MC accepted
$ 1.26   Tax for D.C. residents
$ 3.50   Postage and handling

Make check payable to Junior League of Washington
ISBN 0-9649444-0-5

THE CHESAPEAKE COLLECTION

Woman's Club of Denton, Maryland
Tidewater Publishers   800-638-7641
P. O. Box 456   Fax 410-758-6849
Centreville, MD 21617   cornell4@crosslink.net

Created by the Woman's Club of Denton, Maryland, in 1983, this collection of 460 recipes captures the "tads" and "smidgens" by which accomplished Eastern Shore cooks often describe their delicious concoctions and translates them into a readable form that any capable cook can use and enjoy serving to family and friends.

$ 14.95   Retail price   Visa/MC/Amex
$ .75   Tax for Maryland residents

Make check payable to Tidewater Publishers
ISBN 0-87033-431-X

CHESAPEAKE'S BOUNTY

Katie Moose
Conduit Press   410-280-5272
111 Conduit Street   Fax 410-263-5380
Annapolis, MD 21401   Kamoose@erols.com

The Chesapeake Bay region offers an abundance of food from the Bay, fields and woods. Recipes come from the earliest Native Americans to the influx of international flavors. The recipes in this 240-page book are elegant and easy, designed for many different occasions. Over 300 recipes, menus included, make for easy planning and good eating.

$ 16.95   Retail price
$ 3.20   Postage and handling

Make check payable to Conduit Press
ISBN 0-9666610-3-6

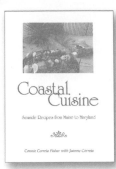

COASTAL CUISINE
SEASIDE RECIPES FROM MAINE TO MARYLAND

by Connie Correia Fisher with Joanne Correia
Small Potatoes Press   856-869-5207
1106 Stokes Avenue   Fax 856-869-5247
Collingswood, NJ 08108   cuizine1@aol.com

Coastal Cuisine celebrates the regional influences, seasonal ingredients, and ocean-born bounty that make Upper East Coast travel and dining so special. Over 100 recipes from seaside restaurants, inns, and hotels, capture the flavors of summer, the taste of travel, and the places that create memorable vacation meals.

$ 11.95   Retail price
$ 2.00   Postage and handling
Make check payable to Small Potatoes Press
ISBN 0-9661200-2-7

COLLECTED RECIPES
YOURS, MINE, OURS

by Linda Channell   908-852-3286
P. O. Box 156
Allamuchy, NJ 07820

My personal recipe collection started when I was 8 years old. Many of these recipes have been handed down generation to generation. They are a gathering of tastes ranging from simple hearty fare to the more fanciful gourmet dishes.

$ 6.95   Retail price
$ .42   Tax for New Jersey residents
$ 2.00   Postage and handling
Make check payable to Cash or Linda Channell

COME, DINE WITH US!

The Gravenor's
c/o Mrs. Iva Mae Gravenor   410-742-5174
168 Morris Mill Road
Salisbury, MD 21804

Come, Dine With Us was created in celebration of the Gravenor's 25th annual family reunion. It honors the living and is in memory of the deceased. Many recipes have been passed down through several generations. Good ole' country eatin'. 400 recipes in 160 pages.

$ 8.00   Retail price
$ 3.20   Postage and handling
Make check payable to Iva Mae Gravenor

CONDUCTING IN THE KITCHEN

The Monmouth Civic Chorus   732-933-9333
P. O. Box 16
Red Bank, NJ 07701

Conducting in the Kitchen is a collection of recipes contributed by the members and friends of The Monmouth Civic Chorus. Designed as a fund raiser to support our musical activities the book presents a full range of recipes from appetizers (Overtures) to main dishes (Main Themes) and desserts (Suites). Over 450 recipes in 257 pages.

$ 10.00   Retail price
$ 2.50   Postage and handling
Make check payable to Monmouth Civic Chorus

THE CONGRESSIONAL CLUB COOKBOOK

The Congressional Club
2001 New Hampshire Avenue NW   Fax 202-797-0698
Washington, DC 20009

This new and unique collection of 662 recipes represents the diverse ethnic backgrounds, regional customs and family traditions of our members and their spouses. In addition to fabulous recipes, this 437-page cookbook features world class photographs of the fifty state flowers in breathtaking beauty. The wild flowers theme truly captures the spirit of our club.

$ 35.00   Retail price   Visa/MC accepted
$ 7.00   Postage and handling   by fax only

Make check payable to The Congressional Club

CONVENIENTLY VEGAN

Debra Wasserman
The Vegetarian Resource Group   410-366-8343
P. O. Box 1463   Fax 410-366-8804
Baltimore, MD 21203   vrg@vrg.org • www.vrg.org

Conveniently Vegan: Turn Packaged Foods into Delicious Vegetarian Dishes is a 208-page book containing 150 healthy recipes using convenience foods along with fresh fruits and vegetables. Included are menu ideas, food definitions and sources for various products. These recipes are easy to prepare, yet delicious.

$ 15.00   Retail price   Visa/MC accepted
$ .75   Tax for Maryland residents
$ 3.00   Postage and handling

Make check payable to The Vegetarian Resource Group
ISBN 0-931411-18-1

A COOKBOOK OF TREASURES

Carol Luzak
Trinity Presbyterian Church   302-798-2626
68 South Avon Drive
Claymont, DE 19703   kakeladi@aol.com

A Cookbook of Treasures is a 101-page book containing 250 tried-and-true recipes from Trinity Presbyterian Church. The book was compiled by the Naomi Circle with recipes from families and friends of Trinity.

$ 8.00   Retail price
$ 3.00   Postage and handling

Make check payable to Trinity Presbyterian Church Cookbook

COOKING ALONG THE SUSQUEHANNA

Susquehanna Museum of Havre de Grace   410-272-3017
P. O. Box 253
Havre de Grace, MD 21078   dswoo@erols.com

Cooking Along the Susquehanna is a compilation of favorite recipes of members and friends of the Susquehanna museum. Each recipe was carefully considered before being included. The 500 recipes on 176 pages is a reflection of our efforts.

$ 10.00   Retail price
$ .50   Tax for Maryland residents
$ 1.50   Postage and handling

Make check payable to Susquehanna Museum of HDG

COOKING SECRETS
MID-ATLANTIC & CHESAPEAKE

by Kathleen DeVanna Fish
Bon Vivant Press
1271 Tenth Street, Suite D
Monterey, CA 93940

800-524-6826
Fax 831-373-3567
www.millpub.com

Take a delectable journey through the Mid-Atlantic and Chesapeake Regions as area chefs share their secrets and menus for all occasions and taste. Explore the rich cooking heritage of each state through signature dishes and special places— romantic inns, hide-aways and fine restaurants.

$ 19.95   Retail price
$ 4.50   Postage and handling
Make check payable to Bon Vivant Press
ISBN 1-883214-28-9

COOKING THROUGH THE YEARS

Clara Maass Medical Center Auxiliary
1 Clara Maass Drive
Belleville, NJ 07109

973-450-2150
Fax 973-844-4945

Consisting of 144 pages, plus several pages of handy hints and basic kitchen information our book includes 300 recipes. All recipes have been tested and approved by the staff at the hospital, including nutritionist and dietitians.

$ 10.00   Retail price
$ 2.00   Postage and handling
Make check payable to Clara Maass Auxiliary

COOKING WITH THE ALLENHURST GARDEN CLUB

The Allenhurst Garden Club
P. O. Box 282
Allenhurst, NJ 07711

Cooking with the Allenhurst Garden Club is filled with 300 recipes from members, families, friends, local business owners and government officials. The recipes reflect the rich diversity of our small historic seaside town, offering Greek, Italian, Russian and Irish dishes among others. The proceeds from sales fund garden related community projects and garden club activities.

$ 12.00   Retail price
$ 3.50   Postage and handling
Make check payable to The Allenhurst Garden Club

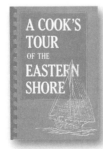

A COOK'S TOUR OF THE EASTERN SHORE

Junior Auxiliary of the Memorial Hospital at Easton, Maryland
Tidewater Publishers
P. O. Box 456
Centreville, MD 21617

800-638-7641
Fax 410-758-6849
cornell4@crosslink.net

Maryland's famed tidewater region is a wellspring of gourmet delights. Since the first edition was published in 1948, this compilation of 460 outstanding recipes by the Junior Auxiliary of Easton's Memorial Hospital, has earned a reputation as *the* cookbook of epicurean fare so characteristic of this area.

$ 15.95   Retail price
$ .80   Tax for Maryland residents
Make check payable to Tidewater Publishers
ISBN 0-87033-001-2

Visa/MC/Amex

COUNTRY CHIC'S HOME COOKIN
by Christine C. Milligan   410-673-2109
6181 Harmony Road   Fax 410-770-8163
Preston, MD 21655   milligans@goeaston.net

This book is a personal collection of treasured recipes of mine, family & friends;
nothing fancy, just good home cookin'! There are well over 600 recipes in this
collection. Laminated, spiral binding. It's a "must have" for every good cook.

$ 15.00   Retail price
$ .75   Tax for Maryland residents
$ 3.00   Postage and handling

Make check payable to Christine C. Milligan

DAPI'S DELECTABLE DELIGHTS
Delaware Adolescent Program, Inc.
Kent Center   302-697-0356
185 South Street   Fax 302-697-1318
Camden, DE 19934

DAPI's Delectable Delights is a 66-page collection of 200 recipes that range from
elegant to easy. The cookbook represents "generations of good cookin'" in a
readable format that is simple to follow. Hearty home cooking, comfort foods,
cakes and treats await the cook. Enjoy!

$ 7.00   Retail price
$ 2.00   Postage and handling

Make check payable to Delaware Adolescent Program, Inc.

DR. JOHN'S HEALING PSORIASIS COOKBOOK...PLUS!
Dr. John O. A. Pagano
The Pagano Organization, Inc.   201-947-0606
35 Hudson Terrace, Box 1215   Fax 201-947-8066
Englewood Cliffs, NJ 07632   Info@psoriasis-healing.com

This is the perfect sequel to the Award-winning book, *Healing Psoriasis: The
Natural Alternative*. The principle behind both books rests on overwhelming
evidence that psoriasis, the skin disease afflicting 7 million Americans, can be
alleviated, controlled, and even healed by adhering to certain dietary measures.

$ 32.00   Retail price   Visa/MC/Dis/Amex
$ 1.92   Tax for New Jersey residents
$ 8.00   Postage and handling

Make check payable to The Pagano Organization, Inc.
ISBN 0-9628847-1-5

FAIR HAVEN FARE
Fair Haven PTA
Knollwood School, Hance Road
Fair Haven, NJ 07704

A collection of nearly 400 recipes are included in this cookbook. Members of our
PTA community submitted their family favorites; featuring traditional, ethnic
and seasonal dishes from appetizers to desserts. Recipes include quick and simple meals as well as dinner party menus. Proceeds from this cookbook support
our schools.

$ 12.00   Retail price
$ 3.00   Postage and handling

Make check payable to Fair Haven PTA

A FAMILY TRADITION

Wicomico County Fair
c/o Mrs. Iva Mae Gravenor   410-742-5174
168 Morris Mill Road
Salisbury, MD 21804

Wicomico County is the center of the Delmarva peninsula (Delaware, Maryland, Virginia). This area is well-known for Frank Perdue's chicken, seafood (clams, fish, crabs, oysters), hunting of wildlife and farming. 850 recipes in 330 pages; 18 categories.

$ 12.00   Retail price
$ 3.20   Postage and handling

Make check payable to Wicomico County Fair

FAVORITE RECIPES HOME-STYLE

Shirley A. Sessions   410-557-8297
2315 Northcliff Drive
Janettsville, MD 21084   Bsess618@aol.com

I have been gathering recipes for many years. I have finally taken the step and compiled about 200 of them in this cookbook. I hope that you will enjoy them as much as our family has over the years. It certainly is easier using the cookbook than sifting through hundreds of recipes in a box.

$ 6.00   Retail price
$ .30   Tax for Maryland residents
$ 1.70   Postage and handling

Make check payable to Shirley A. Sessions

FLAVORS OF CAPE HENLOPEN

Village Improvement Association   302-227-4323
P. O. Box 144   Fax 302-227-8478
Rehoboth Beach, DE 19971   shells@seashellshop.net

Rehoboth Beach Resort recipes features Katie Couric of NBC Today Show and her special recipe. The book gathers the best of the best in its 200 pages. Filled with everything from appetizers to desserts. Over 350 recipes including a Healthy Body Cooking Section plus original drawings of the Beach area.

$ 11.99   Retail price
$ 3.50   Postage and handling

Make check payable to VIA

FOOD FABULOUS FOOD

c/o Volunteer Office/Cookbook
The Women's Board to Cooper Health System   856-428-5312
Cooper Hospital   Fax 856-428-0191
Camden, NJ 08103-1489   maddy6@home.com

Within 358 pages you'll find 350 recipes (95% never before in print) that have been tested at least three times and are guaranteed to turn out beautifully! There are appetizers, pastas, entrées, vegetables and desserts. Also a children's section and a great chef's section.

$ 19.95   Retail price
$ 3.50   Postage and handling

Make check payable to The Women's Board to Cooper Health System
ISBN 0-9655229-0-3

GARDENERS IN THE KITCHEN
A SECOND HELPING

New Market Garden Club
Cookbook Publishers, Inc.   301-631-5711
P. O. Box 225
New Market, MD 21774

A Second Helping is the result of our very successful first cookbook, which had three printings. Two hundred twenty-eight pages of our members' favorite, tested recipes.

$ 10.00   Retail price
$ .50   Tax for Maryland residents
$ 3.00   Postage and handling

Make check payable to New Market Garden Club

THE GLEN AFTON COOKBOOK
RECIPES IN GOOD TASTE

The Glen Afton Women's Club   609-393-3890
Lynne Semmel
644 Sanhican Drive
Trenton, NJ 08618

From delicate nouvelle cuisine to ethnic favorites to down-home county fare, taste the flavor of Glen Afton, a wonderful, historic neighborhood tucked into a quiet corner of Trenton, New Jersey. With over 100 pages, the book includes recipes for every occasion representing diverse people and cultures.

$ 8.50   Retail price
$ .51   Tax for New Jersey residents
$ 2.50   Postage and handling

Make check payable to The Glen Afton Women's Club

GOOD THINGS TO EAT

by Lynn Tritremmel
27 Saranac Road
Hamilton, NJ 08619   ltrit@yahoo.com

Good Things to Eat is a 66-page collection of recipes; many passed down from grandmothers, mothers, sisters, friends, co-workers and students whom I have had the pleasure to know, teach and share wonderful foods with during my ten years of teaching cooking at the local adult school.

$ 10.00   Retail price

Make check payable to Lynn Tritremmel

THE GREAT GOURMET

St. Gregory the Great PTA   609-587-1131
4620 Nottingham Way
Hamilton Square, NJ 08690

From the wonderful cooks in our parish family we collected some of their favorite recipes and compiled them into this special cookbook. You are sure to enjoy the eclectic and delightful offerings within these pages.

$ 10.00   Retail price
$ .60   Tax for New Jersey residents

Make check payable to St. Gregory the Great PTA

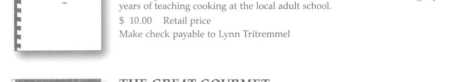

THE HAPPY COOKER 3

Sisterhood Beth Ohr   732-727-0394
19 Shadowlawn Drive
Old Bridge, NJ 08857

Nearly 500 kosher recipes on 200+ pages in all the usual categories, as well as a section of helpful kosher hints. The holiday section is special because each holiday is introduced with a short explanation of the traditions and meanings of the day. Traditional foods and food customs are discussed. There are suggested menus followed by the page numbers. It's a real family cookbook.

$ 15.00   Retail price
$ 4.00   Postage and handling

Make check payable to Sisterhood Beth Ohr

HOBOKEN COOKS
FAVORITE RECIPES FROM THE MILE-SQUARE CITY

United Synagogue of Hoboken   201-659-4000
115 Park Avenue   Fax 201-659-2614
Hoboken, NJ 07030   hoboken.synagogue@usa.net

Hoboken: birthplace of Frank Sinatra and baseball is now home to 35,000 people from Europe, Asia, the Middle East and South America. And we got their favorite recipes! Includes photos of Hoboken and articles from local newspapers from 1880-1920. Special kosher section. 350 pages, over 300 recipes.

$ 18.00   Retail price   Visa/MC accepted
$ 1.08   Tax for New Jersey residents
$ 3.00   Postage and handling

Make check payable to United Synagogue of Hoboken
ISBN 0-9667217-0-5

IN THE KITCHEN WITH KENDI, VOLUME 1

by Kendi O'Neill
Diversions Publications   800-272-2014
6 East Street Suite 301   Fax 301-662-8399
Frederick, MD 21701   www.fredmag.com

In the Kitchen with Kendi, Volume 1 is the ultimate community cookbook for Frederick and all of Mid-Maryland. With more than 100 recipes plus detailed information where to find seasonal produce, historic sites, regional traditions and much more.

$ 19.95   Retail price   Visa/MC/Disc
$ 1.00   Tax for Maryland residents
$ 3.00   Postage and handling

Make check payable to Diversions Publications
ISBN 0-9661278-2-X

IN THE KOMONDOR KITCHEN

Middle Atlantic States Komondor Club, Inc.
102 Russell Road
Princeton, NJ 08540

Our members own Hungarian Komondors, a rare dog breed. We enjoy good food and some of us are avid cooks. Not all recipes are Hungarian—we enjoy the cuisines of many different countries. Some recipes are simple, some are elaborate. Some are loaded with calories; some are low-fat and low-calorie. Some take time; others are quick. 134 pages include 200+ recipes and charming drawings of our unusual dogs.

$ 8.00   Retail price
$ 2.00   Postage and handling

Make check payable to M.A.S.K.C., Inc.

JAYCEE COOKIN'

Annapolis Maryland Jaycees Cookbook Committee
P. O. Box 248
Annapolis, MD 21404   jc_cookin2000@hotm

Jaycee Cookin' is a collection of recipes compiled and edited by the Ana
Jaycees Cookbook Committee. Recipes include local Maryland recipes, a
as hors d'oeuvres and potluck favorites.

$ 12.00   Retail price includes tax and shipping

Make check payable to Annapolis Maryland Jaycees

LA CUCINA CASALINGA
ITALIAN HOME COOKING

c/o Dee Sestito
Italian American Association of the Township of Ocean   732-531-0064
501 Bendermere Avenue   Fax 732-517-0988
Interlaken, NJ 07712   deeses@aol.com

This is no ordinary cookbook! Stories, anecdotes and proverbs have been included to make it very interesting reading. The families of the IAATO have contributed over 350 recipes, some of which have been in their families for generations and have been kept secret until now.

$ 12.00   Retail price
$ .72   Tax for New Jersey residents
$ 2.50   Postage and handling

Make check payable to IAATO

LAMBERTVILLE COMMUNITY COOKBOOK

Kalmia Club of Lambertville   609-397-2537
39 York Street
Lambertville, NJ 08530

This book has 252 pages of over 450 recipes with 12 sections from appetizers to
desserts plus snack and accompaniments and menus. The illustrations, from
beautiful to whimsical are done by well known regional artists. Brief but interesting comments often accompany the recipes.

$ 10.00   Retail price
$ 3.00   Postage and handling

Make check payable to Kalmia Club

LET'S COOK SWISS

c/o Sherry Huber
Swiss Embassy Cookbook
11619 Greenlane Drive
Potomac, MD 20854

Two hundred recipes compiled by the staff of the Embassy of Switzerland in
Washington, D.C. and their spouses, includes traditional Swiss dishes to family
favorites, with a sprinkling of international contributions from multinational
staffers. This is an excellent guide to learning more about Switzerland through
it's multicultural cooking styles.

$ 12.50   Retail price
$ 2.50   Postage and handling

Make check payable to Swiss Cookbook

MARYLAND'S HISTORIC RESTAURANTS AND THEIR RECIPES

by Dawn O'Brien and Rebecca Schenck
John. F. Blair, Publisher   800-222-9796
1406 Plaza Drive   Fax 336-768-9194
Winston-Salem, NC 27103   blairpub@blairpub.com

This guide focuses on 50 restaurants that are housed in buildings at least 50 years old. In addition to a description of the restaurant's building, decor, and cuisine, each entry includes 2-3 recipes from that establishment.

$ 15.95   Retail price
$ 5.00   Postage and handling

Make check payable to John F. Blair, Publisher
ISBN 0-89587-137-8

MARYLAND'S WAY

The Hammond-Harwood House   410-263-4683
19 Maryland Avenue   Fax 410-267-6891
Annapolis, MD 21401   hammondharwood@annapolis.net

This cookbook first printed in 1963—now in it's 14th printing—is dedicated to Maryland cooks who since 1634 have blended the fruits of bay, field, and forest into *Maryland's Way*. 360 pages, historic photographs.

$ 22.00   Retail price   Visa/MC accepted
$ 1.10   Tax for Maryland residents
$ 1.90   Postage and handling

Make check payable to The Hammond-Harwood House
ISBN 0-910688-01-X

A MATTER OF TASTE

The Junior League of Morristown   973-605-5386
7 King Place   Fax 973-539-6724
Morristown, NJ 07960

A Matter of Taste . . . a simple phrase that captures the essence of this collection of stylish and delectable recipes. Highlights include edible floral garnishes, thoughtful wine accompaniments and specialities of the Garden State. In addition, the serving suggestions are certain to tempt even the most seasoned cook, yet they are simple enough to be a success in any kitchen.

$ 21.95   Retail price   Visa/MC accepted
$ 1.33   Tax for New Jersey residents
$ 2.50   Postage and handling

Make check payable to The Junior League of Morristown
ISBN 0-9622230-0-X

MEATLESS MEALS FOR WORKING PEOPLE

Debra Wasserman and Charles Stahler
The Vegetarian Resource Group   410-366-8343
P. O. Box 1463   Fax 410-366-8804
Balitmore, MD 21203   vrg@vrg.org • www.vrg.org

100 quick and easy vegetarian recipes, plus information on 72 fast food and quick service restaurant chains, including which items they serve that are vegetarian or vegan. Learn about convenient frozen food ideas, quick convenience packaged veggie foods, plus more.

$ 12.00   Retail price   Visa/MC accepted
$ .60   Tax for Maryland residents
$ 3.00   Postage and handling

Make check payable to The Vegetarian Resource Group
ISBN 0-931411-19-X

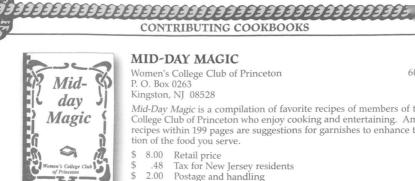

MID-DAY MAGIC

Women's College Club of Princeton   609-73
P. O. Box 0263
Kingston, NJ 08528

Mid-Day Magic is a compilation of favorite recipes of members of the Wom
College Club of Princeton who enjoy cooking and entertaining. Among the 4
recipes within 199 pages are suggestions for garnishes to enhance the present
tion of the food you serve.

$ 8.00   Retail price
$ .48   Tax for New Jersey residents
$ 2.00   Postage and handling

Make check payable to Women's College Club of Princeton

MORE FAVORITES FROM THE MELTING POT

Church of Saint Athanasius   410-355-5740
4708 Prudence St
Baltimore, MD 21226-1298

More Favorites From the Melting Pot contains a variety of recipes. There are
recipes related to the Chesapeake Bay Region, simple home cooking and recipes
from the diverse cultures that comprise St. Athanasius Parish. The cookbook
contains over 650 recipes displayed on 296 pages and is presented in a washable
loose leaf binder.

$ 12.00   Retail price
$ 3.00   Postage and handling

Make check payable to St. Athanasius

MRS. KITCHING'S SMITH ISLAND COOKBOOK

by Frances Kitching and Susan Stiles Dowell
Tidewater Publishers   800-638-7641
P. O. Box 456   Fax 410-758-6849
Centreville, MD 21617   cornell4@crosslink.net

For more than a quarter century, Frances Kitching operated a small restaurant
and inn on tiny Smith Island in the middle of the Chesapeake Bay. Susan Dowell
has gathered more than 100 of Mrs. Kitching's recipes and combined them with
a sensitive telling of the lore and lure of this remote island.

$ 12.95   Retail price   Visa/MC/Amex
$ .65   Tax for Maryland residents

Make check payable to Tidewater Publishers
ISBN 0-87033-264-3

MY FAVORITE MARYLAND RECIPES

by Helen Avalynne Tawes
Tidewater Publishers   800-638-7641
P. O. Box 456   Fax 410-758-6849
Centreville, MD 21617   cornell4@crosslink.net

First published in 1964, this collection of 400 recipes by a former First Lady of
Maryland blends traditional favorites—from Sweet Pickled Watermelon to
Maryland Beaten Biscuits and Panned Oysters—with elegant dishes served to
guests at the governor's mansion, such as Maryland's Finest Crab Imperial and
Lady Baltimore Cake.

$ 9.95   Retail price   Visa/MC/Amex
$ .50   Tax for Maryland residents

Make check payable to Tidewater Publishers
ISBN 0-87033-500-6

OF TIDE & THYME

Junior League of Annapolis
134 Holiday Court Suite 306
Annapolis, MD 21401

410-573-9235
Fax 410-573-9236
jlannapolis@toad.net
www.jlannapolis.org

Of Tide & Thyme is a product of Annapolis's casual lifestyle. This 414-page cookbook is filled with recipes that provide quick, elegant meals using the fresh vegetables and local seafood that are traditional Maryland fare. We invite you to enjoy our recipes and our cooking secrets.

$ 18.95   Retail price
$ .95   Tax for Maryland residents
$ 4.50   Postage and handling

Visa/MC accepted

Make check payable to Junior League of Annapolis
ISBN 0-9642139-0-7

OUR FAVORITE RECIPES

Damascus United Methodist Women
9700 New Church Street
Damascus, MD 20872

301-253-0022
Fax 301-253-2321
dumc@erols.com

Our Favorite Recipes cookbook contains a collection of recipes submitted by members and friends at Damascus United Methodist Church. 236 pages with 600 recipes including everything from appetizers to desserts.

$ 8.00   Retail price

Make check payable to Damascus United Methodist Women

OUR FAVORITE RECIPES
BOOK THREE

Enterprise Fire Co. Ladies Auxiliary
118 Trenton Avenue
Mercerville, NJ 08619

Tried and true favorite recipes from members of our auxiliary members. Our two previous cookbooks were so popular that we decided to carry on with book three as our fund raiser. 78 pages, ring bound, laminated cover.

$ 6.00   Retail price
$ 2.00   Postage and handling

Make check payable to Enterprise Ladies Auxiliary

OUT OF THE FRYING PAN INTO THE FIRE!!!

Berkeley Heights Fire Department Ladies Auxiliary
Anne Manganelli
206 Berkeley Avenue
Berkeley Heights, NJ 07922

908-464-0268
Fax 908-464-0268
Jdimaggio5@home.com

This 2nd edition (1st edition was a sell out) from the Ladies Auxiliary of the Berkeley Heights Fire Department contains over 477 all new, easy and quick recipes. The "Old Time Favorites" section contains many original Italian family specialties. Profits from this book will help the Ladies Auxiliary, who during the course of the year donate to many needy organizations in their community.

$ 10.00   Retail price
$ 2.50   Postage and handling

Make check payable to BHFD Ladies Auxiliary

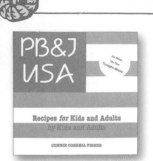

PB&J USA

by Connie Correia Fisher
Small Potatoes Press   856-869-
1106 Stokes Avenue   Fax 856-869-
Collingswood, NJ 08108   cuizine1@aol.c

PB&J USA is a quirky, one-of-a-kind collection of children's and adult's favo
sandwich combinations. Along with the kid's creations, chefs from 25 resta
rants have contributed gourmet PB&J-inspired recipes such as MacNut Breakfas
Sandwich, PB&J Quesadillas, and PB&J Double Decker Crepe that take readers
from breakfast to bedtime and way beyond the basic brown bag.

$ 10.95   Retail price
$ 2.00   Postage and handling
Make check payable to Small Potatoes Press
ISBN 0-9661200-1-9

THE QUEEN VICTORIA® COOKBOOK

Joan and Dane Wells   609-884-8702
102 Ocean Street
Cape May, NJ 08204   www.queenvictoria.com

The Queen Victoria® Bed and Breakfast Inn, located in the center of historic
Cape May, New Jersey, has been serving guests since 1980 and has compiled
over 80 recipes in a popular cookbook for easy, elegant entertaining at breakfast
or brunch plus a selection of sweets and savories for tea time.

$ 7.95   Retail price
$ 3.00   Postage and handling
Make check payable to The Queen Victoria

RECIPES FROM THE SKIPJACK MARTHA LEWIS

Chesapeake Heritage Conservancy, Inc.
121 N. Union Avenue, Suite C   Fax 410-939-4121
Havre de Grace, MD 21078   www.skipjackmarthalewis.org

Fifty-eight pages of 150+ great recipes from the captain, crew, volunteers and
friends of the MARTHA LEWIS with a light seasoning of "oyster talk." Such
delights as Drudgeman's Stew, Oysters Martha Lewis, Dredge Boat Pork Chops,
Roasted Asparagus, and Hummingbird Cake are to be found.

$ 10.00   Retail price   Visa/MC accepted
$ .50   Tax for Maryland residents
$ 2.00   Postage and handling
Make check payable to CHC, Inc.

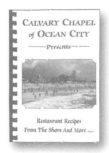

RESTAURANT RECIPES FROM THE SHORE AND MORE...

Calvary Chapel Christian Center   410-723-7098
P. O. Box 3173   Fax 410-723-7098
Ocean City, MD 21843   CalvaryChapelOC@cs.com

Calvary Chapel of Ocean City presents recipes from local restaurants and locals
themselves! They reflect the variety of foods prepared on the Shore of
Delmarva. This unique cookbook includes authentic seafood recipes and more
from such well-known restaurants as Phillips, Reflections and the Wharf.

$ 5.00   Retail price
$ 2.00   Postage and handling
Make check payable to Calvary Chapel

SEALED WITH A KNISH

by Loryn S. Lesser
Micahmatt Press   410-486-8127
14 Ruby Field Court   Fax 410-486-5231
Baltimore, MD 21209   kleid@ix.netcom.com

A kosher cookbook geared for the busy, health-conscious family. Over 200 pages of mostly very simple to prepare, low fat dishes. The recipes presented are either original, adapted or family favorites courtesy of grandmothers, mothers and aunts. Ingredients used are easily found on supermarket shelves.

$ 11.95   Retail price
$ .60   Tax for Maryland residents
$ 5.00   Postage and handling

Make check payable to Micahmatt Press, Inc.

A SECOND HELPING

New Egypt Historical Society   609-758-8111
Box 295
New Egypt, NJ 08533

A Second Helping is a followup to our successful first edition. There are ninety two pages with over 200 tried-and-true recipes from our members, friends and family.

$ 5.00   Retail price

Make check payable to New Egypt Historical Society

SIMPLE PLEASURES
HEALTHFUL EVERYDAY KOSHER RECIPES FOR BODY & SOUL

Jewish Caring Network
17 Warren Road, Suite 7A   410-602-6075
Baltimore, MD 21208

Proceeds from sale of this cookbook are used to expand the many services the all-volunteer Baltimore-based JCN provides to families facing catastrophic illnesses. Over 700 quick and easy recipes compiled by busy mothers, all excellent cooks in their own right. Special emphasis on kid-friendly and healthful meals.

$ 22.50   Retail price
$ 2.50   Postage and handling 1.00 each addt'l book

Make check payable to Jewish Caring Network
ISBN 0-9679787-1

SIMPLY VEGAN—QUICK VEGETARIAN MEALS

Debra Wasserman and Reed Mangels, Ph.D., R.D.
The Vegetarian Resource Group   410-366-8343
P. O. Box 1463   Fax 410-366-8804
Baltimore, MD 21203   vrg@vrg.org • www.vrg.org

224 pages filled with over 160 vegan recipes, an extensive vegan nutrition section, sample menus and meal plans for vegans, food definitions and origin of common and uncommon vegan foods. You'll also find a list of mail order companies offering vegan items. Over 70,000 copies have already been sold.

$ 12.95   Retail price   Visa/MC accepted
$ .65   Tax for Maryland residents
$ 3.00   Postage and handling

Make check payable to The Vegetarian Resource Group
ISBN 0-931411-20-3

SOUTH COASTAL CUISINE

Friends of the South Coastal Library   302-53?
P. O. Box 1617
Bethany Beach, DE 19930

Recipes for *South Coastal Cuisine* were contributed by year-round and summ[er]
residents as well as visitors to our beach community, Delaware political figur[es]
and a few local "celebrities." A popular local artist designed the front cover; fu[ll]
color dividers and pen and ink sketches were done by members of the Bethany
Beach Watercolor Society. 184 pages; 474 recipes.

$ 15.00   Retail price
$ 2.50   Postage and handling
Make check payable to Friends of the South Coastal Library

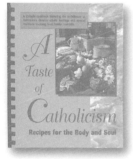

STEPPINGSTONE COOKERY

Steppingstone Museum Association, Inc.   410-939-2299
461 Quaker Bottom Road
Havre de Grace, MD 21078   steppingstonemuseum@msn.com

Steppingstone Cookery features over 300 recipes all categories. Museum members, volunteers, and Harford County residents contributed recipes for this 150-
page, spiral bound book complete with measurement guide, substitutions, and
nutritional tips for your everyday cooking needs.

$ 7.13   Retail price   Visa/MC accepted
$ .37   Tax for Maryland residents
$ 3.50   Postage and handling
Make check payable to Steppingstone Museum Assn., Inc.

A TASTE OF CATHOLICISM

Cathedral Foundation Press   410-547-5324
320 Cathedral Street   Fax 410-332-1069
Baltimore, MD 21201   pmedinger@catholicreview.org

A Taste of Catholicism hi-lites the region's rich ethnic heritage, drawing from
Italian, Lithuanian, German, Irish, Polish, and many other cultures. This spiral-
bound, classic cookbook contains over 200 pages of mouth-watering recipes.
Personal reflections and family traditions are "sprinkled" throughout. Bon
Appetite!

$ 15.00   Retail price
$ 3.00   Postage and handling
Make check payable to Cathedral Foundation Press
ISBN 1-885938-05-5

A TASTE OF GBMC

Greater Baltimore Medical Center Volunteer Auxiliary
Attn: Charlene Glatfelter   410-828-2050
6701 North Charles Street
Baltimore, MD 21204

Our 208-page cookbook is a 3-ring hard bound collection of 550 recipes. It was
compiled by the volunteers, medical staff and employees of Greater Baltimore
Medical Center. All proceeds benefit patient care.

$ 15.00   Retail price
$ .75   Tax for Maryland residents
$ 4.25   Postage and handling
Make check payable to GBMC Volunteer Auxiliary

A TASTE OF HEAVEN

Ministry of Light Outreach Church   856-728-9717
1292 Janvier Road
Williamstown, NJ 08094

Among the angels are a wide variety of recipes such as Mexican Stuffed Peppers, Mother's New England Baked Beans, Oriental Crab Cakes and Tex-Mex Stir Fry; 120 recipes altogether. You are sure to enjoy them all, plus 16 pages of helpful hints.

$ 7.00   Retail price
$ 2.00   Postage and handling

Make check payable to Ministry of Light Outreach

A TASTE OF TRADITION

Sandra Nagler   302-684-1870
24908 Prettyman Road   Fax 302-684-1870
Georgetown, DE 19947

It took me about 25 years to collect the recipes for this cookbook. These recipes have been handed down for many years from family to family and friend to friend. Some of the recipes are over 50 years old. They are cherished and loved by my family and friends.

$ 15.00   Retail price
$ 4.00   Postage and handling

Make check payable to Sandra Nagler

A TASTING TOUR THROUGH THE 8TH DISTRICT

Woman's Club of Arlington EMD   201-997-3446
86 Hedden Terrace   Fax 201-964-3208
North Arlington, NJ 07031

The purpose of the Woman's Club of Arlington, Evening Membership Department, a non-political, non-sectarian and non-profit organization, is to promote civic, cultural, educational and recreational improvements in the community. Proceeds from the sale of our cookbook will go to support the various projects of the 8th District Evening Membership Department.

$ 10.00   Retail price
$ 5.00   Postage and handling

Make check payable to Woman's Club of Arlington EMD

225 YEARS IN PENNINGTON & STILL COOKING

First United Methodist Church   609-737-1374
60 South Main Street
Pennington, NJ 08534   GraceAmazed@aol.com

Published in celebration of the congregation's 225th anniversary, this book includes wonderful recipes and historical anecdotes. A wide variety is offered in 327 recipes presented in 156 pages, with an equal number of recipes for vegetables, salads, and desserts.

$ 7.00   Retail price
$ 3.50   Postage and handling

Make check payable to United Methodist Women

VEGAN MEALS FOR ONE & TWO
YOUR OWN PERSONAL RECIPES
by Chef Nancy Berkoff, R. D.
The Vegetarian Resource Group   410-366-8343
P. O. Box 1463   Fax 410-366-8804
Baltimore, MD 21203   vrg@vrg.org • www.vrg.org

Whether you live alone, are a couple, or are the only one in your household that is vegan, this 216-page book is for you. Each recipe is written to serve one or two people. Information on meal planning and shopping is included.

$ 15.00   Retail price   Visa/MC accepted
$ .75   Tax for Maryland residents

Make check payable to The Vegetarian Resource Group
ISBN 0-931411-23-8

WHAT'S COOKIN'
Arlene Luskin   623-925-2526
16726 West Pierce Street   Fax 623-925-2528
Goodyear, AZ 85338   arlenc@chenandsnoscookbook.com

There are over 300 favorite recipes from co-workers, friends and neighbors. There are original drawings, numerous stories about the origin of foods, food stories. I did this cookbook in memory of a dog I had gotten at the humane society and this is my way of giving something back to them.

$ 7.00   Retail price
$ 3.00   Postage and handling

Make check payable to Arlene Luskin

WHERE THERE'S A WILL . . .
by Evelyn Will   410-820-7449
7300 Waverly Island Road
Easton, MD 21601   dewill@goeaston.net

This cookbook contains a collection of recipes from family and friends! Every effort has been made to acknowledge the source, where known, of each recipe. Book contains 222 pages of recipes plus section on household hints, etc.

$ 25.00   Retail price
$ 1.25   Tax for Maryland residents

Make check payable to Evelyn Will

WHY NOT FOR BREAKFAST?
by Nan Hawkins   609-884-5381
238 Perry Street
Cape May, NJ 08204   bargood@bellatlantic.net

All—over 200—recipes in this book have been enjoyed by the guests of the Barnard-Good House. We have won awards for our unique approach to breakfast—hence the title. Just consider Deep Dish Chili Cheese Pie, always a "gold star" for the "clean plate club."

$ 15.00   Retail price   Visa/MC/Amex
$ .90   Tax for New Jersey residents
$ 1.50   Postage and handling

Make check payable to Nan Hawkins

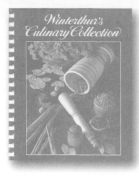

WINTERTHUR'S CULINARY COLLECTION

Winterthur Museum, Garden & Library   800-448-3883
Rt. 52   Fax 302-888-4890
Winterthur, DE 19735   mkrussmahn@winterthur.org

A compilation of treasured recipes from Winterthur, the American country estate of Henry Francis du Pont, which is located just north of Wilmington, Delaware. Recipes for Delaware Crab Puffs and Kennett Square Mushrooms take advantage of our abundant supply of local delicacies. Also enjoy a few forgotten favorites from the Winterthur archives.

$ 15.95   Retail price   Visa/MC/Amex
$ 3.00   Postage and handling
Make check payable to Winterthur
ISBN 0-912724-14-5

INDEX

The first boardwalk was built in Atlantic City in 1870 to prevent sand from the beaches from being tracked into seaside hotel lobbies. The first saltwater taffy was produced at the Jersey Shore in the 1870s as well.

Best of the Best State Cookbook Series

Best of the Best from
ALABAMA
288 pages, $16.95

Best of the Best from
ALASKA
288 pages, $16.95

Best of the Best from
ARIZONA
288 pages, $16.95

Best of the Best from
ARKANSAS
288 pages, $16.95

Best of the Best from
BIG SKY
Montana and Wyoming
288 pages, $16.95

Best of the Best from
CALIFORNIA
384 pages, $16.95

Best of the Best from
COLORADO
288 pages, $16.95

Best of the Best from
FLORIDA
288 pages, $16.95

Best of the Best from
GEORGIA
336 pages, $16.95

Best of the Best from the
GREAT PLAINS
North and South Dakota,
Nebraska, and Kansas
288 pages, $16.95

Best of the Best from
HAWAI'I
288 pages, $16.95

Best of the Best from
IDAHO
288 pages, $16.95

Best of the Best from
ILLINOIS
288 pages, $16.95

Best of the Best from
INDIANA
288 pages, $16.95

Best of the Best from
IOWA
288 pages, $16.95

Best of the Best from
KENTUCKY
288 pages, $16.95

Best of the Best from
LOUISIANA
288 pages, $16.95

Best of the Best from
LOUISIANA II
288 pages, $16.95

Best of the Best from
MICHIGAN
288 pages, $16.95

Best of the Best from the
MID-ATLANTIC
Maryland, Delaware, New
Jersey, and Washington, D.C.
288 pages, $16.95

Best of the Best from
MINNESOTA
288 pages, $16.95

Best of the Best from
MISSISSIPPI
288 pages, $16.95

Best of the Best from
MISSOURI
304 pages, $16.95

Best of the Best from
NEVADA
288 pages, $16.95

Best of the Best from
NEW ENGLAND
Rhode Island, Connecticut,
Massachusetts, Vermont,
New Hampshire, and Maine
368 pages, $16.95

Best of the Best from
NEW MEXICO
288 pages, $16.95

Best of the Best from
NEW YORK
288 pages, $16.95

Best of the Best from
NO. CAROLINA
288 pages, $16.95

Best of the Best from
OHIO
352 pages, $16.95

Best of the Best from
OKLAHOMA
288 pages, $16.95

Best of the Best from
OREGON
288 pages, $16.95

Best of the Best from
PENNSYLVANIA
320 pages, $16.95

Best of the Best from
SO. CAROLINA
288 pages, $16.95

Best of the Best from
TENNESSEE
288 pages, $16.95

Best of the Best from
TEXAS
352 pages, $16.95

Best of the Best from
TEXAS II
352 pages, $16.95

Best of the Best from
UTAH
288 pages, $16.95

Best of the Best from
VIRGINIA
320 pages, $16.95

Best of the Best from
WASHINGTON
288 pages, $16.95

Best of the Best from
WEST VIRGINIA
288 pages, $16.95

Best of the Best from
WISCONSIN
288 pages, $16.95

Cookbooks listed above have been completed as of December 31, 2004. All cookbooks are comb bound.

Special discount offers available! *(See previous page for details.)*

To order by credit card, call toll-free **1-800-343-1583** or visit our website at **www.quailridge.com**.
Use the form below to send check or money order.

Call 1-800-343-1583 or email <u>info@quailridge.com</u> *to request a free catalog of all of our publications.*

 **Order form**   Use this form for sending check or money order to:
QUAIL RIDGE PRESS • P. O. Box 123 • Brandon, MS 39043

❑ Check enclosed
Charge to: ❑ Visa ❑ MC ❑ AmEx ❑ Disc

Card # _____

Expiration Date _____

Signature _____

Name _____

Address _____

City/State/Zip _____

Phone # _____

Email Address _____

Qty.	Title of Book (State) or Set	Total

Subtotal _____

7% Tax for MS residents _____

Postage ($4.00 any number of books) + 4.00

Total _____